Commendations for *Reformation Lette*

'In this fascinating monograph on Calvin's letters, Michael Parsons compares the personal responses of Calvin to life's difficult circumstances, found in his letters to close friends, with his doctrinal theology written for the church. For instance, in one particularly engrossing chapter, Parsons probes how Calvin dealt with his own pervasive grief over the death of his wife and close friends in light of Calvin's firm conviction of the complete sovereignty of God in human affairs found in other writings. The humanity and piety of Calvin is demonstrated equally so in Parsons' exploration of Calvin's correspondence addressing the subjects of vocation and calling, marriage, the fiery execution of Servetus, and the persecution of believers of the evangelical faith in France. I loved this book. Its real strength is in revealing the humanity of Calvin against his official theology.'
Mary Patton Baker, *All Souls Anglican Church, Wheaton, Il.*

'Michael Parsons' latest volume that explores the letters of John Calvin on pertinent subjects (as current as martyrdom) shows us the unnoticed, compassionate side of the Genevan reformer. Like discovering a previously blocked social media account from the Sixteenth Century, the chapters on grief, calling, marriage, affliction, and other topics, reveal to a modern audience the *pathos* of an earlier generation—admirable in so many respects—that is not gleaned from merely reading tracts and volumes. Parsons is a careful and caring guide, who seems to understand the sentiments of a giant of the faith that others studiously miss. Rather than slogging through all Calvin's letters with little thematic guidance, this fine volume does the work for the reader to get to the heart of matters. At times, each paragraph of Parsons' well-written narrative shouts (or whispers) to read slowly . . . for the matters covered herein are well worth reading thoughtfully. This is history at its finest—we know the reformer through these letters, thanks to an expert avatar. A fantastic and interesting work!'
David W. Hall, *Executive Director, Calvin500; and Sr. Pastor, Midway Presbyterian Church, Powder Springs, Georgia, USA.*

'Through his exploration of John Calvin's letters, Michael Parsons' work offers important insights into the life and mind of the great Genevan reformer. Parsons succeeds in correcting misperceptions of Calvin as drastically different in his theological and polemical writings than in his personal correspondence by offering a complex portrait of Calvin as "essentially a pastoral theologian". He adeptly demonstrates how Calvin's letters and theological writings consistently reveal his pastoral heart. Covering a variety of topics in discrete essays, Parsons offers a realistic picture of Calvin as a husband, a friend, a pastor, a statesman, and a struggling follower of Christ who wrote with empathy, passion, anger, trepidation, tenderness, and wisdom. At heart, Calvin was a man seeking to glorify God and encouraging others to do the same, whether it be in their theological beliefs, marriage, or when facing persecution, grief, or prison.'
Karin Spiecker Stetina, *Lecturer in Theology, Wheaton College.*

'Michael Parsons has done an excellent job in making Calvin's letters accessible to us, and helping us listen to Calvin in his personal and pastoral life and role. . . . The book is both scholarly and informative, and will be of benefit to everyday readers and scholars alike. It is a notable example of the combination of scholarship and usefulness!'
From the Foreword by Peter Adam, *Former Principal of Ridley Theological College, Melbourne.*

Reformation Letters

Reformation Letters

A Fresh Reading of John Calvin's Correspondence

Michael Parsons

Foreword by Peter Adam

☙PICKWICK *Publications* · Eugene, Oregon

REFORMATION LETTERS
A Fresh Reading of John Calvin's Correspondence

Copyright © 2018 Michael Parsons. All rights reserved. Except for brief quotations in critical publications or reviews, no part of this book may be reproduced in any manner without prior written permission from the publisher. Write: Permissions, Wipf and Stock Publishers, 199 W. 8th Ave., Suite 3, Eugene, OR 97401.

Pickwick Publications
An Imprint of Wipf and Stock Publishers
199 W. 8th Ave., Suite 3
Eugene, OR 97401

www.wipfandstock.com

PAPERBACK ISBN: 978-1-5326-5665-1
HARDCOVER ISBN: 978-1-5326-5666-8
EBOOK ISBN: 978-1-5326-5667-5

Cataloguing-in-Publication data:

Names: Parsons, Michael, 1949, author. | Adam, Peter, foreword.

Title: Reformation letters : a fresh reading of John Calvin's correspondence / Michael Parsons, with a foreword by Peter Adam.

Description: Eugene, OR : Pickwick Publications, 2018 | Includes bibliographical references and index.

Identifiers: ISBN 978-1-5326-5665-1 (paperback) | ISBN 978-1-5326-5666-8 (hardcover) | ISBN 978-1-5326-5667-5 (ebook)

Subjects: LCSH: Calvin, Jean, 1509–1564. | Calvin, Jean, 1509–1564—Correspondence. | Reformation—France. | Reformed Church—Switzerland—Geneva—History—16th century.

Classification: BX9418 P37 2018 (print) | BX9418 (ebook)

Manufactured in the U.S.A.   05/04/18

for my wife, Becky

STUDIES IN CHRISTIAN HISTORY AND THOUGHT

Series Preface

This series complements the specialist series of Studies in Evangelical History and Thought and Studies in Baptist History and Thought for which Paternoster is becoming increasingly well known by offering works that cover the wider field of Christian history and thought. It encompasses accounts of Christian witness at various periods, studies of individual Christians and movements, and works which concern the relations of church and society through history, and the history of Christian thought.

The series includes monographs, revised dissertations and theses, and collections of papers by individuals and groups. As well as 'free standing' volumes, works on particular running themes are being commissioned; authors will be engaged for these from around the world and from a variety of Christian traditions.

A high academic standard combined with lively writing will commend the volumes in this series both to scholars and to a wider readership

Series Editors

Alan P.F. Sell	Visiting Professor at Acadia University Divinity College, Nova Scotia
D.W. Bebbington	University of Stirling, Stirling, Scotland
Clyde Binfield	Professor Associate in History, University of Sheffield, UK
Gerald Bray	Anglican Professor of Divinity, Beeson Divinity School, Samford University, Birmingham, Alabama, USA
Grayson Carter	Associate Professor of Church History, Fuller Theological Seminary SW, Phoenix, Arizona, USA
Dennis Ngien	Professor of Theology, Tyndale University College and Seminary, Founder of the Centre for Mentorship and Theological Reflection, Toronto, Canada

Contents

Preface
Foreword by Peter Adam

Introduction	The 'relentless drive to relate theory and practice'. John Calvin's letters	1
Chapter 1	'May the Lord overrule it for good.' Calvin's letters on his calling and return	8
Chapter 2	'For the good of the whole Church.' Calvin's letters on marriage	29
Chapter 3	'Nothing was farther from my mind.' Calvin's prefatory letter to Francis I	50
Chapter 4	'Such is our consciousness of the truth': Calvin's letter to Cardinal Sadoleto	74
Chapter 5	'Even in your criticisms, judge me with equity': Calvin's letters on Servetus	100
Chapter 6	'To find consolation in the Lord': Calvin's letters on grief	124
Chapter 7	'It is too late to think of shrinking back': Calvin's letters to contemporary martyrs	143
Chapter 8	Conclusion	165
Appendix	'The gospel is set before us in his name': A final comment	172
Bibliography		174
Indexes		189

Full Contents

Preface
Foreword by Peter Adam

Introduction	The 'relentless drive to relate theory and practice'. John Calvin's letters	1
Chapter 1	**'May the Lord overrule it for good.'**	
	Calvin's letters on his calling and return	8
	Preliminaries	8
	The city of Geneva	8
	Calvin's doctrine of calling	13
	Calvin's letters on his return to Geneva	15
	to the Church of Geneva, Strasbourg, October 1, 1538.	17
	to the Church of Geneva, Strasbourg, June 25, 1539	18
	to the Seigneury of Geneva, Strasbourg, October 23, 1540	20
	to Farel, Strasbourg, October 27, 1540	20
	to the Seigneury of Geneva, Worms, November 12, 1540	22
	Recurrent themes	23
	The strength of divine calling	24
	Inadequacy for ministry	25
	Conclusion	28
Chapter 2	**'For the good of the whole Church.'**	
	Calvin's letters on marriage	29
	John Calvin on marriage	31
	Letters on Calvin's own marriage	34
	To Farel, February 23, 1539	35
	To Farel, May 19, 1539	36
	To Farel, February 6, 1540	37
	To Viret, July, August 19, 1542; June 15, 1548	38
	To Viret, April 7, 1549	38
	Reflections	39
	Calvin's understanding of marriage	40
	The importance of friendship	43
	The complex context	44

	Letters on Viret's second marriage	44
	To Monsieur de Falais, July 4, 1546	44
	To Viret, July 25, 1546	45
	To Monsieur de Falais, October 4, 1546	46
	Letters on Farel's second marriage	46
	To the Ministers of Neuchâtel,	
	September 26, 1558	47
	To Farel, September 1558	48
	Reflections	48
Chapter 3	**'Nothing was farther from my mind.'**	
	Calvin's prefatory letter to Francis I	**50**
	Calvin's letters 1533-1547	52
	The prefatory letter: recent interpretation	55
	Ford Lewis Battles: Calvin at face value	57
	Don Compier: authorial intent	60
	Serene Jones: rhetoric of otherness	62
	The prefatory letter: the text	65
	Reflections	72
Chapter 4	**'Such is our consciousness of the truth':**	
	Calvin's letter to Cardinal Sadoleto	**74**
	Critical interpretation of the letters	77
	The consensus	77
	Trajectories for ecumenical engagement?	79
	Sadoleto's letter to the Genevan authorities	81
	Rhetoric of fear	82
	Jesus Christ, faith and salvation	84
	The significance of the Church in salvation	85
	John Calvin's reply to Sadoleto	89
	Reflections	96
	Calvin's sense of call	97
	The believer's first consideration	97
	The nature and purpose of the Church	98
	The centrality of Jesus Christ	98
	The final tribunal	99
	A matter of truth	99
Chapter 5	**'Even in your criticisms, judge me with equity':**	
	Calvin's letters on Servetus	**100**
	Michael Servetus (1511-1553)	102
	Heresy and *Concerning Scandals*	106
	Scandals	107
	The pattern of history and Satan's	

	Activity	107
	Sects and heresies	109
	Calvin's letters and Servetus	111
	To John Frellon, February 13, 1546	111
	To Farel, August 20, 1553	112
	To Bullinger, September 7, 1553	113
	To Melanchthon, March 5, 1555	114
	Calvin's reasons for having Servetus put to death	114
	Calvin was a man of his time	115
	The historical situation	118
	Calvin's theology	119
	Calvin's pastoral urgency	120
	Reflections	122
Chapter 6	**'To find consolation in the Lord':**	
	Calvin's letters on grief	**124**
	Calvin's pastoral letters to those who grieve	125
	To Monsieur de Richebourg, 1541	125
	To the Budé family, 1547	129
	To Pierre Viret and to Guillaume Farel, 1549	130
	To Madame de Cany, 1549	132
	Calvin's approach to those who grieve	133
	Grief is to be expressed, in moderation	133
	Comfort in the face of death	136
	Exhortations to those who grieve	138
	Reflections	140
Chapter 7	**'It is too late to think of shrinking back':**	
	Calvin's letters to contemporary martyrs	**143**
	Protestant martyrdom	144
	Calvin's letters to contemporary martyrs	146
	Letters to the five prisoners of Lyons	147
	A letter to prisoners in Cambery, September 5, 1555	154
	A letter to women detained in Paris	157
	Reflections	158
	The centrality of God in the situation	160
	The importance of Christian community	161
	Witnesses of God's truth	161
Chapter 8	**Conclusion**	**165**
	Important themes	165
	The significance of God	165

	The significance of Jesus Christ	166
	Faith amidst suffering	167
	The community, the Church	168
	The importance of vocation	169
	The significance of the cross	170
	Intimate relationships	171
Appendix	**'The gospel is set before us in his name': A final comment**	**172**
Bibliography		**174**
Indexes		**189**
	Author index	189
	Letters index	192
	Scripture index	195
	Persons index	196
	Subject index	198

Preface

The Reformation period is fascinating: a period of upheaval and violence, a time of change and entrenchment, and a Church that really should have known better. A few good men and women, who clung to Christ and to his gospel of grace, changed the course of European and ecclesiastical history. Amongst the second generation, and preeminent in many ways, was the reformer, John Calvin. A refugee from his beloved France, a displaced person (in human terms), but 'placed' by divine purpose, a pastor and teacher of the Scriptures, he epitomises what it is to be called and to be determined to answer that call with courage and fortitude. Certainly not without weaknesses and faults, he laboured for Christ and for his people.

Above all, I think, Calvin was a pastor. His letters show this—at least, the ones I've chosen for this book do. Whether he's writing on marriage or calling, on suffering or grief, he exemplifies this characteristic. His defence of the Huguenots to Francis I and his rigorous defence of the Reformation, itself, against Cardinal Sadoleto, indicate as much. Though he's a distinguished theologian, of course, his letters are well worth studying. I trust the following pages will demonstrate that. I hope, too, that through them we will see something of Calvin's faith and of his God. Though clearly 'of his time,' the contemporary Church could learn a lesson or two from this great man.

I am grateful to Mary Patton Baker, David W. Hall and Karin Spiecker Stetina for reading the entire manuscript and commending it. I am also grateful to John Rupnow, Director of Edwin Mellen Press, for permission to use and to revise material from my earlier book, *Luther and Calvin on Grief*, for chapter 6 of the present work. Thank you to Paternoster, for publishing this work. Thank you, too, to Peter Adam for generously reading the manuscript, giving kind feedback and for writing the Foreword for the present work.

As this is my final academic work on the Reformation (see the Appendix), I would like to thank one or two scholars who have encouraged me in the past and continue to do so through personal conversation and through their own scholarship: John L. Thompson, Donald K. McKim, Dennis Ngien, Mark Thompson, Peter Matheson, Neil R. Leroux, Andre A. Gazal, David W. Hall and Mary Patton Baker. Fellowship in the scholarly endeavor is a wonderful and enriching thing!

Finally, the work is entirely my own!

I dedicate *Reformation Letters* to my wife, Becky, whom I love.

Michael Parsons
November, 2015

Foreword

We have much to learn from Christians who live in other places and other times. We can do this by listening to people from other countries. We can also do it by listening to people from other ages. It is especially useful to listen to people who lived in formative times in the history of Christianity. As we come to the 500th anniversary of the Reformation, we have good reason to look again at that age and that movement. We need to understand our past to understand our present. And we need to see that past with new eyes and ears, with new questions, and with new insights. And so it is beneficial to listen to John Calvin, not only in his *Institutes*, not only in his commentaries, but also in his letters. Michael Parsons has done an excellent job in making Calvin's letters accessible to us, and helping us listen to Calvin in his personal and pastoral life and role.

From Calvin's letters we gain deep insights into the answers of two important questions: What was it like to be a gospel believer in the 16th century in Europe? And, What was it like to be a gospel minister in the 16th century in Europe? As we learn about the person, we also learn about his friends, his church, his ministry, his daily life, his frustrations, hopes and joys, as we also learn about the world in which he lived, the church in which he served, and the day-by-day issues, problems, tragedies and triumphs of the Reformations in different places and countries in Europe.

Michael Parsons serves as an excellent guide and interpreter. He provides the background necessary for us to understand the letters, and also to see their significance for Calvin, and for the church and the world in which he lived and served. He places the letters under the useful themes of Calvin on ministry; Calvin on marriage; his letter to Francis 1 king of France, which introduces *The Institutes*; his reply to Cardinal Sadoleto; letters concerning the heretic Servetus; letters about grief; and letters about and to martyrs. This covers a wide range of Calvin's interests and activities, and provides new and fascinating perspectives on the great reformer, and on the church in Europe. The book is both scholarly and informative, and will be of benefit to everyday readers and scholars alike. It is a notable example of the combination of scholarship and usefulness!

In the words of Kevin Vanhoozer, 'The Golden Rule, for hermeneutic and ethics alike, is to treat others—texts, persons, God—with love and respect.' Those who treat Calvin and his letters with love and respect cannot but be enriched by reading them. And in this book Michael Parsons proves to be a useful and perceptive guide to help us understand and appreciate them.

Peter Adam
Former Principal of Ridley Theological College, Melbourne.

INTRODUCTION

The 'relentless drive to relate theory and practice'.[1]
John Calvin's letters

John Calvin's writings and, indeed, his theology generally, has always been the subject of extreme views and prejudiced judgement—ever since he put pen to paper in the sixteenth century. This partisan thinking can happen in either direction, as it were. Some enthusiastic writers champion the reformer and his views no matter what, others certainly do not. As an example of the latter, negative approach we might take Henry F. Henderson's early, short work on John Calvin's letters, *Calvin in his Letters*, published in 1909.[2] In the introductory chapter to that work he shows his hand rather overtly, it seems to me. By that remark I mean to intimate that at times he makes it clear that he writes in order to show something of the humanity of a man *he simply does not like*. For instance, he speaks of Calvin as a man who 'awes and repels us' through his theology, revealed in the *Institutes of the Christian Religion* and elsewhere. He continues, 'His teaching seems forbidding, some of his public acts are barbarous.' Then, he concedes a point in relation to the reformer's correspondence: 'But,' he says, 'in his letters we see a better side to his nature. . . . In his letters, it is like seeing him face to face, and speaking to him as a man speaks to a friend.'[3] This qualified negativity becomes a recurrent theme that runs throughout the whole book. Later, for example, Henderson states that we are apt to think of Calvin as 'an unlovable and unsympathetic man. We associate him in our minds with hard and gloomy theological ideas. . . . [But],' he says, 'besides the stern and unyielding figure that repels and alarms us there is a Calvin who wins us by his

---

[1] A.E. McGrath, *A Life of John Calvin* (Oxford: Blackwell, 1993), 220.
[2] Henry F. Henderson, *Calvin in his Letters* (Eugene: Wipf and Stock, 1996; originally published by J.M. Dent in 1909). On Calvin's letters, generally, see Douglas Kelly, 'The Transmission and Translation of the Collected Letters of John Calvin,' *Scottish Journal of Theology* 30.5 (1977), 429-37. See, also, two excellent, though more narrowly-focused essays by C.J. Blaisdell: 'Calvin's Letters to Women: The Courting of Ladies in High Places,' *Sixteenth Century Journal* 13 (1982), 67-85; and, 'Calvin's and Loyola's Letters to Women' in R.V. Schnucker (ed.), *Calviniana: Ideas and Influence of Jean Calvin* (Kirksville: Sixteenth Century Journal Publishers, 1988), 235-53.
[3] Henderson, *Calvin in his Letters*, 16. One imagines that Henderson has in mind here the apparently harsh sentence against the heretic, Michael Servetus. See chapter 5 of the present volume for an examination of this tragic situation.

large-hearted humanity, and even by his betrayal of attractive human weakness.'[4] So, he suggests that we read and study the reformer's letters *in order* to appreciate that there is another side to the reformer, a side that softens the daunting and dislikeable characteristics disclosed in his major writings and public reforming career.

I want to distance myself straightaway from such an extreme and largely ludicrous view; one that so artificially divides between the theology and the letters, one that implies two Calvins, as it were. I neither want to attack nor to advocate for the reformer. That is adamantly *not* the reason for this present short volume on John Calvin's letters. However, in decades of reading and writing on the Reformation I have found John Calvin, and Martin Luther, for that matter, to be passionate for what they considered to be truth, but also generally to be pastoral and compassionate in their response to others—men and women, kings and commoners, ecclesiasts and laity, evangelical and those of a different persuasion. John Calvin was a man of great strength and character and, sometimes, of obvious weakness and failure, and lacking in self-confidence. We are at times forcefully reminded of the scriptural comment about another: 'he was a human being, even as we are'.[5] That needs to be remembered.

In my work, *Luther and Calvin on Grief* (2013)[6] I demonstrate the reformers' humanity as they come to terms with their own loss and grief and as they struggle to find a pastoral path through that of others. In my earlier published doctoral research, *Reformation Marriage* (2011), I argue their humanity in the familial (albeit, patriarchal) sphere.[7] Indeed, a careful reading of Calvin's major writings—including the *Institutes*, his polemical writings, his sermons, and so on—reveals him to be as he is in his correspondence. It seems to me that there is no substantial difference. Calvin is essentially a pastoral theologian; or, in reverse, his theology is fundamentally pastoral. And, of course, this much has been incrementally accepted over the years since Henderson wrote on the reformer's letters at the turn of the last century.[8]

---

[4] Henderson, *Calvin in his Letters*, 26.
[5] James 5.17—a comment referring to Elijah in the original instance, of course.
[6] Michael Parsons, *Luther and Calvin on Grief. Life Experience and Biblical Text* (Lewiston: Edwin Mellen, 2013).
[7] Michael Parsons, *Reformation Marriage. The Husband and Wife Relationship in the Theology of Luther and Calvin* (Eugene: Wipf and Stock, 2011; originally published by Rutherford House in 2005).
[8] See, for example, the excellent early work by Richard Stauffer, *L'humanité de Calvin* (Neuchâtel: Delachaux and Niestlé, 1964). Also, amongst others, P.E. Hughes, 'John Calvin: The Man Whom God Subdued' in J.I. Packer (ed.), *How Shall They Hear?* (Stoke-on-Trent: Tentraker, 1960), 5-10; D. Hourticq, *Calvin, mon ami* (Geneva: Labor et Fides, 1963); Stanford Reid, 'John Calvin, Pastoral Theologian,' *Reformed Theological Review* 42.3 (1982), 65-72; A. Perrot, *Le visage humain de Calvin* (Geneva: Labor et Fides, 1986); Takasaki Takeshi, 'Calvin's Theology as Pastoral Theology,' *Reformed Review* 57.3 (1998), 220-41; W. Robert Godfrey, 'The Counsellor

Having said that, however, the present volume is not simply a championing of the reformer. That, too, would be misguided; a misreading of the history and the corpus. The present work recognises his weakness and failings, as well as his many strengths. Nor am I unaware of William Naphy's critique that Calvin's letters are over-rated and that they are merely a 'masterful', propaganda for the Reformed city of Geneva.[9] Nevertheless, even if we take on board that somewhat exaggerated comment in our reading and interpretation of the reformer's correspondence on the more political matters (which I am not necessarily fully inclined to do), we find that the letters *are* significant in discerning the reformer's career and pastoral theology and concerns.

There is in his letters vulnerability and warmth that surface at times in other works, but which appear more clearly when he writes to friends and colleagues, or to those in distress. We would expect this, of course. In his letters, there are grand moments of decisiveness and, at times, instances of reticence, too. Calvin writes as a husband, a friend, a pastor, a statesman; he writes with compassion, anger, insight, deference, but always with theological and exegetical acumen. John Thompson's comment on Calvin's biblical writing is perhaps relevant to his letters. He remarks that 'Virtually every aspect of daily life—not just preaching and sacraments, but also marriage and divorce, family life, commerce and consumption, as well as politics on every scale—was charged with theological and thus exegetical implications.'[10]

The following chapters certainly attempt to recognise this aspect of the reformer's letter-writing. Each chapter is a discrete essay, as such, but, of course, the volume as a whole offers a cumulative perspective on the Genevan reformer. It will be seen that each chapter argues a point, sometimes against the perspective of relevant secondary literature, at other times simply attempting to

---

to the Afflicted' in Burk Parsons (ed.), *John Calvin. A Heart for Devotion, Doctrine and Doxology* (Lake Mary: Reformation Trust, 2008), 83-93; Christoph Strohm, 'Beobachtungen zur Elgenart der Theologie Calvins' *Evangelische Theologie* 69.2 (2009), 85-100; Sinclair B. Ferguson, 'Calvin the Man: A Heart Aflame' in J.R. Beeke and G.J. Williams (eds), *Calvin. Theologian and Reformer* (Grand Rapids: Reformation Heritage, 2010), 7-24.

[9] William G. Naphy, 'Calvin's Letters: Reflections on their Usefulness in Studying Genevan History,' *Archiv für Reformationsgeschichte* 86 (1995), 89.

[10] John L. Thompson, 'Calvin as a biblical interpreter' in Donald K. McKim (ed.), *The Cambridge Companion to John Calvin* (Cambridge: Cambridge University Press, 2004), 59. In a similar way Alister E. McGrath, *A Life of John Calvin* (Oxford: Blackwell, 1993), 220, emphasises that, generally, Calvin shows a 'relentless drive to relate theory and practice'. See also, B. Armstrong, '*Duplex cognitio Dei*, Or the Problem and Relation of Structure, Form and Purpose in Calvin's Theology' in E.A. McKee and B. Armstrong (eds), *Probing the Reformed Tradition* (Louisville: Westminster John Knox, 1989), 142, who is correct in saying that, 'Calvin simply does not understand theology to be partly theoretical and partly practical. It is always at once practical and edifying.'

observe more carefully what Calvin says on a particular topic. In outline, the volume covers the following subjects.

Chapter 1 examines the reformer's letters on his calling and recall (after expulsion) to pastoral ministry in Geneva and demonstrates that Calvin felt inadequate for the task of leading the Church in that city. I argue—against the background of the reformational importance of the city and Calvin's intransigent theory of calling (*vocatio*)—that the situation around the reformer's recall was more complex than saying, as some do, that somehow he just 'hated' Geneva per se—the city, the people or the politics.

Having written at length on the subject,[11] chapter 2 takes another look at Calvin's theology of marriage and, particularly, his now (in)famous words after Idelette's untimely death that 'From her I never experienced the slightest hindrance.'[12] The brief essay argues against a superficial reading and for a more nuanced understanding of his comment, viewing it through the 'second lens' of public or Church good, as opposed to the 'first lens' of private or personal good. It is argued that the reformer's view of marriage (or of his wife, specifically) is not cold and utilitarian as has sometimes been suggested,[13] but that his wider and controlling consideration is the overall good of the Church to which both he and his wife are called by divine grace.

Chapter 3 is an examination of Calvin's prefatory letter to Francis I, King of France, which he penned for his first edition of the *Institutes*, but perhaps surprisingly retained in every further edition—even long after Francis' death. Against secondary literature that appears to define the purpose of the *Institutes* by that letter, this chapter argues that the letter may have been retained in subsequent editions in order to demonstrate and to underline the Church's continued perseverance against the troublesome persecution in France. By grace, the Church remains though the king's existence is short-lived.

Chapter 4 discusses, against some current innovative ecumenical interpretation, the reformer's response to the Catholic Cardinal Sadoleto. It shows that the theological differences between the two scholars are both real and substantial, precluding the possibility that emphases in language and rhetoric are the main differences. Against the Cardinal's continual rhetoric of fear directed towards the Genevan leaders and population, Calvin presents the gospel of the God of grace and of Jesus Christ, revealed in his Word and preached by the Reformed leadership.

---

[11] See footnote 7 above.

[12] Letter to Viret, April 7, 1549, Calvin, *Letters*, 2.216. For the most part, throughout this present volume I am employing John Calvin, *Letters*, 4 volumes (edited by Jules Bonnet; translated by Marcus R. Gilchrist; Philadelphia: Presbyterian Board, 1858). See, also, John Calvin, *Lettres françaises*, 2 volumes (edited by Jules Bonnet; Paris: Meyrueis, 1854) and *Ioannis Calvini Opera quae supersunt omnia* [CO] (Corpus Reformatorum: Brunswick: Schwetschke et Filium, 1863–1900).

[13] See, for example, the absurd conclusion of R.H. Bainton, *Women of the Reformation* (Boston: Beacon, 1974), 87, that Calvin might as well have married a plank!

Chapter 5 considers the reformer's letters regarding the unfortunate heretic, Michael Servetus, and asks why Calvin acted as he did in this tragic occurrence. Whilst fully accepting the reformer's part in the event, this essay argues that there were several 'reasons' for his response, but that most importantly he had the spiritual welfare of his own Reformed congregation at heart.

Chapter 6 investigates Calvin's letters on his own grief and grieving, and those to others who similarly grieve the loss of loved ones. Some secondary literature suggests that Calvin urges grieving people to consider divine providence and thus to stop lamenting and to 'get on with it,' as it were. We discover that this reading of Calvin cannot be sustained in light of his pastoral correspondence on the subject.

Chapter 7 examines Calvin's involvement with those who wait in prison for execution for their faith, those he terms and, indeed, defines as 'martyrs'. What hope does he offer to those facing death? I argue that he places an *experience* of God in the very centre of his counselling, together with the important reminder that those who wait in this way are surrounded and upheld by a Reformed community in prayer. Calvin struggles with his own empathy, but offers hope for those who wait on the Lord.

In a helpful essay on the realism of Calvin's theology, John Leith suggests nine characteristics of the reformer's theology that contribute to its realism.[14] In brief, he suggests the following:

1) the rejection of vain speculation;
2) theology's purpose is to edify, not to satisfy idle curiosity;
3) Calvin's biblical interpretation had a 'hard-nosed sense for what was real';[15]
4) theology deals with the concrete realities of life in the language of ordinary human experience;
5) 'simplicity' describes Calvin the person, as well as his theology;
6) the reformer's willingness to face difficulties;
7) Calvin's work has an emphasis on sanctification;
8) Calvin's theology authentically reflects the reformer's faith;
9) the reformer's theological doctrines correspond to reality.

In reading the reformer's letters it becomes very clear that the same characteristics that permeate his theological writing pervade his correspondence, too—some of them, more emphatically than others, of course. Nonetheless, this fact betrays the consistency of his thinking and practice.

---

[14] John Leith, 'Calvin's Theological Realism and the Lasting Influence of his Theology' in D. Willis and M. Welker (eds), *Toward the Future of Reformed Theology* (Grand Rapids: Eerdmans, 1999), 339-45.

[15] Leith, 'Calvin's Theological Realism,' 343.

We might underline, first, that his letters' purpose is so often to edify those who receive them, not to speculate in theology. So, to those suffering in prison and facing certain death by execution he speaks of experiencing God in the situation, not about the subtleties of divine providence or eschatological possibilities. Similarly, to those suffering grief he speaks with empathy of their loss and of the Lord's grace in Jesus Christ. Likewise, his letters on his own calling, on marriage, on Servetus' death rest fundamentally on theological understanding, but seek to edify those to whom he writes; to develop faith in Christ in the concrete situation.

Second, it is certainly true that we find here in Calvin's letters an express pastoral wish to deal with 'the concrete realities of human life in the language of ordinary human experience'.[16] Again, his letters to those being martyred for the Reformed faith, to those suffering the loss of loved ones, on his and others' marriage, show a down-to-earth quality about his writing and engagement with matters of human life in all its fragility and co-dependence.

Third, Calvin shows himself in his correspondence to be a person willing to face diverse difficulties. In a striking phrase, Leith remarks that 'Calvin was vividly aware of the evidences of damnation in the world.'[17] This is never clearer than in his correspondence to those in grief and those facing death in prison. It is there, too, when he writes of Servetus' heresy and, as he sees it, his utter foolishness. His willingness to face difficulties, however, is probably best seen in his readiness to expose his own weaknesses, his own grief and failings, in his letters.

Fourth, Leith is correct in stating that Calvin's theology has an emphasis on the transformation of human beings and the Church. He says the following at length:

> This emphasis upon edification can be carried forward in Calvin's insistence upon the transformation of human life to correspond to the image of God. For Calvin the Christian life is not simply being, not simply believing, but also doing. Theology has as its purpose the transformation of human life so that persons who once lived in fear now live in confidence in God, so that persons who once lived aimlessly now understand their lives as a fulfilment of the purposes of God, so that people who once took what they could from society now seek to live in such a way that human life shall be enhanced to the glory of God.[18]

This, above all, perhaps, is what we glean from Calvin's letters, his continual pastoral drive to encourage others toward Christian piety, 'upon the transformation of human life to correspond to the image of God'. Whether in the more immediately practical situations of wedlock, of grief or the terrible anticipation of death, or whether in the longer 'political' letters to King Francis I of France

---

[16] Leith, 'Calvin's Theological Realism,' 343.
[17] Leith, 'Calvin's Theological Realism,' 344.
[18] Leith, 'Calvin's Theological Realism,' 344.

Introduction: John Calvin's letters

or Cardinal Sadoleto, we discern the reformer's default drive toward transformation, toward godliness and, ultimately, toward the glorifying of the Lord.

Incidentally, one of the underlying themes of the present volume is that Calvin's theology is reflected in and undergirds his letters. That John Calvin's theology has contemporary significance is hardly in doubt.[19] His relevance, then, permeates his correspondence. We need to read Calvin's letters with a realistic perspective, not seeking to deride him, nor attempting to champion him without reason. An authentic reading will help us discern the man, the theologian and the pastor afresh.

---

[19] See, for example, Hans-Joachim Kraus, 'The Contemporary Relevance of Calvin's Theology' in Willis and Welker, *Toward the Future of Reformed Theology*, 323-38; Brian A. Gerrish, 'Sovereign Grace. Is Reformed Theology Obsolete?' *Interpretation* 57 (2003), 45-57.

CHAPTER 1

'May the Lord overrule it for good.'[1]
Calvin's letters on his calling and return

It is sometimes said, or at least implied, that John Calvin hated Geneva and that he dreaded the possibility of a return there after being expelled from the city with his friend and colleague William Farel, between April 23 1538[2] and September 2 1541. This chapter briefly examines this assumption, demonstrating that it is, in fact, only partially true, and that there is more than that going on in the situation. It is clear that the reformer did indeed dread his return to Geneva, but it was both the troubles he envisaged upon the resumption of his ministry there and also what he considered to be a call to an overwhelming amount of pastoral and administrative work, coupled with his own sense of inadequacy or insufficiency for the task that concerned him. As it turned out, both of these concerns proved to be more real than imagined, particularly in the light of his subsequent issues with prolonged ill-health.

Preliminaries

Two important matters might be addressed as background to the present examination: first, the importance and centrality of the city of Geneva—that is, its importance in its own right, its centrality for the work and expansion of the Reformation—and, second, the reformer's almost obsessional sense of his own calling.[3] As we will see, both of these greatly influenced Calvin's response to his recall to minister in Geneva.

The city of Geneva

First, then, we might consider Geneva as an important city. Cities, generally, were of vital importance to the Reformation; in each generation the movement

---

[1] To Farel, September 16, 1541; Calvin, *Letters*, 1.284. For the most part, throughout this present volume I am employing John Calvin, *Letters*, 4 volumes (edited by Jules Bonnet; translated by Marcus R. Gilchrist; Philadelphia: Presbyterian Board, 1858). See, also, John Calvin, *Lettres françaises*, 2 volumes (edited by Jules Bonnet; Paris: Meyrueis, 1854) and *Ioannis Calvini Opera quae supersunt omnia* [CO] (Corpus Reformatorum: Brunswick: Schwetschke et Filium, 1863–1900).

[2] Calvin and Farel's expulsion was confirmed on May 26 1538.

[3] Bernard Cottret, *Calvin. A Biography* (Grand Rapids: Eerdmans / Edinburgh: T&T Clark, 2000), 154, understandably speaks of Calvin's 'obsession with calling'.

was, of course, essentially an urban phenomenon.[4] Geneva, itself, became central to both the Reformation—particularly in its second generation[5]—and within that to John Calvin's own reforming career. McGrath reflects on the closeness of this relationship when he writes that to 'speak of Calvin is to speak of Geneva'. Explaining, he continues, 'Calvin would shape, and be shaped by, Geneva. The interaction of this man and his adopted city is one of the great symbiotic relationships in history.'[6] Apparently called through the insistence of the early reformer, William Farel,[7] in 1536 as 'Doctor' or 'Reader of Holy Scriptures' the reformer remained for most of his life (with the exception of the three years' expulsion) ministering the Scriptures on an almost daily basis in (what was for him) the foreign city of Geneva.[8] Therefore, as with all the major reformers of the period, Calvin was and remained essentially an urban reformer; committed to the city of Geneva.[9]

Alister McGrath embraces a very broad view in answer to the question of why cities were so significant for the Reformation. He argues that the Refor-

---

[4] B. Moeller, 'What was Preached in German Towns in the Early Reformation?' in C.S. Dixon (ed.), *The German Reformation* (Oxford: Blackwell, 1999), 36. See, also, B. Moeller, *Imperial Cities and the Reformation* (Philadelphia: Fortress, 1972); O. Chadwick, *The Early Reformation on the Continent* (Oxford: Oxford University Press, 2001), 82; Andrew Pettegree (ed.), *The Reformation of the Parishes: The Ministry and the Reformation in Town and Country* (Manchester: Manchester University Press, 1993); P. Collinson, 'The Late Medieval Church and its Reformation (1400-1600)' in J. McManners (ed.), *The Oxford History of Christianity* (Oxford: Oxford University Press, 1993), 243-76, particularly, 271-72; W.P. Te Brake, *Shaping History. Ordinary People in European Politics, 1500–1700* (Berkeley: University of California Press, 1998), 35-44; Scott Hendrix, *Recultivating the Vineyard. The Reformation Agendas of Christianization* (Louisville: Westminster John Knox, 2004), 69-96.

[5] See R.M. Kingdon, 'International Calvinism' in T.A. Brady, H.A. Oberman and J.D. Tracy (eds), *Handbook of European History 1400–1600. Late Middle Ages, Renaissance and Reformation* (Leiden: Brill, 1995), particularly, 229-36.

[6] A.E. McGrath, *A Life of John Calvin. A Study in the Shaping of Western Culture* (Oxford: Blackwell, 1993), 79. See, also, Susanne Selinger, *Calvin Against Himself* (Hamden: Archon, 1984), 88-91; Hendrix, *Recultivating the Vineyard*, 86-96.

[7] It should be remembered, though, that, according to Farel himself, Calvin was constrained 'by many'—see David N. Wiley, 'Calvin's Friendship with Guillaume Farel' in David Foxgrover (ed.), *Calvin Studies Society Papers 1995, 1997* (Grand Rapids: Calvin Studies Society, 1998), 191. See, also, Calvin's letter to Francis Daniel, Lausanne, October 13, 1536; Calvin, *Letters*, 1.44-45, in which he speaks of 'the brethren' (plural) detaining him at Geneva.

[8] An important essay puts this into a significantly wider context: Robert R. Vosloo, 'The Displaced Calvin: "Refugee Reality" as a Lens to Re-Examine Calvin's Life, Theology and Legacy,' *Religion and Theology* 16.1/2 (2009), 35-52. See, also, Alister E. McGrath, *In the Beginning* (New York: Anchor, 2002), 107-14, on the subject of refugees in Geneva at the time of Calvin.

[9] H.O. Old, *The Reading and Preaching of the Scriptures in the Worship of the Church* (Grand Rapids: Eerdmans, 2002), 4.113.

mation in the cities appears to have been a response to some form of popular pressure for change—a change in which he discerns religious, social, economic and political grievances, together with a number of historical contingencies, such as political relationships with other cities and trading relations.[10] His realistic (though, admittedly, rather global) conclusion positions the reformer's place within the movement as follows:

> The reformer, by presenting a coherent vision of the Christian gospel and its implications for the religious, social and political structures and practices of a city, was able to prevent a potentially revolutionary situation from degenerating into chaos. . . . Someone had to give religious direction to a movement which, unchecked and lacking direction, might fall into disorder, with momentous and unacceptable consequences for the existing power structures of the city, and the individuals who controlled them.[11]

McGrath's option has the advantage of realistically involving *every* area of the city's life, without unnecessarily prioritizing one in particular, and of discerning the reformer's position in the very centre of the tension of the social and historical situation—a centre that Calvin, unfortunately, found terribly troublesome.[12]

Geneva, itself, if only superficially, adopted the Reformation before Calvin arrived, at the age of twenty-six or twenty-seven. The city already had newly minted coins with reformational mottoes on both sides: '*Post tenebras lux*' ('After darkness, light') and '*Deus noster pugnat pro nobis*' ('Our God fights for us').[13] It appears that the reforming work in that city began as anticlerical revolution,[14] and was well under way before Calvin came in 1536.[15] However,

---

[10] McGrath, *A Life of John Calvin*, 83. See 80-84. See, also, B. Hall, 'The Reformation City', *Bulletin of the John Rylands Library* (1971/72), 103-48; Collinson, 'The Late Medieval Church,' 271-72; Carter Lindberg, *The European Reformations* (Oxford: Blackwell, 1996), 35.

[11] McGrath, *A Life of John Calvin*, 85.

[12] See W.G. Naphy, 'Calvin's Geneva' in D.K. McKim (ed.), *The Cambridge Companion to John Calvin* (Cambridge: Cambridge University Press, 2004), 25-37.

[13] F. Bonivard, *Advis et devis de l'ancienne et nouvelle police de Genève* (Geneva: J.G. Fick, 1865), 135.

[14] See C.M.N. Eire, 'Antisacerdotalism and the Young Calvin' in P.A. Dykema and H.A. Oberman (eds), *Anticlericalism in the Late Medieval and Early Modern Europe* (Leiden: Brill, 1994), 583-603.

[15] See D.W. Hall, *The Genevan Reformation and the American Founding* (New York: Lexington, 2003), chapters 2 and 3. Also, J. Rilliet, *Le vrai visage de Calvin* (Toulouse: Pensée/Privat, 1982), 57-59; H. Naef, *Les Origines de la Réforme à Genève* (Geneva: La Société d'Histoire et d'Archéologie de Genève, 1936); A. Roget, *Histoire du Peuple de Genève depuis la Réforme jusqu'a l'escalade* (Nieuwkoop: B. de Graaf, 1976), vol. 1; R.M. Kingdon, 'Was the Protestant Reformation a Revolution? The Case of Geneva' in R.M. Kingdon (ed.), *Transition and Revolution: Problems and Issues of European Renaissance and Reformation History* (Minneapolis: Burgess, 1974), 53-107; William J. Bouwsma, *John Calvin. A Sixteenth Century Portrait* (New York: Oxford University Press, 1988), 19.

because of the anticlericalism that gave it impetus at its inception (that is, before Calvin's entry into the city) Wallace is understandably cynical of its depth, being of the opinion that 'Geneva had reformed in name but not entirely in heart.' His critique is that 'many of its citizens . . . wanted rather freedom from the restraints of the old regime than the guidance of the Word of God'. Thomas Lambert, in his doctoral dissertation, concludes similarly that the reform in Geneva was not as perfect or absolute as it is sometimes reputed to have been.[16] David Chidester writes that Calvin found that the city was reformed 'only to the extent that the council had formally adopted a policy of iconoclasm'.[17] And it was always this religious and social discrepancy and resultant tension that Calvin felt so acutely.

It is well documented that John Calvin had no real wish to come to or to stay in the city of Geneva.[18] As mentioned above, initially, he had to be constrained by Farel's forceful intimidation and that of others,[19] though as an exile he went to Geneva of his own free choice (*in exilum voluntarium*), of course. Some few years later, when the reformer had been called to return after his brief and humiliating expulsion, Calvin intimated in personal correspondence that he dreaded the thought of going again into that arena. We will turn to that more thoroughly below. Between his return in 1541 to his death over twenty years later, in 1564, the reformer certainly did not have it all his own way.[20] In fact, most commentators suggest 1555 as pivotal, as the year in which the reformer began to have some sort of peace in and with the city, though he became a citizen somewhat later.[21] It was at that crucial point (the year 1555) that Calvin had at least some support from the Council. Lester De Koster reminds us that 'It was safer thereafter, less physically threatening, but no less strenuous.' Perhaps, as

---

[16] R.S. Wallace, *Calvin, Geneva, and the Reformation. A Study of Calvin as Social Reformer, Churchman, Pastor and Theologian* (Edinburgh: Scottish Academic, 1988), 15; T. Lambert, 'Preaching, Praying and Policing the Reform in Sixteenth-Century Geneva' (unpublished doctoral dissertation, University of Wisconsin-Madison, 1998), 526, cited by Karen Spierling, *Infant Baptism in Reformation Geneva. The Shaping of a Community, 1536–1564* (Aldershot: Ashgate, 2005), 27n.68.

[17] David Chidester, *Christianity. A Global History* (London: Penguin, 2000), 351.

[18] This may have been reciprocal, of course. T. George, *Theology of the Reformers* (Nashville: Broadman, 1988), 180, points out that the first mention of Calvin in the city's records is as 'Ille Gallus'—'that Frenchman'. See, also, D. Crouzet, *Jean Calvin: Vies parallèles* (Paris: Fayard, 2000), 15.

[19] See A. Ganoczy, *The Young Calvin* (Edinburgh: T&T Clark, 1988), 106-109.

[20] Michael Mullett, *Calvin* (London: Routledge, 1989), 38. See, also, N.R. Needham, *2000 Years of Christ's Power*; Part 3 'Renaissance and Reformation' (London: Grace Publications, 2004), 224-27.

[21] See, for example, M.J. Larson, 'John Calvin and Genevan Presbyterianism,' *Westminster Theological Journal* 60 (1998), 43-69; McGrath, *A Life of John Calvin*, 125; P.G. Wallace, *The Long European Reformation. Religion, Political Conflict, and the Search for Conformity, 1350–1750* (Basingstoke: Palgrave MacMillan, 2004), 104-105.

he puts it somewhat colloquially, 'The Word was given more elbow-room to work.'[22]

Apart from the personal problems that Calvin faced as almost intolerable there were numerous social pressures within Geneva's historical circumstances. These, generally, are well enough known. In his brief summary, Kearsley speaks of the 'claustrophobic and xenophobic atmosphere of a city which lived only on the knife-edge of Christian freedom', and of 'Geneva and its unruly crosswinds'.[23] He further writes concerning tensions between clerical and secular powers, citizens and non-citizens, native Genevans and, what he terms, incomers.[24] Karen Spierling speaks of the complexity of Genevan society and loyalties, making the point that they clashed outright when, for example, 'native Genevans resisted and fought against the growing power of the ministers and the Reformed Church in the 1540s and 1550s'.[25] Neither was Geneva an exception to the violence that permeated sixteenth century European society— civil and familial, political and domestic.[26] Together with this, Robert Kingdon speaks of extreme overcrowding in the city. He says that Genevan overcrowding was 'even greater than in most cities of the time', which must have made things a great deal worse.[27] Bernard Cottret adds to this impression, saying that Geneva was 'in the true sense a city of refuge, to which flowed the unsatisfied, the insatiable, the lovers of Jesus Christ, desiring of building an ideal Christian society, still inaccessible fifteen centuries after the preaching of Jesus Christ'.[28] We need to remember this context in considering the reformer's comments on his calling and his reticence to serve the city.

The city of Geneva, then, was important as it developed into a Reformed centre in Europe. Cornelis Augustijn, in arguing for Strasbourg as a model for

---

[22] Lester de Koster, *Light for the City. Calvin's Preaching, Source of Life and Liberty* (Grand Rapids: Eerdmans, 2004), 15.

[23] R. Kearsley, 'Calvin and the Power of the Elder: A Case of the Rogue Hermeneutic' in A.N.S. Lane (ed.), *Interpreting the Bible. Historical and Theological Studies in Honour of David F. Wright* (Leicester: Apollos, 1997), 125, 129, respectively. Also, T.H.L. Parker, *John Calvin. A Biography* (London: Dent, 1975), 51-66; A. Biéler, *La Pensée Economique et Sociale de Calvin* (Geneva: Librairie de l'Université, 1959), 138-79; S. Ozment, *The Age of Reform 1250-1550. An Intellectual and Religious History of Late Medieval and Reformation Europe* (New Haven: Yale University, 1980), 358-62.

[24] Kearsley, 'Calvin and the Power of the Elder,' 122.

[25] Karen Spierling, *Infant Baptism*, 17.

[26] On this subject, see D. Kagay and L.J.A. Villalon (eds), *Final Argument: The Imprint of Violence on Society in Medieval and Early Modern Europe* (Woodbridge: Boydell, 1998); J.R. Ruff, *Violence in Early Modern Europe 1500–1800* (Cambridge: Cambridge University Press, 2001). See, also, the fascinating essay, William G. Naphy, 'Baptism, Church Riots and Social Unrest in Calvin's Geneva', *Sixteenth Century Journal* 26 (1995), 87-97.

[27] R.M. Kingdon, *Adultery and Divorce in Calvin's Geneva* (Cambridge: Harvard University Press, 1995), 96.

[28] Cottret, *Calvin*, 109.

the later Geneva, lists, 'the mediating role played by Geneva between both Reformed and Lutheran churches and theology; Geneva as a center for refugees, as a center for the establishment and development of the French Church . . . ; the University; [and] the diplomatic threads that met in Geneva'.[29]

Calvin's doctrine of calling

Second, by way of introduction, we need to consider Calvin's doctrine of *vocatio*. The concept of calling (vocation, *vocatio*) in the sixteenth century was a significant, practical and, in some ways, a defining idea. For example, in Luther's teaching on vocation he stresses the horizontal relationship and its divinely-given utilitarian purpose of maintaining peace and harmony in the community. For him, *vocatio* is the particularization of God's broader temporal government in the life of an individual. Calvin's idea of *vocatio*[30] is similar in its out-working, but it seems to stem more naturally from the concept of God's initial spiritual calling of the person to faith in Jesus Christ. It appears, therefore, most often employed with reference to the divine choosing of the elect. Indeed, Alister McGrath emphasizes that Calvin's view of social *vocatio* is that it is inherently entailed in God's election to salvation. In Calvin's theology, then, *vocatio* 'expresses primarily the fact that an individual has been elected by God, and only secondarily the worldly vocation (*un vocation juste et approuvée*) in which this calling finds expression'.[31]

An integral link between divine election to spiritual life in Christ and vocation as the outworking of that life in society is established by Calvin: '[I]t is one proof that we have been really elected,' he says, 'if a good conscience and integrity of life *correspond with* our profession of faith.'[32] This is seen most clearly worked out in the *Institutes*, for example.[33] Calvin stresses that the object of regeneration in believers is to confirm their adoption by living 'a rightly ordered life'. In the next two chapters of his major work, Calvin spells out that this pattern for the conduct of life (*Rationem vitae formande*) is to be modelled on God, himself. Later, the reformer comes to the point at which he emphasizes

---

[29] Cornelis Augustijn, 'Calvin in Strasbourg' in Wilhelm H. Neuser (ed.), *Calvinus Sacrae Scripturae Professor. Calvin as Confessor of Holy Scripture* (Grand Rapids: Eerdmans, 1994), 169.

[30] Generally, see, for example, Michael L. Monheit, '"The ambition for an illustrious name". Humanism, Patronage, and Calvin's Doctrine of the Calling,' *Sixteenth Century Journal* 23.2 (1992), 267-87.

[31] McGrath, *A Life of John Calvin*, 251-52. See, also, G. Harkness, *John Calvin: The Man and his Ethics* (Abingdon, New York, 1981), chapters 8-10; *Inst.* 3.9.4 (OS 4.173). Also, G.D. Badcock, *The Way of Life: A Theology of Christian Vocation* (Grand Rapids: Eerdmans, 1998), 55-56.

[32] *Comm. 2 Pet.* 1.10 (CO 55.449), emphasis added. Calvin says that the apostle 'uses "calling" here in the sense of result or evidence of election'. See, also, *Inst.* 3.14.19-20 (OS 4.237-38), 3.17.1, 4-5 (OS 4.253-54, 4.256-58), 3.24.4 (OS 4.4.414-15); *Comm. Matt.* 25.24 (CO 45.570).

[33] *Inst.* 3.6.1 (OS 4.146-47).

that the Christian's life is to be a reflection of the spiritual calling they have received:

> [God] has appointed duties for every man [sic] in his particular way of life. And that no-one may thoughtlessly transgress his limits, he has named these various kinds of living "callings".[34]

As a result of divinely-constituted duties Calvin remarks, '[N]o task will be so sordid and base, provided you obey your calling in it, that it will not shine and be reckoned very precious in God's sight.'[35] Calvin's definition of 'calling' or 'vocation' is revealing: 'We call vocation the duty to which God binds us.'[36] Elsewhere, he speaks of vocation as 'a lawful mode of life'.[37] It is apparent that a sense of duty pervades his understanding. There is clearly, then, a twofold emphasis that seems to underline his thought. The first emphasis is that vocation is a duty for people to perform; the second is that vocation is that to which God 'binds' people, both men and women. He says,

> The Lord bids each one of us in all life's actions to look to his calling. For he knows with what great restlessness human nature flames, with what fickleness it is borne hither and thither, how its ambition longs to embrace various things at once.... Therefore, each individual has his own kind of living assigned to him by the Lord *as a sort of sentry post so that he may not heedlessly wander about throughout life.*[38]

Two important points are worth underlining here. First, Calvin is aware of humanity's sinfulness that tends towards individual and, subsequently, social and civil instability. Human nature 'flames' with 'great restlessness'. He says that it is fickle and ambitious. Second, God has appointed vocations to keep each person under control and within limits: men and women must not overstep the boundary lines (the 'limits') of their particular vocation. Consequently, one of the reformer's constant applications is that everyone must persevere within the calling given to them by God.[39] So, on preaching about the story of the ill-fated Uzzah reaching out to steady the ark of God and his subsequent death, for example, he applies the particular situation in a general principle (as he almost invariably does, of course): 'Let us note that we must undertake nothing outside of our vocation. For what might seem a virtue to us will be considered vice before God *if we go beyond our limits*'.[40]

---

[34] *Inst.* 3.10.6 (OS 4.181).
[35] *Inst.* 3.10.6 (OS 4.181). This is reminiscent of Luther's view of mundane tasks. See, for example, *LW* 45.39-41 (*WA* 10².295-97).
[36] *Serm. 2 Sam.* 6:6-12. See *Sermons on 2 Samuel, chapters 1-13* (translated by Douglas Kelly; Edinburgh: Banner of Truth, 1992), 246—hereafter, Kelly.
[37] 'vocatio in scripturis est legitima vivendi ratio,' *Comm. 1 Cor.* 7.20 (CO 49.415).
[38] *Inst.* 3.10.6 (OS 4.180-81), emphasis added.
[39] See, for example, *Serm. 2 Sam.* 5.6-12 (Kelly, 198); *Comm. Col.* 3.18 (CO 52.125).
[40] *Serm. 2 Sam.* 6.1-12 (Kelly, 246), emphasis added. See on this difficult passage, Michael Parsons, '"Let us not . . . call God to account." John Calvin's reading of some

Calvin concludes that pride is at the centre of people going beyond their vocation. He exhorts his congregation,

> In sum, *let us be modest enough* to pay attention to that to which God calls us, which he strictly requires from us and which belongs to our office. Let everyone openly devote himself to it, so that we will not go beyond our boundaries *like wild horses.*[41]

We must foster modesty and humility (*modestia et humilitate*)[42] and we must live in moderation (*moderatio*) within our calling. This is part of what we might call the inner boundary, the self-imposed restrictions of a believer within their vocation. There are external boundaries, as well, of course, such as the implied threat of the judgement—an implication from which Calvin does not shy away. In his sermons on Job, for example, we find Calvin persuading people to persevere in following their vocation and he adds, significantly, that in so doing everyone would glorify God, 'the great Lord and Master, who is the common Judge of all (*qui est le Iuge common de tous*)'.[43]

In subsequent sections, we need, then, to keep in mind that the city from which the reformer is expelled and to which he is recalled was considered significant both in its own right and in the wider cause of the gospel. We also need to remember that as Calvin considers his recall it is within the context of his acute understanding of his former, initial call to ministry in Geneva – a call defined by duty and divine constraint; a call requiring of the reformer modesty and humility, obedience and perseverance.

Calvin's letters on his return to Geneva

Somewhat superficially we might say that William Farel and John Calvin were expelled from the city of Geneva because of differences of opinion on the subject of excommunication and the ministers' refusal to administer communion on Easter day, 1538. But there was much more going on, of course, as Bernard Cottret suggests in his helpful treatment of the situation. For example, he says, 'That a Frenchman, and therefore a foreigner, could arrogate to himself the right to excommunicate respectable Genevans seemed highly presumptuous.'[44] His removal to Basel and then to Strasbourg gave Calvin time to think and his

---

difficult deaths' in Michael Parsons (ed.), *Aspects of Reforming. Theology and Practice in Sixteenth Century Europe* (Milton Keynes: Paternoster, 2013), particularly 208-13.

[41] *Serm. 2 Sam.* 6.1-12 (Kelly, 246), emphases added. See, also, *Comm. Ps.* 127 (CO 32.322).

[42] See *Catechismus Ecclesiae Genevensis* (OS 2.104).

[43] *Serm. Job* 31.9-15 (CO 34.660).

[44] Cottret, *Calvin*, 130. See, also, Herman J. Selderhuis, *John Calvin. A Pilgrim's Life* (Downers Grove: IVP, 2009), 83-84; Lindberg, *The European Reformations*, 257.

thoughts are captured in a few significant letters and in dispersed comments over the next few years.

As early as May (1538) Calvin and Farel accompanied a disputation, charged to entreat for their return to Geneva. Two months later, in July, it was resolved to call an assembly in which pastors of the Reformed churches of Zurich, Bern, Basel, Strasbourg and Geneva would inquire about the circumstances of their dismissal. Calvin was hoping that this same assembly would declare 'that we have duly and faithfully administered our charge, to the end that such a testimony may stand as a lawful judgement'[45] against those who malign the reformers.

By August Calvin wrote to Farel commenting on the divisions in Geneva, caused partly by the fact that the nomination of their successors was approved only by a part, not the whole, of the church. Together with this, these new ministers appear to have thought it best for their own ministry if they 'tear in pieces our estimation, publicly and privately,' as Calvin puts it. He calls upon both himself and his friend Farel to humble themselves and to 'wait upon God' and his good timing.[46]

By September 1538 Calvin had had time to think about his dismissal and to come to a more considered opinion, perhaps. He wrote, again to Farel, saying that Martin Bucer had corresponded with the Genevans about reconciliation with the reformers. The magistrates appear to have wanted Calvin to admit his part in the fracture of relations; perhaps to admit the primary part in the breakdown. On his part, Calvin is willing only to acknowledge the following: '[I]t is in some measure owing to our unskilfulness, indolence, negligence, and error, that the Church *committed to our care* has fallen into such a sad state of collapse.' However, he continues, '[B]ut it is also our duty to assert our innocence and our purity against those who, by their fraud, malignity, knavery, and wickedness, have assuredly brought about this ruin.' He refuses to have fixed upon him 'the smallest particle of blame',[47] by which, in the context, he appears to mean as the material cause of the rift. This becomes clearer when, in writing to Louis du Tillet in October, 1538, he admits again that regarding the situation his conscience accuses him of fault, of ignorance and blame, and 'peculiar faults'—that is, specific failings. 'I do not perceive the greatest of them,' he readily concedes.[48]

Calvin wrote several letters to the Genevan church and to others, most notably Farel, over a number of years. In them he remains open and naturally appears vulnerable. This section examines them and discerns important themes: calling,

---

[45] To Louis du Tillet, Strasbourg, July 10, 1538; Calvin, *Letters*, 1.72.
[46] To William Farel, Basel, August 4, 1538; Calvin, *Letters*, 1.75.
[47] To Farel, Strasbourg, September 1538; Calvin, *Letters*, 1.81. The added emphasis stresses the reformer's thought that the ministry in Geneva was committed to Calvin by God, himself.
[48] To Louis du Tillet, Strasbourg, October 20, 1538; Calvin, *Letters*, 1.95.

return, pastoral concern for the church, feelings of inadequacy and insufficiency, and so on. The next section concludes by reflecting on these themes, employing Calvin's letters over the period May 1538 to March 1542.

To the Church of Geneva, Strasbourg, October 1, 1538.[49]

Five months after his expulsion Calvin wrote a somewhat lengthy letter to the estranged church, addressing them as 'the relics of the dispersion of the Church of Geneva'—those who had remained on his departure and after divisions had begun to appear. Several important themes emerge in this, his first letter to his former pastoral charge.[50]

It is clear, first, that the reformer holds them in high esteem and affection. He addresses them as 'my dearly-beloved brethren in the Lord' and concludes with the words 'Your brother and servant in the Lord'.[51] Even allowing, as we must, for rhetoric and conventional ecclesiastical formality, it is worth remembering that the reformer does not see the *whole* church as his adversary; that much is evident. He clearly distinguishes throughout the letter between those who are against him—presently causing divisions, the church's enemies, too[52]—and those who continue in fellowship with him through the gospel. Though it may be misconstrued, Calvin is determined to assure the brethren of his love:

> I have been unable . . . to refrain from writing to you to assure you of the affection with which I do ever regard you, and my remembrance of you in the Lord, as it is my bounden duty. . . . Our whole study has been to keep you together in happy union and concord of agreement.

We note, of course, how affection and duty are bound together in vocation. He further hopes that they might keep him in their memory.[53]

Second, Calvin speaks briefly, but clearly, of his calling to the ministry of the Genevan church. He states that his own conscience before God is clear on the matter: '[I]t has been by him [God] that we have been called to the fellowship of this ministry among you.' And, significantly, given the present situation, he adds, 'For which reason it cannot be in the power of men to break asunder such a tie.'[54] Given his strong view of vocation or calling as that duty to which God binds his people, this comment seems to be saying that he believes that his call to Geneva still remains intact and unharmed, at least as far as its *divine* intention is concerned. Indeed, his affection and his continuing call

---

[49] To the Church of Geneva, Strasbourg, October 1, 1538; Calvin, *Letters*, 1.82-88.
[50] He notes, however, that William Farel had already written to them on behalf of them both.
[51] Calvin, *Letters*, 1.82 and 1.88, respectively.
[52] In the same month Calvin wrote to Louis du Tillet, calling these same enemies, 'the manifest enemies of God and of his majesty'—to Louis du Tillet, Strasbourg, October 20, 1538; Calvin, *Letters*, 1.97.
[53] Calvin, *Letters*, 1.83.
[54] Calvin, *Letters*, 1.83.

appear to undergird his writing to them. Later, Calvin suggests that insofar as he has already 'duly and faithfully' discharged his duty to the church, he is ready to do so again.[55]

Third, the reformer mentions the divisions that have disrupted the church since his dismissal, but he does so in order both to reveal something of the Lord's providential ways and to admonish the church in the situation. Concluding that Satan lies at the back of the difficulties, Calvin employs fighting imagery from Paul's letter to the Ephesians, chapter 6,[56] for example, to suggest that in reviling men they resist 'the wiles of our spiritual enemy': therefore, he advises, 'be guided solely by your zeal for the service of God, moderated by his Spirit according to the rule of his word'.[57] Again, we see clear pastoral concern shown by Calvin in this situation. Then, in a rather lengthy passage, he states that this trouble is happening to punish and to rebuke both the church *and* the reformers, Calvin and Farel: the church, he says, 'to chastise, your negligence, your contempt, or even your careless slighting of the word of God *which you had among you*' (note, the past tense); the reformers, 'to make us acknowledge our ignorance, our imprudence, and those infirmities which, for my own part, I feel in myself, and do make no difficulty in confessing before the Church of the Lord'.[58] Assuring the church that God's anger lasts for a short time only, but that his mercy is eternal, he calls for humility and submission, prayer and expectation, comfort and hope. He appears to speak to both the church and to himself:

> [God] exalts the humble and the despised, and lifts them out of the dunghill; . . . to those who are in weeping and in tears he gives a crown of joy; . . . he gives light to those who sit in darkness, and raises up to newness of life those who have dwelt in the valley of the shadow of death.[59]

There can be no doubting Calvin's earnest pastoral heart and concern for the church in Geneva, even at this early point of disjunction.

To the Church of Geneva, Strasbourg, June 25, 1539.[60]

Just over twelve months after his expulsion Calvin demonstrates that same pastoral concern again.[61] On hearing about more of the divisions within the church

---

[55] Calvin, *Letters*, 1.86.
[56] See, for example, Ephesians 6.11, 'Put on the full armour of God, so that you can take your stand against the devil's schemes' (TNIV).
[57] Calvin, *Letters*, 1.85.
[58] Calvin, *Letters*, 1.85 and 86, respectively, emphasis added.
[59] Calvin, *Letters*, 1.87.
[60] To the Church of Geneva, Strasbourg, June 25, 1539; Calvin, *letters*, 1.142-49.
[61] We should remember that only three months later Calvin was busy with his important letter to Bishop Sadoleto. He wrote this, in effect, because of his concern for the Genevan church. See his letter to Farel, September 1539; Calvin, *Letters*, 1.150-151: 'Sulzer [the minister of the church in Bern] had brought hither the epistle of Sadolet,' Calvin says. 'I was not very much concerned about an answer to it, but our friends

he writes, greatly saddened, to recommend peace. Calvin writes to help restore the church to harmony and integrity. His priority in this is that the kingdom of God may be promoted through unity and mutual respect, and there is a sense throughout of the fact that the church and the city of Geneva, itself, are struggling to maintain reformational truth and values at this tenuous time of transition.[62] 'I felt myself compelled to write to you,' Calvin states, 'that I might endeavour, so far as lay in me, to find a medicine for this disease, which without great sin against God, it was not possible for me to conceal.'[63] The medical image, though common enough, of course, is telling in this context. His spiritual and pastoral sense of compulsion is significant. 'My only object is to lead you into the right way.'[64]

Having been made aware of the rift that has formed between the new pastors and some of the church, Calvin asks them to consider the honour in which the Lord holds his servants. He outlines what he calls the accepted and established rule:

> That those who hold the office of ministers of the word, since the guidance and rule over your souls is entrusted to their care, are to be owned and acknowledged in the relation of parents, to be held in esteem, and honoured on account of that office which, by the calling of the Lord, they discharge among you.[65]

Notice the importance of the office here. It is in relation to the clerical office that these men hold that they are to be esteemed. And, significantly, Calvin makes the point that there is a reciprocal accountability between pastors and their people. He asks the church, then, to consider two important matters. First, 'that the calling of your ministers does not happen without the will of God'; and, second, 'that there may be due inspection of their regular discharge of duty, that they may fulfil the ministry of the Church'—that is, that pastors may not be able simply to stand on their calling or office as important as that is, but that a pious and dedicated life might clearly demonstrate its truth.[66]

Again, the reformer's pastoral concern for the church in Geneva is clear, even during his sustained and forced absence. He speaks of his 'kindly affec-

---

have at length compelled me. At the present moment I am entirely occupied upon it. It will be a six days' work' (151). See chapter 4 of the present volume.

[62] Calvin, *Letters*, 1.143. For example, Calvin reminds the church that they are in danger of falling back 'under the yoke of Antichrist, *from which he has once rescued you already*' (Calvin, *Letters*, 1.145), italics added. See the interesting essay by William Naphy, 'Calvin's Church in Geneva: Constructed or Gathered? Local or Foreign? French or Swiss?' in Irena Backus and Philip Benedict (eds), *Calvin and His Influence, 1509-2009* (Oxford: Oxford University Press, 2011), 102-118.

[63] Calvin, *Letters*, 1.143-44. For similar imagery, see Calvin's letter to Louis du Tillet, Strasbourg, July 10, 1538; Calvin, *Letters*, 1.72-73.

[64] Calvin, *Letters*, 1.144.

[65] Calvin, *Letters*, 1.145.

[66] Calvin, *Letters*, 1.145 and 146, respectively.

tion' towards them,[67] and entreats and admonishes them to submit to Christ as the head of the church.[68] 'In conclusion, therefore,' he writes, 'accept this admonition, if you wish me to be held by you as a brother.'

To the Syndics and Council of Geneva, Strasbourg, October 23, 1540.[69]

This short letter is a reply to letters received from the Syndics and the Council in Geneva in which they entreated the reformer to take up again the ministry of the church in the city. The reformer's concern is obvious again, but he faces a problem ('a singular perplexity'[70]): he wishes to help the church but 'cannot slightingly quit the charge or lay it down to which the Lord has called,' by which he presumably refers to his work in Strasbourg and beyond.[71] He underlines this thought:

> [W]hen our Lord appoints a man as pastor in a church to teach in his word, he ought to consider himself as engaged to take upon himself the government of it, so that he may not lightly withdraw from it without the settled assurance in his own heart, and the testimony of the faithful, that the Lord has discharged him.[72]

Earlier, he had spoken of this combination of internal and external call as the 'regular and lawful means' which God employs in such situations.[73] To alleviate the church's present troubles Calvin advises them to call Peter Viret to a temporary ministry amongst them, assuring them that he himself will do his utmost to serve the church 'so far as God permits'.[74]

To Farel, Strasbourg, October 27, 1540.[75]

Four days after the previous letter Calvin wrote to his friend Farel, having considered the request to return to minister in Geneva and clearly having been greatly troubled by it. He speaks of being 'scarcely half myself' for two days, given the perplexity that the invitation had caused in him.[76] He speaks in depressing terms concerning Geneva: 'Whenever I call to mind the state of wretchedness in which my life was spent when there, how can it be otherwise but that my very soul must shudder when any proposal is made for my re-

---

[67] Calvin, *Letters*, 1.146.
[68] Calvin, *Letters*, 1.148.
[69] To the Syndics and Council of Geneva, Strasbourg, October 23, 1540; Calvin, *Letters*, 1.208-209. According to the editor (1.208n.2) this letter was directed to 'the Magnificent and Honourable Lords Messieurs the Syndics and Council of Geneva'. He reminds us that of the four Syndics who pronounced the expulsion of Calvin and Farel, two were exiled to Bern and two had perished by a violent death.
[70] Calvin, *Letters*, 1.209.
[71] Calvin, *Letters*, 1.209.
[72] Calvin, *Letters*, 1.209.
[73] See, also, *Inst.* 4.3.7 (OS 5.49-50), and, particularly, *Inst.* 4.3.10-16 (OS 5.51-57).
[74] Calvin, *Letters*, 210.
[75] To Farel, Strasbourg, October 27, 1540; Calvin, *Letters*, 1.210-14.
[76] Calvin, *Letters*, 1.210.

turn?'[77] He admits that if he is to live for Christ then the world must become a scene of 'trial and vexation . . . the field of conflict'. However, his memory of Geneva suggests that it exceeded even that. With graphic imagery he compares it to torturing his soul on the rack, concluding, 'I dread that place as having about it somewhat of a fatality in my case.'[78] He brings Farel (and, indeed, God, himself) in as witness

> that I dared not to throw off the yoke of my calling, which I was well assured had been laid upon me by the Lord. So long, therefore, as I was thus bound hand and foot, I preferred to suffer even to the utmost extremity, than for one moment to entertain those thoughts that were apt to arise in my mind of changing my place of abode.[79]

No-one, he says, would excuse him if he refused to return to such a place. What we have here, then, is a minister of the Word who is wrestling between the extreme poles of his divine calling to ministry ('the yoke of my calling'; 'bound hand and foot') and his very human experience of ministerial hardship and distress ('the utmost extremity'). Given the difficult, but liberating, circumstances of his departure, that much is understandable, of course.

However, we should notice that the letter takes a significant turn at this point, a turn in which Calvin shows a pastoral vulnerability which has been common amongst sensitive ministers throughout history, even to today. He asks a number of significant, probing and poignant questions in this regard: '[H]ow can I have any reasonable expectation that my ministry can be of any use to them?' '[H]ow shall I ever be able to restrain and keep within due bounds so great a multitude?' What if they are only recalling him to avoid becoming a laughing-stock; not out of any regard for the reformer, himself?[80] In Strasbourg, Calvin says, he takes the oversight of only a few,[81] compared with what he terms 'the multitude' in Geneva.[82] Having been out of that context for some time, he says he has lost 'the arts' required for guiding a large number of people. There is definitely, then, a growing sense of a feeling of inadequacy, of insufficiency in the reformer's words. Though, as he sees it, the basic trouble arose from the Genevans, he asks whether his own ministry was really adequate to the task. And in this questioning reticence there is recognition of shared culpability, perhaps.

Not trusting in his own reasoning in this situation, he calls on others—specifically, Farel, Bucer, Capito—to help him. His conclusion, though, is ad-

---

[77] Calvin, *Letters*, 1.211.
[78] Calvin, *Letters*, 1.211.
[79] Calvin, *Letters*, 1.211.
[80] Calvin, *Letters*, 1.212, 1.213, respectively. In his letter to Farel, Worms, November 13, 1540; Calvin, *Letters*, 1.218, the reformer simply asks, '[W]hat is there in me to recommend me?'
[81] Calvin admits that he finds it difficult enough to oversee a few teachable people in Strasbourg— Calvin, *Letters*, 1.212.
[82] On overcrowding in Geneva, see Kingdon, *Adultery and Divorce*, 96.

amant: 'It is my desire that the Church of Geneva may not be left destitute; therefore, I would rather venture my life a hundred times over than betray her by my desertion.'[83] We note, in passing, that he speaks here of 'desertion' when in reality he refers to his continued forced absence.

To the Syndics and Council of Geneva, Worms, November 12, 1540.

This short letter[84] begins with affirmation of both the reformer's vocational duty towards and pastoral love for the church in Geneva:

> It is the special love which I bear to your Church, having always in remembrance that she has been formerly recommended to my care and intrusted to my oversight by God, and on that account I am for ever obliged to seek her welfare and prosperity.[85]

However, having said that, the reformer tells them that he is going to be necessarily delayed from returning. He is needed to attend a diet, for the good of the churches more generally. Nevertheless, he continues,

> I assure you, that in every manner of way that it shall be possible to employ me to help your Church in her time of need, I will therein do my duty, just the same as if I had already accepted the charge to which you have called me—exactly as though I was already in the midst of you doing the office of pastor.[86]

There is in this letter, perhaps, a sense of defensiveness about the reformer's words. The Genevan authorities have recalled him to his former position, but Calvin appears to be delaying that return. He assures them that it is for a good and genuine reason, that his primary duty is towards them, that ultimately his calling is to the ministry in Geneva, and that his 'heart and mind, [his] whole

---

[83] Calvin, *Letters*, 1.213.
[84] To the Syndics and Council of Geneva, Worms, November 12, 1540; Calvin, *Letters*, 1.214-17. The present letter is Calvin's response to the following correspondence from Geneva:

> 'To Doctor Calvin, Minister of the Gospel. Monsieur, our good brother and special friend, We commend ourselves affectionately unto you, for that we are thoroughly informed that you have no other desire than the growth and advancement of the glory and honour of God, and of his sacred and holy word. On the part of our lesser, great and general councils (which hereupon have strongly admonished us) we pray you very earnestly that you would transfer yourself hitherward to us, and return to your old place and former ministry; and we hope, with the help of God, that this shall be a great benefit, and fruitful for the increase of the holy Evangel, seeing that our people greatly desire you among us, and will conduct themselves toward you in such sort, that you shall have occasion to rest content—Your good friends, The Syndics and Council of Geneva (October 22, 1540). With the seal, *Post tenebras spero lucem* ('After darkness, I hope light').

[85] Calvin, *Letters*, 1.215.
[86] Calvin, *Letters*, 1.216.

soul', is engaged to prove to them that he is thoroughly prepared to assist the church in their time of need.[87]

Interestingly, Calvin had still not arrived in Geneva by February of the following year (three months later). In a short letter, written in that month, the reformer states that he is at the divine disposal; he recognizes their confidence in him and assures them of his love and willingness to return to the Genevan ministry.[88] But, again, he excuses himself from immediate return because he has been summoned to the Diet of Ratisbon, 'which call I could not avoid,' he says.[89] Part of his conclusion reads, 'I am always allied to you in heart and affection, and hope, besides, never more to be separated from you. . . . Your humble servant and assured friend.'[90]

Eight months later (September 7, 1541), Calvin wrote again to the Genevans relating to them how he had finally left Strasbourg at the end of August and that he would be with them soon—having explained that he had been delayed in Basel and in Neuchâtel on the journey.[91] Finally, on September 16, 1541, Calvin wrote to William Farel to inform him that he had settled in Geneva—his wife and furniture would come sometime after.[92]

Recurrent themes

Not surprisingly, Calvin's letters demonstrate the struggle that the reformer went through at the time of his expulsion from Geneva and beyond into the time of recall. It should, of course, be remembered how young John Calvin was at this time. He was just around 29 years of age. And, as a young pastor with very little experience in ministry, no theological or pastoral training, believing strongly in the determinative calling of God, it must have been devastating to his faith and sensibility when he and his older and trusted colleague, William Farel, were expelled from the scene of what they probably considered to be their future life's work. The difficulties thus aroused were considerably exacerbated by Geneva's decision to recall Calvin without his colleague, and, as far as we can tell from the correspondence, with little by way of apology, either. This short study concludes with brief reflections on two significant recurring themes

---

[87] Calvin, *Letters*, 1.217.
[88] To the Syndics and Council of Geneva, Strasbourg, February 19, 1541; Calvin, *Letters*, 1.225-26.
[89] Calvin, *Letters*, 1.226. The comment by Heiko A. Oberman, 'Calvin and Farel: the Dynamics of Legitimation in Early Calvinism,' *Journal of Early Modern History* 2.1 (1998), 38, is relevant here and should perhaps be noted. He says that the three years in Strasbourg 'transformed Calvin from a local city reformer, preoccupied with Geneva—and from this perspective concerned with developments in Bern, Zurich, and Basel—into one of Europe's spokesmen'. See, also, 40.
[90] Calvin, *Letters*, 226.
[91] To the Syndics and Council of Geneva, Neuchâtel, September 7, 1541; Calvin, *Letters*, 1.281.
[92] To Farel, Geneva, September 16, 1541: Calvin, *Letters*, 1.284-85.

that arise from the correspondence of this short, turbulent period in the young reformer's life.

The strength of divine calling

We saw above[93] that Calvin believed in the strength of divine calling (*vocatio*), both to life in Christ, as well as to vocations in which God requires that life to be spent and demonstrated—in Calvin's case, of course, primarily in the ministry.[94] In essence, divine calling undergirds his understanding of the whole situation of dismissal and recall as far as the reformer is concerned. His struggle with both the expulsion and the recall was a struggle with his sense of divine vocation versus his present experience of failure and of loss. As we have noted, time and again in his correspondence he comes back to this fundamental belief in vocation.

Early in the period, on July 10 1538, Calvin wrote to Louis du Tillet[95] the following about his sense of being freed from his calling to minister in Geneva, but we should notice the confusion in his thinking:

> Above all, however, on looking back and considering the perplexities which environed me from the time I first went thither, there is nothing I dread more than returning to the charge from which I have been set free. For while, when I first entered upon it I could discern the calling of God which held me fast bound, with which I consoled myself, now, on the contrary, I am in fear lest I tempt him if I resume so great a burden, which has already felt to be insupportable. . . . Nevertheless, I know assuredly that our Lord will guide me in that so very doubtful a deliberation, the more so because I shall look rather to what he will point out to me than to my own judgment, which beyond measure drawing me contrariwise, I feel ought to be suspected.[96]

This paragraph is significant for a number of reasons. First, it is clear that Calvin believes that his calling to ministry was from God and that God will now lead him into future ministry. Indeed, he suspects his own judgement as being too subjective, biased and fearful.[97] Second, the reformer says he dreads a return to Geneva. However, it is important to note that when he speaks of his problems with his ministry there he looks not simply to the troublesome months previous to his expulsion, but to the very beginning of his ministry in the city: 'from the time I first went thither', 'when I first entered upon it'. He speaks of 'so great a burden . . . already felt to be insupportable'. There is, perhaps, the

---

[93] Under 'Preliminaries', pages 13-15 of the present chapter.

[94] I say 'primarily' the ministry, but we should underline that, along with the other reformers of his time, Calvin believed in many other legitimate and significant callings, including those of marriage and parenthood, too. See chapter 2 of the present work.

[95] To Louis du Tillet, Strasbourg, July 10, 1538; Calvin, *Letters*, 1.71-73.

[96] Calvin, *Letters*, 1.72-73. On this topic, see, also, Calvin's reply to Sadoleto in *A Reformation Debate. Sadoleto's Letter to the Genevans and Calvin's Reply* (edited by John C. Olin; New York: Fordham University Press, 2000), 45.

[97] Calvin speaks of his fear of following his own reasoning again in a letter to Nicolas Parent, Worms, December 14, 1540; Calvin, *Letters*, 1.224.

implication, then, that he found ministry itself to be a burden right from the beginning. Is he hinting at his own sense of inadequacy for the task in such a place rather than simply the difficulties he found in Geneva? It appears to be the case. This seems confirmed later in the year. In October, 1538, Calvin wrote again to du Tillet, repeating his comment that he was well aware of his own insufficiency and inadequacy for the office of minister.[98] Third, at this early stage he feels freed from the responsibility of ministry in Geneva, but, as we have already seen, by October of the same year—just three months later—he is speaking with confidence about the Lord's call to his pastoral role in the city.[99] Later, in March 1539, the reformer wrote to Farel, 'If our calling is indeed of the Lord, as we firmly believe that it is, the Lord himself will bestow his blessing, although the whole universe may be opposed to us.'[100]

On being urged by James Bernard, one of the interim ministers in Geneva, to return to the pastorate there, Calvin again speaks of his sense of divine call.[101] He declares that he has never rejected the call to Geneva, because he had been afraid to withstand God. He speaks of his determination never to enter into ecclesiastical office again, 'unless the Lord himself, by a clear and manifest call, should summon me to it'.[102]

Inadequacy for ministry

We have found that in his letters Calvin reflects between the strong sense of divine calling (*vocatio*) and his equally strong sense of his own inadequacy for ministry. We see that he wavers in his opinion of the former, but that is to be expected, given the circumstances. Regarding the latter, however, the reformer admits to himself, and to others, that he is insufficient for such a task. Though there are numerous examples in both Scripture and history of this overwhelming sense of inadequacy to which he could have referred, this is clearly more than rhetoric in Calvin, of course. Suggestions of a return to ministry awaken in him feelings of fear and dread, of hell[103] and the cross,[104] seen, partly, as we

---

[98] To Louis du Tillet, Strasbourg, October 20, 1538; Calvin, *Letters*, 1.96.
[99] Calvin, *Letters*, 1.83.
[100] To Farel, March 1539; Calvin, *Letters*, 1.128-31 (131). See, also, Calvin's letter to Farel, Strasbourg, February 6, 1540; Calvin, *Letters*, 1.172.
[101] To James Bernard, Ulm, March 1, 1541; Calvin, *Letters*, 1.234-37.
[102] Calvin, *Letters*, 1.235. See, also, his letter to Farel, Ratisbon, May 4, 1541; Calvin, *Letters*, 1.258-60. Selinger, *Calvin Against Himself*, 61, suggests that, like his conversion, Calvin's call and recall to Geneva were 'imposed from without, an intervention demanding total submission and acquiescence . . . a response, based upon evaluation vis-à-vis the divine, of obedience of a life-constituting nature'.
[103] To Louis du Tillet, Strasbourg, October 20, 1538; Calvin, *Letters*, 1.97.
[104] Calvin speaks of Geneva as a cross: to Farel, Strasbourg, March 1540: Calvin, *Letters*, 1.175: '[B]ut rather would I submit to death a hundred times than to that cross, on which I had to perish daily a thousand times over'; and, to Peter Viret, Strasbourg, May 19, 1540: Calvin, *Letters*, 1.187: '[Y]ou . . . recommend Geneva. Why could you not have said at the cross? For it would have been far preferable to perish once for all than to be tormented again in that place of torture.'

have noted, in the use of the imagery of torture (the rack), and so on. We should note here, though, his emphatic statement late on in the period under consideration:

> [T]here is no place under heaven of which I can have a greater dread, *not because I have hated it*; but because I see so many difficulties presented in that quarter which *I do not feel myself far from being equal to surmount*.[105]

We must notice the italicized words. Calvin declares that he hasn't hated Geneva, but that his main problem is his feeling of not being equal to the task that Geneva represents. If it was simply to oversee the church, then he would be less anxious, he says, but he realises that there is much more to it than that in a city like Geneva.

Calvin, then, feels inadequate to perform the duties that would fall upon him in a calling to ministry. Another thread that runs through Calvin's correspondence seems to insinuate this too; that is, his longing to work with other men in ministry rather than to work on his own. In August 1538, Calvin says that he had to excuse himself from the early reconciliatory deliberations because the authorities in Geneva would not include his colleague, William Farel. They would allow his older colleague to go into ministry elsewhere, but 'will not suffer both [Calvin and Farel] . . . to labour together'.[106] His natural reticence and anxiety are clearly increased by this: '[T]he thought which chiefly alarms me,' he says to Farel, 'is that which presents itself, when I set before my eyes the great gulf into which I must enter, where surely I felt that it would swallow me up entirely, when notwithstanding *it would be less by a half*.'[107] He dreads to think what ministerial life in Geneva ('the great gulf') would be like without his former colleague and mentor.[108] Of course, as his frequent correspondence with William Farel reveals, the older reformer remained his mentor and adviser in the faith throughout his later ministry.[109]

In similar fashion, Calvin relies on his friend, the more moderate reformer Peter Viret,[110] for pastoral support. In February 1541, Calvin informs Farel that

---

[105] To Viret, Ulm, March 1, 1541; Calvin, *Letters*, 1.231, emphasis added.

[106] To Farel, Basel, August 20, 1538; Calvin, *Letters*, 1.77-78.

[107] To Farel, Strasbourg, April 1539; Calvin, *Letters*, 1.134, emphasis added. Again, in his letters: to Farel, Strasbourg, October 24, 1538; Calvin, *Letters*, 1.121; to Farel, Strasbourg, May 1540; Calvin, *Letters*, 1.179. Calvin speaks of William Farel's 'piety, learning and sanctity'—letter to James Bernard, Ulm, March 1, 1541; Calvin, *Letters*, 1.236.

[108] But see his letter to Farel, Strasbourg, May 1540; Calvin, *Letters*, 1.178-79, in which the reformer says that he is not 'entirely frightened' at the prospect of ministering without his colleague, Farel.

[109] Though, see Oberman, 'Calvin and Farel,' 43.

[110] Cottret, *Calvin*, 272. See, also, Robert D. Linder, 'Brothers in Christ: Pierre Viret and John Calvin as Soul-Mates and Co-Laborers in the Work of the Reformation' in David Foxgrover (ed.), *Calvin Studies Society Papers 1997* (Grand Rapids: Calvin Studies Society, 1998), 145.

Viret is to go to Geneva as an interim pastor in Calvin's absence and until his return.[111] He writes to Viret a month later to encourage him in that work and to confirm his own imminent return,[112] and again to Farel in April: 'You must keep up the spirits of Viret, by frequent encouragement, that he may not be too much cast down. Nevertheless, I was glad when lately I heard that he had removed his wife and household furniture to Geneva.' This presumably implied a longer stay or even potential permanence in the city for the Viret family. 'On receiving this intelligence,' Calvin admits, 'I became less anxious.'[113] 'I must retain Viret,' Calvin says, 'whom I shall not suffer *on any account* to be dragged away from me.'[114] Two and a half months after his return, Calvin writes the following to Farel, regarding Viret, who he claims to be vital for the success of the gospel in Geneva:

> Should Viret be taken away from me I shall be utterly ruined, and this Church will be past recovery. On this account it is only reasonable that you and others pardon me if I leave no stone unturned to prevent his being carried off from me. . . . Only let Viret remain with me.[115]

Farel and Viret, then, become Calvin's indispensable supporters, colleagues, mentors and friends for his ministry—inside and away from Geneva. One more reformer takes some of the load for Calvin; that is, the reformer of the city of Strasbourg, Martin Bucer. It is obvious from the history that in Strasbourg Bucer became Calvin's mentor.[116] However, it is clear from the correspondence, too, that the younger man wanted his older colleague to retain that position in order to help in Calvin's ministry. In October, 1541, Calvin wrote to Bucer:

> I must ask, however, that you will not form any estimate from my letters to you either of my sayings or doings here. Until I shall have declared that I could bear

---

[111] David N. Wiley, 'Calvin's Friendship with Guillaume Farel' in *Calvin Studies Papers (1997)* (Grand Rapids: Calvin Studies Society, 1998), 192, believes that Calvin wanted Peter Viret to assume the pastorate in Geneva, so that Calvin himself might stay in Strasbourg—noted, too, by David W. Hall, 'Calvin's circle of friends: propelling an enduring movement' in Michael Parsons (ed.), *Reformation Faith. Exegesis and Theology in the Protestant Reformations* (Milton Keynes: Paternoster, 2014), 196n.28. This seems unlikely, however, given Calvin's correspondence at this time, as we have noted in this present chapter. Rather, he appears to be bringing Viret into the Genevan ministry to help as an interim measure until his (Calvin's) return and, perhaps, even beyond that.

[112] To Viret, Ulm, March 1, 1541; Calvin, *Letters*, 1.230-33.

[113] To Farel, Ratisbon, April 24, 1541; Calvin, *Letters*, 1.257.

[114] To Farel, Geneva, September 16, 1541; Calvin, *Letters*, 1.284, emphasis added.

[115] To Farel, Geneva, November 11, 1541; Calvin, *Letters*, 1.307.

[116] Cottret, *Calvin*, 134, speaks of this relationship, at least in Calvin's Strasbourg years as a distinguished patronage, but it clearly became more than that as time went on. See Hall, 'Calvin's circle of friends,' 197; also, Willem van 't Spijker, 'Calvin's Friendship with Bucer: Did it make Calvin a Calvinist?' in David Foxgrover (ed.), *Calvin Studies Society Papers 1995, 1997* (Grand Rapids: Calvin Studies Society, 1998), 170-72.

no more, you need not question my faithful performance of what I have promised you. And if in any way I do not answer your expectation, you know that I am under your power, and subject to your authority. Admonish, chastise, and exercise all the powers of a father over his son.[117]

Some clear elements of mentorship are alluded to in this short passage. Clearly and understandably (given the circumstances), Calvin has promised the older reformer faithfully to undertake his ministry in Geneva. The mentor clearly expects certain things and, in a situation of accountability, is given authority to admonish, chastise and so on. Calvin requires the relationship to be one of father-son, which appears to be in accord with Martin Bucer's own wishes. He concludes the letter with the ascription to Bucer, 'honoured father in the Lord'.[118]

Conclusion

To conclude briefly, we see that Calvin's letters around the time of his expulsion from Geneva (May 1538-September 1541) reveal a great deal of vulnerability, as one would expect, and ambivalence towards his calling and to the city of Geneva, itself. However, because of his strong sense of divine vocation—reflecting for Calvin our call into salvation in Christ—he is largely ready to take up the yoke again, believing that in *vocatio* God binds us to his purpose for our lives. However, understandably, given the circumstances, the reformer dreads his return into the Genevan ministry. What we *cannot* say, though, is simply that he dreads this because he hates Geneva. I have argued that it is clear from his correspondence that he fears return to ministry in Geneva essentially because he realizes the inadequacy, the insufficiency of his own resources to do that ministry well. He feels deficient and unequal to the task. This is not that 'grand' humility that rests faithfully in God's power and innate ability; rather it appears to be a genuine sense of being overwhelmed by the task in hand.

Perhaps, we need to remember to read his life from beginning to end, not in the reverse direction. That is to say, in this context, it may be because we understand the massive, final influence of John Calvin on the European Reformation and on the city of Geneva (despite its many problems and difficulties) that we presume his dislike to be purely for the city itself. There is that element, too, of course; but, as we have seen, it is so often tied to his feelings of inadequacy. He gains confidence in confiding in and trusting those with whom he shares intimate fellowship—Martin Bucer, William Farel and Peter Viret—two of whom are older colleagues, the other a man after Calvin's own heart.

---

[117] To Bucer, Geneva, October 15, 1541; Calvin, *Letters*, 1.294.
[118] See Karin Spiecker Stetina, *The Fatherhood of God and the Use of Feminine Imagery in John Calvin's Thought* (Milton Keynes: Paternoster, 2016), 13-17, who makes a related point about the mentorship of these three friends.

CHAPTER 2

'For the good of the whole Church.'[1]
Calvin's letters on marriage

In his excellent recent biography of Calvin, historian Michael Mullett states that 'from the time of "The Judgement of Martin Luther on Monastic Vows" and Luther's "Concerning Married Life," both of 1522, the marriage of the clergy became a fundamental Reformation principle'.[2] This principle itself had been preached, demonstrated and reinforced by the marriage of Luther's colleagues and fellow reformers—Philip Melanchthon, Johann Agricola and Bernhardi Bartolomäus as early as 1520; Bartholomew Bernhardi in 1521; Andreas Karlstadt, Justus Jonas and Johann Bugenhagen in 1522; Wenceslas Link, Francis Lambert and Thomas Münster in 1523—and, later, by Luther's own marriage to the former nun, Katherine von Buren, in 1525. So significant was the principle and its concrete application in the lives of the clergy that Steven Ozment makes the following comment:

> No institutional change brought about by the Reformation was more visible, responsive to late Medieval pleas for reform, and conducive to new social attitudes than the marriage of Protestant clergy. Nor was there another point in the Protestant program where theology and practice corresponded more successfully.[3]

Both the principle and the practice were well established by the time that the second generation of reformers, including John Calvin, came to marry. It was deemed crucial to be, and to be seen to be, different to the old Church clergy,[4] but there were other, more personal and pressing reasons for marrying as well, of course.

---

[1] Letter to Christopher Fabri, January 13, 1553, Calvin, *Letters*, 2.387-88. For the most part, throughout this present volume, I am employing John Calvin, *Letters*, 4 volumes (edited by Jules Bonnet; translated by Marcus R. Gilchrist; Philadelphia: Presbyterian Board, 1858). See, also, John Calvin, *Lettres françaises*, 2 volumes (edited by Jules Bonnet; Paris: Meyrueis, 1854) and *Ioannis Calvini Opera quae supersunt omnia* [CO] (Corpus Reformatorum: Brunswick: Schwetschke et Filium, 1863–1900).

[2] Michael Mullett, *John Calvin* (London: Routledge, 2011), 76-77.

[3] Steven Ozment, *The Age of Reform 1250-1550* (New Haven: Yale University Press, 1980), 381.

[4] See Bernard Cottret, *Calvin. A Biography* (Grand Rapids: Eerdmans / Edinburgh: T&T Clark, 2000), 140.

Reformation Letters: A Fresh Reading of John Calvin's Correspondence

It is interesting that, compared with many other areas of Reformation thought and practice, there is, in fact, relatively little major study of the reformers' doctrine of marriage currently available. William Lazareth's otherwise excellent work, *Luther on the Christian Home* (1960), is somewhat dated and confessional, as is W.E. Cocke's later essay, 'Luther's View of Marriage and Family' (1973). André Biéler's invaluable, indeed seminal, work, *L'homme et la femme dans la morale calviniste* (1961), only briefly touches on Calvin's understanding of marriage in a much broader social context.[5]

In more recent years, one or two works have singled out the marital aspect of the reformers' theology. C.M. Baldwin's article, 'Marriage in Calvin's Sermons' (1988), for example, is exceptional but merely suggestive of the important subject matter. B.J. van der Walt's essay on women and marriage in the period (1986), in contrast, is lengthy but covers too much material in general terms.[6] V.N. Olsen, *The New Testament Logia on Divorce* (1971), and Herman Selderhuis' writing on marriage in the thought of Martin Bucer (1999) remain, to my mind, essential reading.[7] My own work, *Reformation Marriage* (2005)— a revised version of my University of Wales doctoral thesis—tackling the theology of Martin Luther and John Calvin specifically on the relationship between the husband and his wife, followed two extraordinarily illuminating, but largely tangential, studies: Jane Dempsey Douglass' *Women, Freedom and Calvin* (1985) and John L. Thompson's *John Calvin and the Daughters of Sarah* (1992).[8]

In general terms, neither Luther nor Calvin brought about any major changes to the doctrine of marriage or to marital or familial relationships. Basically,

---

[5] W.H. Lazareth, *Luther on the Christian Home* (Philadelphia: Muhlenburg, 1960); W.E. Cocke, 'Luther's View of Marriage and Family,' *Religion in Life* 42 (1973), 103-16; A. Biéler, *L'homme et la femme dans la morale calviniste; la doctrine réformée sur l'amour, le marriage, le celibate, le divorce, l'adultère et la prostitution, considerée dans son cadre historique* (Geneva: Labor et Fides, 1961).

[6] C.M. Baldwin, 'Marriage in Calvin's Sermons' in R.V. Schnucker (ed.), *Calviniana: Ideas and Influence of Jean Calvin* (Kirksville: Sixteenth Century Journal Publishers, 1988), 121-29; B.J. van der Walt, 'Woman and Marriage: In the Middle Ages, in Calvin and in our own time' in B.J. van der Walt (ed.), *John Calvin's Institutes: His Opus Magnum* (Potchefstroom: Potchefstroom University for Christian Higher Education, 1986), 184-238.

[7] See V.N. Olsen, *The New Testament Logia on Divorce. A Study of their Interpretation from Erasmus to Milton* (Tübingen: Mohr, 1971); H.J. Selderhuis, *Marriage and Divorce in the Thought of Martin Bucer* (Kirksville: Thomas Jefferson University Press, 1999). See, also, the useful work by C.W. Pfeiffer, 'Heinrich Bullinger and Marriage' (unpublished doctoral thesis, St Louis University, 1981).

[8] Michael Parsons, *Reformation Marriage. The Husband and Wife Relationship in the Theology of Luther and Calvin* (Eugene: Wipf and Stock, 2011; first printed by Rutherford House, Edinburgh, in 2005); Jane Dempsey Douglass, *Women, Freedom and Calvin* (Philadelphia: Westminster, 1985); John L. Thompson, *John Calvin and the Daughters of Sarah* (Geneva: Librarie Droz, 1992).

they remained men of their time and their time was not conducive to fundamental change at this point.[9]

Calvin on marriage

For Calvin, the three significant institutions within society are the church, the state and the family. This was commonplace among the reformers and, previously, within medieval theology, following Augustine amongst others. This order (*la police de ce monde*) is generally said to be *inviolable*. Within that view of the social order Calvin approaches the doctrine of marriage with what appears to be an obsessive concern for the maintenance of order (*ordo*) within the outworking of society's diverse relationships. This general concern was seminally recognised in Joseph Bohatec's early study. He highlights Calvin's 'passion for order' (*Pathos der Ordnung*) which he discerns in the reformer's desire for unity, harmony and order in society and the state, over against his contrasting fear of disorder and chaos. He further delineates Calvin's idea that it is through the church that order (specifically, divine order—*ordinationes Dei*) is restored in the historical, concrete realm.[10] Likewise, more recently, Michael Mullett says that Calvin's passion for order lay 'deep in his personality, fostered ... by the whole of his education'.[11] In the familial realm order begins traditionally, and in Calvin's thought, with the subordination of the wife and the parental control of the children.[12]

---

[9] C.J. Blaisdell, 'The Matrix of Reform: Women in the Lutheran and Calvinist Movements' in R.L. Greaves (ed.), *Triumph over Silence: Women in Protestant History* (Westport: Greenwood, 1985), 35. See, also, C.J. Blaisdell, 'Calvin's Letters to Women: The Courting of Ladies in High Places,' *Sixteenth Century Journal* 13 (1982), 67-85; C.J. Blaisdell, 'Calvin's and Loyola's Letters to Women' in R.V. Schnucker (ed.), *Calviniana: Ideas and Influence of Jean Calvin* (Kirksville: Sixteenth Century Journal Publishers, 1988), 235-53. Also, F.W. Barton, *Calvin and the Duchess* (Louisville: Westminster John Knox, 1989), 30.

[10] J. Bohatec, *Calvin und das Recht* (Feudingen: Buchdruck und Verlags-Anstalt, 1934). While not necessarily positing order as *the* governing principle, others see order as clearly central to specific aspects of Calvin's writing. See F.L. Battles, '*Calculus Fidei*: Some Ruminations on the Structure of the Theology of John Calvin' in R. Benedetto (ed.), *Interpreting John Calvin* (Grand Rapids: Baker, 1996), 139-78; J.M. Gustafson, *Theology and Ethics* (Oxford: Blackwell, 1981), 166; M.L. Monheit, 'The ambition for an illustrious name: Humanism, Patronage, and Calvin's Doctrine of the Calling,' *Sixteenth Century Journal* 23 (1992), 278; C.A.M. Hall, 'With the Spirit's Sword' (unpublished doctoral thesis, Basel University, 1968), 49; L.W. Spitz, *The Protestant Reformation. 1517-1559* (New York: Harper and Row, 1985), 213. See, also, Douglass, *Women, Freedom and Calvin*, chapter 2, who traces his doctrine of order to the late medieval voluntarism of Scotus and Occam, and to Stoicism and Augustine.

[11] Michael Mullett, *Calvin* (London: Routledge, 1989), 13.

[12] See *Comm. 1 Tim.* 2.13 (CO 52.276-77); *Comm 1 Cor.* 11.7 (CO 49.476); 14.34 (CO 49.533); *Comm Acts* 10.2 (CO 48.223); 16.15 (CO 48.378); 18.26 (CO 48.437); *Comm. Gen.* 18.6, 19 (CO 23.252, 258).

A cursory knowledge of both Calvin's epistemology and theology would lead us correctly to expect that from his perspective it is God who takes the initiative in marriage, it is a heavenly calling or vocation (*coelesti vocatione*)[13] and a divine institution (*divinae institutionis*).[14] That is, when a marriage takes place God is intimately involved and central to the event—he presides over the union, his authority joins the man and his wife together, their promises are spoken before him and in his name, he requires a mutual pledge of faithfulness from them both, he sanctions the alliance. Something of the joint divine-human co-operation in marriage is seen by Calvin in the paradigmatic example of Adam and Eve. The reformer stresses that the man (Adam) did not choose his wife (Eve), but he *did*, actively, receive her from God. Eve is a divine gift to the man. In this, Calvin clearly recognizes both God as the author of marriage and also the man's responsibility in that area of life experience.[15] Importantly, if God is the author of marriage, as Calvin suggests, then the on-going obligation and responsibility of men and women is to use that institution or vocation for God's purpose (and his glory) in their lives in the world.

We should note that the reformer speaks in a traditional manner of the three reasons for marrying—first, marriage is seen as a remedy against man and woman's unbridled sexual desire and lust (that is, marriage is a remedy against sin—*remedium peccati*);[16] second, people marry for the legitimate conception and raising of children and, third, marriage is the social, vocational context for men and women to enjoy companionship together. Although Calvin says considerably less on the purposes of marriage than Martin Luther, for example, the reasons he gives exactly parallel Luther's reasons and are the conventional purposes that the medieval church, and indeed the Catholic Church of his own day, would have listed.[17]

The reformer stresses the seriousness of getting married. He insists, for instance, on the presence of witnesses to engagements to ensure that the parties had both consented, on the publication of the banns to avoid bigamous unions, that some solemn, public testimony to marriage should be practised.[18] Indeed,

---

[13] *Comm. Matt.* 19.11 (CO 45.533); *Comm. 1 Cor.* 7.20 (CO 49.415); *Serm. 1 Tim.* 2.13-15 (*sa vocation*—CO 53.229); *Inst* 3.10.6 (OS 4.180-81); *Comm. Exod.* 2.1 (CO 24.21).

[14] *Comm. 1 Cor.* 6.15-20 (CO 49.398); 7.1 (CO 49.401); *Comm. Matt.* 19.5 (CO 45.528); *Inst* 2.8.41 (OS 3.281), 4.19.34 (OS 5.467-68); *Serm. Deut.* 22.13-24 (CO 28.48). See, also, *Lausanne Articles* (1536), article ix, LCC.22, 36. Although this work was prepared by William Farel, Calvin supported the articles.

[15] *Comm. Gen.* 2.22 (CO 23.49, 50).

[16] It should be noted, however, that for Calvin marriage is a positive vehicle for God's gracious, creative activity in the lives of men and women. It is not, intrinsically, a *remedium peccati*. It only becomes that at the fall of Adam and Eve.

[17] However, see Parsons, *Reformation Marriage*, 213-335, for an extensive examination of the subject.

[18] See Jeffrey R. Watt, 'The Marriage Laws Calvin Drafted for Geneva' in Wilhelm H. Neuser (ed.), *Calvinus Sacrae Scripturae Professor. Calvin as Confessor of Holy*

on the basis of the dignity of marriage (*la dignité et excellence de l'estat de Mariage*) and upon scriptural evidence, this stress on the seriousness of marriage is said to be necessary—in fact, it is God's will.[19] In this context, the wedding ceremony is to be bi-focused: it is to reflect the worldly nature of marriage, while it is also to maintain its spiritual significance. And, it is to be conducted with order and seriousness (*tenant ordre et gravité convenable à Chrétiens*). The wedding ceremony was generally celebrated on a Sunday when the congregation met for worship. Calvin stipulates that the ceremony, though it is *not* essentially a spiritual matter, should begin with spiritual songs, it should include a sermon and the exchanging of vows, a blessing, followed by the Eucharist. Though, together with Luther and other reformers, he emphasizes that it is a civil matter, the ceremony should be conducted, insists Calvin, by ministers of the gospel, not by magistrates.[20] The impression given by these requirements is, therefore, that marriage should be considered as extremely important and as the converging point of temporal reality and spiritual significance. It is, after all, a temporal vocation (*vocatio*), graciously instituted by God. It is one of the points in life experience where election to spiritual life in Christ is demonstrated by specific temporal and concrete calling.[21]

Lee Palmer Wandel is of the opinion that Calvin moved weddings into church as both structure and community:[22]

> In communities that looked to Geneva and Calvin for guidance, the wedding was no longer simply a rite joining families, which they and their connections witnessed. The wedding and with it, marriage, moved into the living community of Christians, physically and spatially as well as imaginatively. In Reformed communities, each wedding was itself 'public': witnessed by the community of the

---

Scripture (Grand Rapids: Eerdmans, 1994), 245-55; Christopher Elwood, 'Calvin, Beza and the Defense of Marriage in the Sixteenth Century' in David Foxgrover (ed.), *Calvin, Beza and Later Calvinism* (Grand Rapids: Calvin Studies Society, 2006), 11-34. Heinz Schilling, 'Reform and Supervision of Family Life in Germany and the Netherlands' in R.A. Mentzer (ed.), *Sin and the Calvinists. Morals Control and the Consistory in the Reformed Tradition* (Kirksville: Sixteenth Century Journal Publishers, 1994), 25-26, suggests that the promise of fidelity replaced the bond of sacramental marriage.

[19] *La Forme des Prieres et chantz ecclesiastiques*, 1542-43 (OS 2.50). He insists on 'bon et decent ordre' (51); *Comm. Gen.* 24.59 (CO 23.339), respectively.

[20] *Les ordonnances ecclesiastiques*, 1541 (OS 2.345-55). See, also, G. Harkness, *John Calvin: The Man and his Ethics* (New York: Abingdon, 1981), 138; Herman J. Selderhuis, *John Calvin. A Pilgrim's Life* (Downers Grove: IVP Academic, 2009), 179.

[21] Occasionally, Calvin fails to follow the implications of his own teaching. This is so, for example, when he seems to put commercial considerations before the importance of the marriage ordinance. See *Comm. Exod.* 21.1-6 (CO 24.700-701)—pointed out by D.F. Wright, 'Calvin's Pentateuchal Criticism: Equity, Hardness of Heart, and Divine Accommodation in the Mosaic Harmony Commentary,' *Calvin Theological Journal* 21 (1986), 41.

[22] Lee Palmer Wandel, *The Reformation. Towards a New History* (Cambridge: Cambridge University Press, 2011), 123.

faithful, within the space devoted to the collective and public worship of God, the vows now binding not only before God, but also before the entire congregation.[23]

This is an extremely important point and much more could be said, of course, but this brief section simply introduces the topic of marriage in Calvin's thought and Calvinist Genevan practice before moving on to his letters on the subject. We will return to the subject generally in the reflections that conclude this next section.

Letters on Calvin's own marriage

Calvin married Idelette von Buren in the same month and year as he became a citizen of Strasbourg (August, 1540), suggesting at this point a sense of or, at least, a longing for permanence and stability, perhaps. Apparently, he was influenced towards marriage partly by observing Martin Bucer's happy marriage and, as we will see, partly for other reasons, too. Idelette was somewhat older than Calvin but, evidently, according to Herman Selderhuis, she looked young.[24] She was the widow of the Anabaptist, John Stordeur of Liège. Both had converted to the Reformed faith before the husband tragically fell ill and died of the plague. The reformer clearly saw in Idelette a woman of exceptional qualities (*singularis exempli femina*)—an important point to which we will return below. With her, Calvin had three children, none of whom survived. Nevertheless, as far as we are able to tell, his rather short marriage to Idelette was significantly more than a *mariage de convenance*. His grief over her death, though somewhat controlled, reveals the importance of their relationship together and his own love towards her.[25] The first letters refer to plans for his forthcoming marriage; the next refer to his wife's illness and death. From these we can glean something of the reformer's view of clerical marriage.

---

[23] Wandel, *The Reformation*, 124.
[24] Selderhuis, *John Calvin*, 169.
[25] See chapter 6 of the present volume. Also, Michael Parsons, *Luther and Calvin on Grief. Life Experience and Biblical Text* (Lewiston: Edwin Mellen, 2013), 42-62, 237-54. It should be noted though, that several writers complain that Calvin's love for Idelette was less close than this suggests. For example, at one extreme, R.H. Bainton, *Women of the Reformation* (Boston: Beacon, 1974), 87, suggests that Calvin might as well have married a plank! For a more positive reading, see R.N. Carew-Hunt, *Calvin* (London: Centenary, 1933), 101; J.H. Alexander, *Ladies of the Reformation* (Harpenden: Gospel Standard Strict Baptist Trust, 1978), 90-92; William J. Bouwsma, *John Calvin. A Sixteenth Century Portrait* (New York: Oxford University Press, 1988), 23; A.E. McGrath, *A Life of John Calvin* (Oxford: Blackwell, 1993), 16; William Edgar, 'Ethics: The Christian Life and Good Works according to Calvin (3.6-10, 17-19)' in David W. Hall and Peter A. Lillback (eds), *A Theological Guide to Calvin's Institutes. Essays and Analysis* (Phillipsburg: P&R, 2008), 320-46 (334-35). And, generally, see Karen E. Spierling, 'Women, Marriage and Family' in David M. Whitford (ed.), *T&T Clark Companion to Reformation Theology* (London: T&T Clark, 2012), 178-96.

To Farel, February 23, 1539

The background to this letter is important, as will become clear below. Calvin had been asked by the ministers of Strasbourg—Capito, Sturm and Claude (in the absence of Martin Bucer)—to write to his colleague, William Farel, in Neuchâtel concerning the possibility of union between the churches in Germany and Switzerland.[26] However, according to the editor of Calvin's letters, those in Zurich were more inclined 'to exalt the memory of Zwingli at the expense of Luther'.[27] 'The good men,' says Calvin, 'flame up into a rage if any one dares to prefer Luther to Zwingli. . . . I ask you, dear Farel, if any one extolled Luther in this manner, would not the Zurichers have grumbled, and complained that Zwingli had been overborne?'[28] The complexity and sensitivity of the situation is clear from the reformer's brief comments.

At this important juncture Calvin declares that he is tired of discussing Pierre Caroli and that he wants a private word with his friend, Farel, and he proceeds to speak of his forthcoming marriage—a marriage, it must be said, more planned in his thinking and imagination than in concrete reality at this moment.[29] He says,

> An excellent opportunity will occur for your repairing hither, if, as we hope, the marriage shall come to pass. We look for the bride to be here a little after Easter. But if you will make me certain that you will come, the marriage ceremony might be delayed until your arrival. We have time enough beforehand to let you know the day. First of all, then, I request of you, as an act of friendship, that you would come. Secondly, that you assure me that you will come. For it is altogether indispensable that someone from thence be here to solemnize and ask a blessing upon the marriage. I would rather have you than anyone else. Therefore, resolve whether you think it is worth while, on my account, to undertake this journey.[30]

This paragraph clearly indicates the importance of Calvin's friendship with William Farel, a friendship not merely of ecclesial cooperation, but of personal warmth and appreciation.[31] He is eager to know if Farel will make the journey to be at the wedding—he asks him twice in as many lines—even to the point of re-arranging the whole wedding event if need be to accommodate Farel's later arrival. Calvin needs reassurance of his friend's intention, requesting it even in a letter of some ecclesial and ecumenical significance.

The remainder of the letter speaks of 'these disturbances by which Geneva is at present thrown into a state of commotion,' 'desperate circumstances' and mentions the very real possibility of war. The next paragraph informs Farel

---

[26] Letter to Farel, Strasbourg, February 23, 1539, Calvin, *Letters*, 1.107-112.
[27] Calvin, *Letters*, 1.107n.1.
[28] Calvin, *Letters*, 1.109.
[29] Calvin, *Letters*, 1.110.
[30] Calvin, *Letters*, 1.110.
[31] See David N. Wiley, 'Calvin's Friendship with Guillaume Farel' in David Foxgrover (ed.), *Calvin Studies Society Papers 1995, 1997* (Grand Rapids: Calvin Studies Society, 1998), 187-204. See page 26 of the present volume.

about 'our little church here' and two men who have returned to the congregation: Hermann of Liège, a former critic of the reformers, Calvin and Farel, in Geneva; also, Hans in Ulm who now 'appears to be penitent'.[32]

To Farel, May 19, 1539

Again, this later letter,[33] written three months after the previous one, begins with comments about the state of the Swiss church. Calvin writes of Gasper Grossman, who had been discharged by the Senate of Bern for having composed an inferior catechism—that is, one not entirely agreeing with Martin Bucer's theology—and Zebedee, minister of Orbe, who had been censured for the same reason.[34]

Later, in this relatively long letter, he speaks of his friends' concern for his marital well-being and of their active involvement in attempting to bring about his marriage. Then the reformer (in)famously lists the characteristics of the woman he would agree to marry; a list of which he desires his friend to be aware.

> But always keep in mind what I seek to find in her; for I am none of those insane lovers who embrace also the vices of those they are in love with, where they are smitten at first sight with a fine figure. This only is the beauty which allures me, if she is chaste [Latin *castus*—'pure'], if not too nice or fastidious, if economical, if patient, if there is hope that she will be interested about my health.[35]

Apparently, beauty and good looks generally are of no consequence to Calvin, particularly when they might divert him from the characteristics he really values in a wife. Rather, he seeks those attributes that would tend to harmony and that might realistically enhance and reflect the reformer's sense of piety, that suit his ministry and, he adds, his own health.[36]

> [T]herefore if you think well of it, set out immediately, in case some one else get beforehand with you. After this, I shall not write again until you come. Do, however, come. You are of all persons the most desired. Come, then; you will show your well-disposedness in a remarkable way by making this journey.[37]

Again, we observe Calvin's desire to have William Farel at the wedding: 'You are of all persons the most desired,' he says. He also wants to confirm in his own mind Farel's readiness and willingness to be at his friend's side at this

---

[32] Calvin, *Letters*, 1.110, 111, respectively.
[33] Letter to Farel, Strasbourg, May 19, 1539, Calvin, *Letters*, 1.139-42.
[34] Calvin, *Letters*, 1.141n.1.
[35] Calvin, *Letters*, 1.141.
[36] Selderhuis, *John Calvin*, 167, appears overly cryptic in suggesting that Calvin needed a housekeeper more than a wife—a point to which we return in the reflections later. Robert L. Reymond, *John Calvin. His Life and Influence* (Geanies House, Fearn: Christian Focus, 2000), 69, seems entirely to miss the point in saying, simply, that Calvin finds bachelorhood 'an inconvenience' and that because of this he marries Idelette.
[37] Calvin, *Letters*, 1.141.

important life-changing event. Bernard Cottret, Calvin's recent biographer, may well be correct in suggesting that it is quite possible that the union was celebrated by Farel in Strasbourg.[38]

To Farel, February 6, 1540

Before broaching the subject of marriage again—now a year since the first letter to his friend Farel—Calvin speaks of what he sees as their indulgent response to Pierre Caroli: '[T]here is not among us that severity of discipline which ought to exist.'[39] He mentions the Emperor Charles V and the French king's proposed meeting at Amiens and the very real possibility of war in Europe. Then, surprisingly, perhaps, he states that 'in the midst of such commotions as these, I am so much at my ease [relaxed, rather than with time to spare, perhaps], as to have the audacity to think of taking a wife'. The reformer then recounts the proposal of a certain woman 'of noble rank' and 'with a fortune above my condition' coming from a well-meaning and devout brother and his wife. He recalls that he may even have been prevailed upon, such was their earnestness and their love of him, 'unless the Lord had otherwise appointed'. How does the Lord appoint in such circumstances? Interestingly, the reformer continues, 'Two considerations deterred me from that connection—because she did not understand our language, and because I feared she might be too mindful of her family and education.' Calvin explains that he asked that the woman, to be considered, should learn the French language. Bernard Cottret, rather sarcastically, perhaps, suggests that Calvin told the woman to learn French as 'a subterfuge,' taking advantage 'of the young girl's hesitations to sneak away'.[40] This seems unlikely, given the trouble the reformer goes to in order to secure a suitable companion. It is more probable that Calvin said in earnest he would marry her on the proviso that she would learn French. It appears that he expected an immediate answer, for then, on being asked for time to think, he turned his attention to someone else. 'If she answers her repute,' he says of this next woman, 'she will bring a dowry large enough, without any money at all.' Again, he pleads with Farel to come but at this stage appears reluctant to insist upon it:

> I wish you might then be present, that you may bless our wedlock. As, however, I have troubled you so much more than I ought during the past year, I dare not insist upon it. . . . I make myself look very foolish if it shall so happen that my hope again fall through. But as I trust the Lord will be present to help me, I express myself as though I spoke of a certainty.[41]

By this time, a year into marriage negotiations, Calvin is clearly beginning to feel embarrassed, but trusts in God to help him.

---

[38] Bernard Cottret, *Calvin*, 140.
[39] Letter to Farel, Strasbourg, February 6, 1540, Calvin, *Letters*, 1.171-75 (171). He says, '[W]hatever may happen, the work of the Lord is never to be deserted' (1.172).
[40] Cottret, *Calvin*, 141.
[41] Calvin, *Letters*, 1.174.

To Viret, July, August 19, 1542; June 15, 1548[42]

In July 1542, two years after marrying Idelette, the reformer writes a very short letter to his friend Peter Viret to say that he was 'in great anxiety' because Idelette 'has been delivered prematurely, not without extreme danger,' adding, characteristically, 'but may the Lord have a care over us'.[43] Their son, Jacques, was born on July 28; however, his premature death caused great grief and sorrow to both John and Idelette Calvin. The latter, particularly, was unable ever to fully recuperate from the loss and suffered thereafter with ill health, so much so that in August Calvin writes to say that his wife is unable to put pen to paper nor even to dictate a greeting to Viret's wife. 'The Lord,' he says, 'has certainly inflicted a severe and bitter wound in the death of our infant son. But,' he adds poignantly, 'he is himself a Father, and knows best what is good for his children.'[44]

Sadly, illness was part of their lives together. Six weeks after their wedding, for example, they were both unwell. Calvin's remark at that time seems peculiarly characteristic of him, though, by implication, it does indicate that he could envisage contentment and delight in marriage as well: 'In truth, out of fear that our marriage would be too happy, the Lord from the beginning moderated our joy.'[45] Later in their marriage Calvin is not slow to show concern for his wife's ill-health. In a letter to Madame de Falais, in September 1545, he offers the 'humble commendations of my wife, who lies sick in bed'. Again, in a letter to Peter Viret in 1548 he apologises for his wife's illness during her recent stay with the Viret family.[46]

To Viret, April 7, 1549[47]

Here Calvin writes poignantly to his friend, Peter Viret, about the death of his wife, asserting that it is 'exceedingly painful to me, yet,' he continues, 'I subdue my grief as well as I can'.[48] Then he makes the following important remarks:

> I have been bereaved of the best companion of my life, of one who, had it been so ordered, would not only have been the willing sharer of my indigence, but even of my death. During her life she was the faithful helper of my ministry. From her I never experienced the slightest hindrance. She was never troublesome to me

---

[42] Letter to Viret, Geneva, July, 1542, Calvin, *Letters*, 1.335-36; Letter to Viret, Geneva, August 19, 1542, Calvin, *Letters*, 1.340-44; Letter to Viret, Geneva, June 15, 1548, Calvin, *Letters*, 2.167-68.
[43] Calvin, *Letters*, 1.335.
[44] Calvin, *Letters*, 1.344.
[45] OC 11, col 83, cited by Cottret, *Calvin*, 142.
[46] Letter to Madame de Falais, Geneva, September 18, 1545, Calvin, *Letters*, 2.19-20 (20); Letter to Viret, Geneva, June 15, 1548, Calvin, *Letters*, 2.167-68, respectively.
[47] Letter to Viret, April 7, 1549, Calvin, *Letters*, 2.216-17.
[48] Calvin, *Letters*, 2.216. See chapter 6 of the present work for a more detailed engagement with this letter.

throughout the entire course of her illness; she was more anxious about her children than about herself.[49]

At the point of terrible loss and grief the reformer speaks of Idelette with obvious affection, with sorrow and appreciation of one who would have journeyed into exile and even to death (a suggestion of the possibility of martyrdom, perhaps?[50]) with her husband. He underlines the fact that she had never been 'a hindrance' to his ministry. Referring to this letter, Herman Selderhuis, in his generally warm and positive portrait of Calvin, says, 'Still, although it is to be hoped that everyone might claim his or her partner was no hindrance, we might also wish that Calvin had simply dropped this remark.'[51] One would have to question whether this really does justice to the reformer's intention here. It seems to me that the phrases 'the slightest hindrance' and 'faithful helper of my ministry' are to be held together. The former may sound somewhat negative; the latter a positive depiction of Idelette's work, albeit in a patriarchal context. Interestingly, in his letter to Farel in April, 1549, Calvin recounts his wife's last hours, including these words about his last conversation with her: 'I, having spoken a few words about the love of Christ, the hope of eternal life, *concerning our married life*, and her departure, engaged in prayer.'[52] Note that he speaks concerning their married life just moments before Idelette's death. This surely indicates a positive, companionate relationship within the context of mutual gospel ministry.

Reflections

It is somewhat commonplace at this point to be rather negative about Calvin in the context of marriage. Michael Mullett, for example, though he concedes that the reformer eventually falls in love with his wife, speaks of the match in an adverse way in which the 'obsessively egocentric bachelor is dragged into the married state with a woman of the most conventional bourgeois virtues who is ready to act as his nurse'.[53] This seems to me to come from a rather one-dimensional reading of the matter. By that, I mean that it implies a reading of Calvin's notorious comment about Idelette not having been a hindrance, for example, in a way that allows little positive interpretation as such. On the whole, a reading like this might make sense and is, perhaps, allowable from the

---

[49] Calvin, *Letters*, 2.216. See his further comments in his letter to Farel, Geneva, April 11, 1549, Calvin, *Letters*, 2.217-19.

[50] In an earlier generation, the prospect of possible (or, perhaps, probable) martyrdom appears to have made Martin Luther at first reluctant to marry. See, for example, his letter to Spalatin, Wittenberg, November 30, 1524, *LW* 49.93 (*WA Br.* 3.393-94), in which he states that his 'mind is far removed from marriage since *I expect the death and punishment due to a heretic*' (emphasis added). See Parsons, *Reformation Marriage*, 176.

[51] Selderhuis, *John Calvin*, 171. See, also, 172.

[52] Calvin, *Letters*, 2.219, emphasis added.

[53] Mullett, *John Calvin*, 78.

very limited evidence, but I wonder if there is a better and a more three-dimensional way to look at the situation. I think there is, and the present reflections will propose that.

In a later letter (1553) to Christopher Fabri, encouraging him on his forthcoming marriage,[54] Calvin says the following:

> I am exceedingly glad that you are about to get married, not only because it will be for your own private good, but also because *the brethren have considered it to be for the good of the whole Church*. And while I do not indeed know enough of the lady, yet I confidently trust, from various conjectures, that each of you will turn out according to our wishes. We have good reason, therefore to congratulate you, and we feel thankful to God in no ordinary degree.[55]

The reformer goes on to say that he would have been happy to have come to the wedding, but that present troubles in Geneva keep him from doing so—indicating again that complicated broader context, political and religious—noted several times above.

It is significant that the reformer speaks of Fabri's marriage as being for his own personal good and also 'for the good of the whole Church'. It is of interest, too, that the brethren *together* are said to have considered this latter conclusion to be the case. That is, in Calvin's view, marriage is about personal benefit (directly related, of course, to the three traditional purposes of marriage: a remedy against lust, the legitimate conception and raising of children, and mutual companionship), but it also concerns the Church's benefit. That is, marriage is both personal and public—personal in terms of the husband's wellbeing (in this case), public in terms of the Reformed community, the Church of Christ. Importantly, it is the public, the ecclesial good that 'the brethren' are said to consider and to evaluate. Now, perhaps we should ask ourselves whether this is the bifocal lens through which we need to read Calvin's letters on marriage, and particularly prioritising, as he seems to, the communal perspective? Will the employment of this lens add to our understanding? Will this lens give a specific context in which to comprehend and to appreciate the reformer's correspondence—correspondence which has often been seen to be somewhat reluctant and negative on the subject of marriage? It will be helpful to delineate his thinking in a number of brief points through this lens of the Church's good.

Calvin's understanding of marriage

At this point, it is important to remember two foundational considerations. The first foundational consideration is that Calvin believes that the image of God in individuals expresses itself through order, which is not something static and engraved *on* people, but is expressed dynamically *by* them. The image in men and women, thus conceived, is seen by the reformer in relation to themselves,

---

[54] Letter to Christopher Fabri, Geneva, January 13, 1553, Calvin, *Letters*, 2.387-88.
[55] Calvin, *Letters*, 2.387, emphasis added.

in relation to the household and, importantly, in service of others[56]—living in thankful response to God's grace in Christ. Calvin insists that each person is essentially formed *for others*.[57] The second foundational consideration is that marriage, itself, is divinely instituted in order that each person should be able to find their own vocation and to help the other to fulfill theirs.[58] Calvin knew at this time his vocation to be that of pastor of the church and preacher of the Word in the French-speaking church in Strasbourg (and later, of course, in Geneva).[59]

This brings us back to Calvin's (in)famous words to William Farel concerning the characteristics of a potential wife. Of course, there is clearly self-consciousness and self-interest in the reformer's comments. We would have to say that that, after all, is of the nature of marriage and of choice, generally. To concentrate only on that, however, is to prioritise the first lens, that of private or personal interest, above the second. Conversely, if we look through the second lens, that of the good of the whole Church—a lens that the reformer appears to have given precedence to—we may see the wisdom of Calvin's words. He does not wish to 'embrace also the *vices*' of a beautiful woman simply because he is smitten by her looks. He wishes to marry someone who is not promiscuous (that is, one who is 'chaste' or 'pure'), who is not too demanding or fussy, one who will be careful with the minister's small stipend, someone who is patient and caring.[60] These are the qualities that he deems to be of use to himself as a pastor and through him to the church as a whole.[61] This is true piety in the concrete situation of marriage. Elsewhere Calvin says,

---

[56] See *Serm. 1 Tim.* 3.3-5 (CO 53.271-82); *Comm. Gen.* 2.18 (CO 23.46). In the context of the restoration of society, André Biéler, *L'Humanisme Social de Calvin* (Geneva: Labor et Fides, 1961), 94, stresses that Calvin's ethics essentially have a dynamic about them (*L'éthique sociale du Reformateur est une éthique dynamique*).

[57] *Comm. Gen.* 2.18 (CO 23.46)—'*Principium ergo generale est, conditum esse hominem, ut sit sociale animal.*' Also, *Inst* 2.2.13 (OS 3.256-57); *Comm Gen.* 1.27 (CO 23.27); 2.21 (CO 23.48); *Comm. Matt.* 5.43 (CO 45.187); *Comm. Ps.* 127.1 (CO 32.321).

[58] Cottret, *Calvin*, 140, speaks disparagingly of this: 'God created woman so that men could devote themselves to the Lord.' Whether equal or not, the arrangement was clearly reciprocal in some way in the reformer's mind.

[59] See chapter 1 in the present work.

[60] Calvin, *Letters*, 1.141.

[61] Though Calvin does not refer to Scripture here, see, for example, 1 Tim. 3.1-13; particularly, verse 11. Linder, 'Brothers in Christ,' 150, quotes Viret's letter to Nicholas de Wattville, 'The Lord has taken the half of myself from me; he has deprived me of a faithful companion, an excellent homemaker, and *a wife admirably gifted to share my life, my studies, and my ministry.* I am so affected by this blow that I feel like a stranger in my own home' (citing Viret to Nicholas Wattville, 6th March, 1546, CO 12.306). The italicized words are clearly important in the present context.

I, who have the air of being so hostile to celibacy, I am still not married and do not know whether I ever will be. If I take a wife it will be because, being better freed from numerous worries, *I can devote myself to the Lord.*[62]

Calvin is unwilling to compromise his foremost (public, ecclesial) vocation for his personal taste. As we have observed, to make a marriage work in the context of this public vocation the woman may need to learn French, and so on. As we have seen, he can say, therefore, at Idelette's death, 'During her life she was *the faithful helper of my ministry*. From her *I never experienced the slightest hindrance*. She was *never troublesome* to me throughout the entire course of her illness.'[63] Perhaps the italicised words reflect, not his view of Idelette as a woman or a wife, but rather as a partner in the wider, important vocation of gospel ministry: her willingness to go with him into poverty and even to death—martyrdom, perhaps[64]—attest as much.[65]

However, that does not need to insinuate that Calvin's view of marriage, generally, nor of his marriage to Idelette, in particular, was anything other than affectionate.[66] 'I have been bereaved of the best *companion* of my life,' Calvin laments on his wife's death.[67] 'I am no more than *half a man*, since God recently took my wife home to himself.'[68] The italicised words are very significant. On a wider reading we find that Calvin teaches that at creation God appointed male and female to be partners, companions, indeed, 'one whole man [sic]'. Thus, each person is created a 'social animal [*sociale animal*]'.[69] This companionship becomes the man and woman's particular calling when they marry. Elsewhere, Calvin says that 'The husband and wife live together in such a way as to cherish either the other no less than half himself.'[70] Again, more fully in the reformer's commentary on 1 Corinthians 7.1:

---

[62] OC 10-1, col 228, cited by Richard Stauffer, *L'humanité de Calvin* (Neuchâtel: Delachaux and Niestlé, 1964), 19; and, again, by Cottret, *Calvin*, 140, emphasis added.
[63] Calvin, *Letters*, 2.216, emphasis added.
[64] See chapter 7 of the present work.
[65] Calvin, *Letters*, 2.216.
[66] After suggesting that the reformer's attitude to marriage was 'resoundingly unromantic,' N.R. Needham, *2000 Years of Christ's Power*. Part 3, 'Renaissance and Reformation' (London: Grace Publications Trust, 2004), 216, later admits that it *was* affectionate (217). Interestingly, Bouwsma, *John Calvin*, 137, suggests a 'romantic feeling' in Calvin's view of marriage. He cites *Comm. Jer.* 3.4, *Comm. Dan.* 11.38-39 and *Comm. Gen.* 29.18. On the latter Calvin concludes, 'He who shall be inclined to choose a wife because of the elegance of her shape will not *necessarily* sin' (cited, 137, emphasis added). However, infatuation and lust must never constitute the reason for marriage; on this, he is emphatic.
[67] Calvin, *Letters*, 2.216, italics added.
[68] Cited by Selderhuis, *John Calvin*, 172, italics added.
[69] *Comm. Mal.* 2.14 (CO 44.453-6); *Comm. Gen.* 2.18 (CO 23.46), respectively. See, also, *Comm. Gal.* 5.14 (CO 50.250); *Inst* 2.3.4-6 (OS 3.275-80); 2.8.41; *Comm. 1 Cor.* 6.15-20 (CO 49.398-400).
[70] *Comm. Matt.* 19.5 (CO 45.529). See, also, *Serm. Eph.* 6.5-9 (CO 51.797).

[W]here the wife is a help to her husband, making his life happy [*ad felicem vitam*], then that is in accordance with God's intention. For God so ordered it in the beginning that the man without a wife was half a man [*quasi dimidius homo*], as it were, and felt himself lacking in help which he particularly needed [*seque singulari et necessario auxilio*]; and the wife was, as it were, the completion of the man [*quasi viri complementum*].[71]

Putting aside the obviously patriarchal perspective in Calvin's words,[72] the fact remains that he sees the man as incomplete and, therefore, in need, without his wife. No wonder, then, that Calvin feels only 'half a man' at the death of his divinely-given companion—his theology has come to roost in his tragic experience. So, whilst acknowledging the obvious affection that existed between Calvin and Idelette, we need also to realise that in her death the reformer lost the companion of his ministerial vocation. Though we must not separate the two artificially, we can say the former is his loss in the private realm, the latter in the public realm of gospel and reform.

The importance of friendship

The letters that we have so far considered were written to William Farel and Peter Viret—Calvin's closest life-long friends,[73] both reformers in their own right, leaders in the Reformation and of the Reformed Church, in particular. We might add Martin Bucer to this short list as one who, together with the other two men, searched for a suitable wife for their friend. This was not unusual, George Spalatin and Argula von Grumbach, amongst others, had encouraged Martin Luther to marry earlier in the century.[74] It is not unusual, but it *is* significant. They are searching for a suitable wife: suitable for the reformer, personally (for they knew him well) and, conceivably, suitable for the Church over which he had been called as an overseer.

Calvin writes several times over a twelve-month period to Farel to encourage him to come to the wedding, and to give his blessing—this is more than 'form' or formality. His persistent encouragement almost becomes a refrain. Calvin is insistent. Of all his friends, Farel is the one Calvin wants to attend.[75] On May 19, 1539, Calvin speaks of Farel's hoped-for attendance as showing not simply his friendship, but that he is well disposed towards the marriage, itself. Farel, the older reformer, his colleague in gospel ministry, must be in attendance to demonstrate that the marriage is seen to be and acknowledged as

---

[71] *Comm. 1 Cor.* 7.1 (CO 49.401).

[72] See Parsons, *Reformation Marriage*, for a full exposition of this aspect of reformational thought on the subject of the husband and wife relationship.

[73] See A. Perrot, *Le Visage humain de Calvin* (Geneva: Labor et Fides, 1986), for a good account of Calvin's friendships, and his ability to have and to keep friends. See, also, the earlier but less useful work, D. Hourticq, *Calvin mon ami* (Geneva: Labor et Fides, 1963).

[74] See Parsons, *Reformation Marriage*, 149-53.

[75] See Calvin's letters to Farel, February 23, 1539, Calvin, *Letters*, 1.107-12; May 19, 1539, Calvin, *Letters*, 1.139-42; February 6, 1540, Calvin, *Letters*, 1.171-75.

good for the whole Church, perhaps. And to Viret he is able to write that Idelette was never a hindrance to him, that is, to his ministry and to the reforming work in the city of Geneva.

The complex context

We have seen that comments from Calvin about marriage are rarely full letters. He does not write letters about his marriage. Rather, the comments form short or longer paragraphs in the middle of lengthy and sometimes complex correspondence, coming in the context of theological and ecclesial matters, of rumours of possible war and international disruption, of troubles in Geneva, of his own poverty, and so on. It is important for us to realise therefore, albeit briefly, that the reformer's concern about marriage was significant, significant enough to take up time in his extremely busy schedule as a pastor and preacher in Strasbourg and, later, in Geneva. Even a cursory glance at the varied and involved context in which the reformer was thinking and writing about marriage adds to the weight of the subject in his consideration. This is not simply about finding a wife for personal satisfaction or companionship (though it clearly involves that); nor is it a light distraction; it is about making sure that he finds a wife who is entirely suited to the divinely-given vocation she will enjoy with her husband ('one whole man') in the Church as a whole.

Letters on Viret's second marriage

We have observed that we can interpret Calvin's letters on marriage with fresh insight using the double or bifocal lens of private and public wellbeing. This section and the next simply apply this, first, to the reformer's letters on Peter Viret's second marriage and, then, on William Farel's marriage to a much younger woman, a marriage of which Calvin thoroughly disapproved. Do these new historical scenarios add to our perspective, making it more viable as a device for getting closer to Calvin's ideas? Remembering what has gone before, here, we can be brief.

To Monsieur de Falais, July 4, 1546[76]

Letters from Calvin to Viret in February and March, 1546, show the reformer's pastoral concern for his friend on, first, the incurable illness and, second, the death of his beloved wife, Elizabeth.[77] From our twenty-first century perspective, no doubt, we find it surprising that in July of that same year (just over

---

[76] Letter to Monsieur de Falais, Geneva, July 4, 1546, Calvin, *Letters*, 2.63-64. Henry F. Henderson, *Calvin in his Letters* (Eugene: Wipf and Stock, 1996), 91, 'Turning aside from the more serious occupations of his life, he seeks to find a partner for the widower Viret.' In the light of what we have learned it is quite inappropriate to speak of the subject of marriage as in some way *less* serious.

[77] Letter to Viret, Geneva, February 22, 1546, Calvin, *Letters*, 2.36-37; Letter to Viret, Geneva, March 8, 1546, Calvin, *Letters*, 2.37-38. See chapter 6 of the present work on Calvin's response to the grief of his friend.

three months later) Calvin writes to de Falais to mention that Viret 'our brother' is about to look for someone to marry and that he and Viret are rather anxious about the matter. However, the speed of the situation demonstrates, perhaps, less their disrespect and more the importance of the married state in the reformers' minds. It is clear that Calvin has searched for a suitable wife, for he says that none of the potential women in Geneva, Lausanne or Orbe, are satisfactory as far as he can assess. Then he asks de Falais' advice and help, making this comment:

> I am well aware that, for your part, *knowing how much consequence the marriage of such a man is for the Church of God*, you would not spare yourself any pains therein.[78]

In the middle of his own marriage to Idelette Calvin is aware of the consequences of a good, a suitable, marriage. It has repercussions for the whole Church. Clearly, then, at one level, Calvin is asking de Falais to judge potential partners against the public wellbeing of such a marriage. How will this affect the Church and the preaching of the gospel? In a letter from Calvin to Viret in the same month, the reformer closes with the solemn and significant words, 'Adieu; may the Lord govern you by his counsel, and bless us in an undertaking of such moment.'[79]

To Viret, July 25, 1546[80]

In this letter, Calvin writes to explain a disappointing situation with a prospective candidate for marriage. The woman and her father have visited Geneva (note) to discuss the proposal with Calvin, but in conversation it appears that the father would only consent to the marriage if Viret moved to live in Lausanne with the man's daughter. The seriousness of the proposal is seen in Calvin's language as he recounts his response:

> I pointed out how *absurd* it would be if we were to leave our churches to follow whither our wives called us; that a marriage consummated under such a condition would be an *unhappy*, because an *unholy*, alliance, that would not pass without *punishment* falling on both you [Viret] and the girl; finally, that you would never

---

[78] Calvin, *Letters*, 2.64, emphasis added.
[79] Letter to Viret, July 13, 1546, Calvin, *Letters*, 2.65. Calvin actively searched for a wife for his friend Viret, 'interfering,' as he put it. See Letter to Viret, July 15, 1546, Calvin, *Letters*, 2.65-67, 'I will never, however, allow that there is any man on earth who has greater concern about his own matters than I have about the present.' On his interfering in such matters see the following: Letter to Viret, July 1546, Calvin, *Letters*, 2.68; Letter to Monsieur de Falais, November 16, 1546, Calvin, *Letters*, 2.79-84; Letter to Monsieur de Falais, May 1, 1547, Calvin, *Letters*, 2.110-11; Letter to Viret, September 1, 1548, Calvin, *Letters* 4.409-10; Letter to Farel, July 1, 1558, Calvin, *Letters*, 3.427.
[80] Letter to Viret, July 25, 1546, Calvin, *Letters*, 2.68-69.

be prevailed upon to afford the first example of so *disgraceful* a practice, and, therefore, that it was in vain to make the request.[81]

The words in italics indicate what Calvin really thinks. And, again, we can see that he has the public wellbeing in mind here ('so *disgraceful* a practice'), not so much the personal or private, although that is affected by what Calvin would see as disobedience ('an *unhappy* . . . an *unholy* alliance'). As a practical way forward Calvin suggests to the father that Lausanne is not too far for his daughter to travel back and forth, but after three days' consideration the father was unwilling to comply, much to the reformer's annoyance.

To Monsieur de Falais, October 4, 1546[82]

Interestingly, in this letter, Calvin remarks that Viret had previously said that 'it is necessary that the wife he shall take may be informed beforehand of some domestic charges which he is obliged to bear'. The reformer's response to this is significant. He says to de Falais, 'Besides, love requires previous acquaintance, and the household affairs never go well without a private mutual understanding, and a settlement of the conditions required on both sides.'[83] This is simply an oblique reminder of the reformer's understanding that the husband and wife, though in a patriarchal relationship, are mutual partners in the vocation to which they are called in marriage. Calvin believes that a Christian must only marry the woman who would best help him to fulfil the duty of the life of faith.[84] In an age of domestic unrest and violence it was important that the reformers exemplify the love of God in their familial relationships.[85]

Letters on Farel's second marriage

At the age of 69 William Farel, having lived many years in celibacy, determined to marry Marie of Rouen, whose father, Alexandre Turol, was a refugee in Neuchâtel. Together with the rest of the Reformed community, Calvin was set against this from the beginning. Indeed, the ministers of Neuchâtel, distraught by the affair, were determined to intervene to stop the arrangement, but in the end did not. There were several reasons why people objected, as we shall see. However, in the end, William and Marie married on Tuesday December 20, 1558.

It is worth noting in this context that the control of matrimonial morality extended to the age of the spouses. Bernard Cottret explains that the age of marriage depended on the ability to procreate. 'Intimate relations that had only en-

---

[81] Calvin, *Letters*, 2.69, italics added.
[82] Letter to Monsieur de Falais, Geneva, October 4, 1546, Calvin, *Letters*, 2.74-76.
[83] Calvin, *Letters*, 2.75.
[84] Selderhuis, *John Calvin*, 178.
[85] See Spierling, 'Women, Marriage and Family,' 192; Schilling, 'Reform and Supervision,' 37-39; David Keck, 'Sorrow and Worship in Calvin's Geneva: their place in family history' in M.R. Forster and B.J. Kaplin (eds), *Piety and Family in Early Modern Europe* (Aldershot: Ashgate, 2005), 204-205.

joyment as their object,' he tells us, 'were considered fornication.'[86] He gives two examples. The first is that the widow of Claude Richardot (75 years of age) was forbidden to marry the servant Jean Achard (25 or 26 years of age). This was considered to be 'against nature'. Interestingly, the second example he alludes to is that of William Farel, himself.[87] Similarly, Herman Selderhuis quotes Calvin: 'If a frail old man falls in love with a young woman, it must be from shameful lust.'[88]

To the Ministers of Neuchâtel, September 26, 1558[89]

Three months before Farel's marriage Calvin writes to the ministers of Neuchâtel about the inappropriateness, but the seeming inevitability of the union. It appears that the ministers were thinking of making Farel break off the relationship, but Calvin advises them against this as it would cause even more scandal and, anyway, he reminds them, the union is not actually against the law. The reformer then deliberately contrasts the public nature of Farel's marriage against its private or personal face: 'Were it a private person,' he says, 'I should be less at a loss for means.' At the level of personal morality Calvin speaks of the situation as 'this foolish enterprise,' 'an evil that cannot be cured'. He speaks of his friend Farel as 'a man who had lost his wits,' and of 'his weakness'. He refers to the situation as 'his fall' and 'the evil'. However, in relation to the public level of his pastoral office within the Reformed church, Calvin writes the following.

> As it is, what will the sneerers say, and what will the simple think, but that the preachers wish to have a law for themselves; and that, in favour of their profession, they violate the most indissoluble tie in the world? . . . Nevertheless, I cannot help entreating you to remember how he has employed himself, during the space of 36 years and more, in serving God and edifying his church, how profitable his labours have been, with what zeal he laboured, and even what advantages you have derived from him. Let that dispose you to some indulgence, not to approve of the evil, but at least not to proceed with extreme rigour. . . . *that* the scandal may be hushed up and produce as little evil as possible, and that our brother be not overwhelmed with sorrow.[90]

There is evident pastoral concern here for a beloved and foolish brother (so he will not be 'overwhelmed by sorrow'); but the priority as far as Calvin is concerned falls on the public perspective, the ecclesial consequences and the repercussions for gospel ministry. He fears that the preachers will be blamed for being a law to themselves and that the scandal will be ruinous to the Church.

---

[86] This, as it stands, is an exaggeration or oversimplification. See Parsons, *Reformation Marriage*, 267-75.
[87] Cottret, *Calvin*, 253.
[88] Selderhuis, *John Calvin*, 177.
[89] Letter to the Ministers of Neuchâtel, Geneva, September 26, 1558, Calvin, *Letters*, 3.473-75.
[90] Calvin, *Letters*, 3.473, 474-75.

To Farel, September 1558[91]

Having received an invitation to his friend's wedding, Calvin explains to Farel that he has already said to his face that he cannot come to the wedding. He insists that it is 'a thing not possible, and because I judged it inexpedient.'[92] Now he says, somewhat nebulously, that he is 'prevented' from coming because of increased responsibilities in Geneva. The Senate, he says, would not permit his absence! He continues:

> But, should no obstacle stand in my way, yet as my coming would afford an admirable handle for the ungodly and the badly disposed to vent their malice in evil speaking, you neither seem to do prudently in inviting me, nor should I act with due consideration if I complied with your wishes.[93]

Further, he had hoped that Farel had hurried it all up, to get it over with. 'Now, by putting them off, I do not doubt but you have occasioned much clandestine talking, which will break out more freely afterwards. For you are much mistaken in thinking that the affair is quite a secret.'[94] We find again, here, Calvin's fear of gossip and scandal which would tend to spoil, not only Farel's reputation, but the reputation of the Church, the gospel and the work of reform—particularly in light of 'the ungodly and the badly disposed'.

Reflections

Judging by his letters on marriage, it can be seen that Calvin sees it in its fullest and broadest context. By coming to it with a bifocal lens, as such, the reformer is able to divide between the private and the public face of marriage. The former is important: marriage helps the individual in relation to their sexual desires, it forms the godly context for the conception and the raising of children, it shapes pious love and companionship,[95] and more—and these, for Calvin, are no small matters. However, the latter, the public face of marriage, appears to be given the priority in Calvin's letters about his own marriage and those of his reforming friends. The vital and, one would have to say, realistic, questions seem to be: How is this union going to affect the whole Church? What are the likely repercussions for the reforming work of the Church? How is this marriage going to influence this man's ministerial vocation? In what ways does this union reflect something of the love and grace of God in Christ? These are the questions of paramount importance when he considers marrying and, later,

---

[91] Letter to Farel, Geneva, September 1558, Calvin, *Letters*, 3.475-77.
[92] Calvin, *Letters*, 3.475.
[93] Calvin, *Letters*, 3.476.
[94] Calvin, *Letters*, 3.476.
[95] We might note, in passing, that the reformer speaks of marriage as a 'holy friendship [*une amitié saincte*],' 'a friendship of life [*vitae societatem*]' and 'the society of two reasonable creatures [*la compagne de deux creatures humaines*]'—*Serm. Titus* 2.3-5 (CO 54.516), *Comm.* 1 Pet. 3.1-7 (CO 55.256), *Serm. Deut.* 22.13-24 (CO 28.48), respectively.

when he judges the invaluable contribution of Idelette to his own ministry. These are the questions that galvanize his thinking when he 'interferes' in Peter Viret's proposed marriage and in assessing William Farel's ill-chosen tie. In recognising this priority we are given another, a more positive and a culturally realistic way of reading the reformer's correspondence on the subject.

It should be noted that Calvin worked very much in a patriarchal context, of course. This needs to be taken into account. Today, in the twenty-first century, we would be asking the question of both men and women; but, nevertheless, Calvin's questions stand scrutiny, I think. His bifocal approach bears consideration if the church is to fulfil its calling and mission in our generation and beyond.

CHAPTER 3

'Nothing was farther from my mind.'[1] Calvin's dedicatory letter to Francis I

In 1536 John Calvin was just 26 years old. Living in Basel for a short period of time he conceived and wrote what would become perhaps *the* major work of the European reformations—certainly of the Reformed Church within that broad and rigorous movement. The first edition of *Christianae Religionis Institutio* (the *Institutes of the Christian Religion*) was short, merely 6 chapters in length. By 1539 this work was to grow to 17 chapters, with a different readership in view; by 1543-50 it developed to 21 chapters, and in the fifth and final edition (1559) it was five times longer, consisting of four lengthy books and 70 chapters.[2] The original 1536 edition was dedicated to King Francis I of France and one of the matters that remains intriguing is that the reformer used that prefatory letter to the French king (*Praefatio ad Regem Gall*) 'in its original, unaltered form to introduce each successive edition of the *Institutes*'[3] up to and including the definitive 1559 Latin edition (French 1560), though that particular king had died twelve years earlier, in 1547.

T.H.L. Parker states that 'The *Institutio* was written in and for the sixteenth century. It was directed to sixteenth-century readers within sixteenth-century patterns of thought.' John Leith, similarly, says that 'Calvin's intention in writing the *Institutes* was to make not a timeless statement of Christian faith, but a summary of faith for the particular situation in which he lived and to which his

---

[1] Calvin to Francis I, King of France (1536), in John Calvin, *The Institutes of the Christian Religion* (edited by John T. McNeill; translated by Ford Lewis Battles; Philadelphia: Westminster, 1960), 9.

[2] For useful introductory comments on the *Institutes* see Wulfert de Greef, *The Writings of John Calvin. An Introductory Guide* (translated by Lyle D. Bierma; Grand Rapids: Baker / Leicester: Apollos, 1993), 195-97; Wulfert de Greef, 'Calvin's Writings' in Donald K. McKim (ed.), *The Cambridge Companion to John Calvin* (Cambridge: Cambridge University Press, 2004), 42-44; Bernard Cottret, *Calvin. A Biography* (Grand Rapids: Eerdmans / Edinburgh: T&T Clark, 2000), 110-14; Stephen Edmondson, 'The biblical structure of Calvin's *Institutes*,' *Scottish Journal of Theology* 59.1 (2006), 1-13. And, more fully, David W. Hall and Peter A. Lillback (eds), *A Theological Guide to Calvin's* Institutes. *Essays and Analysis* (Phillipsburg: P&R, 2008).

[3] Serene Jones, *Calvin and the Rhetoric of Piety* (Louisville: Westminster John Knox, 1995), 50.

ministry extended in the middle of the sixteenth century.'[4] That specificity is incontrovertible, though, we might note, in passing, Bernard Cottret's intriguing, seemingly contradictory conclusion that 'the *Institutes* did not deal only with existing circumstances. A profoundly original theology was introduced.'[5] Nevertheless, Calvin wrote largely concerning the needs of the time (*quid exigat tempus*)—including political, social and religious needs, if we might separate them in that way, somewhat anachronistically—and largely for the evangelical Christians of his own country of France—hence the dedication to the French king. However, it has to be said that Francis I was 'a most unlikely patron'.[6]

Though there had already been moderate reform in France—Calvin's translator, Ford Lewis Battles, for example, mentions in this context Jacques Lefèvre d'Étaples, Bishop Guillaume Briçonnet and the so-called Cercle de Meaux[7]—the king generally went along with his conservative Parisian theologians at the University of the Sorbonne, and they were openly and aggressively against the new reform movement, hoping to suppress dissenting, nonconformist and heretical factions in France. This antagonism understandably increased after the Affair of the Placards in October, 1534. Persecution was not monolithic, of course; it differed in various areas; it altered in intensity at times. However, though it slackened at times, it never really ceased. Indeed, in reality, the king's treatment of Protestants depended on shifting political circumstances—particularly his fragile relations with both the Pope and the Holy Roman Emperor, Charles V. The context for Calvin's writing the *Institutes* (1536), then, and, specifically, the dedicatory letter to Francis I was one of the persecution of French evangelicals—those who held to the same truths as Calvin, those who came from his homeland, from whence he had been banished. When Francis I died in 1547 his successor, Henry II, was even more vigorously repressive against the French Protestants. Serene Jones describes the whole period (1536-1559) as follows: 'During these years, intervals of increased toleration had occurred, but constantly shifting relations of power . . . kept the threat of persecution a living and often terrifying reality for the evangelical community.'[8]

---

[4] T.H.L. Parker, *Calvin. An Introduction to his Thought* (London: Geoffrey Chapman, 1995), 2; John Leith, 'Calvin's Theological Realism and the Lasting Influence of his Theology' in D. Willis and M. Welker (eds), *Toward the Future of Reformed Theology* (Grand Rapids: Eerdmans, 1999), 339, respectively.

[5] Cottret, *Calvin*, 111.

[6] Lee Palmer Wandel, *The Reformation. Towards a New History* (Cambridge: Cambridge University Press, 2011), 160. See 160-61.

[7] See Ford Lewis Battles, 'The First Edition of the *Institutes of the Christian Religion* (1536)' in R. Benedetto (ed.), *Interpreting John Calvin* (Grand Rapids: Baker, 1996), 94-95. See, also, Heiko A. Oberman, *Initia Calvini*: The Matrix of Calvin's Reformation' in Wilhelm H. Neuser (ed.), *Calvinus Sacrae Scripturae Professor: Calvin as Confessor of Holy Scripture* (Grand Rapids: Eerdmans, 1994), 150-52.

[8] Jones, *Calvin*, 50-51. See, also, D. Nicolls, 'The Theatre of Martyrdom in the French Reformation,' *Past and Present* 121 (1988); Philip Benedict, 'Settlements: France' in

Calvin's letters, 1533-1547

It is clear from the reformer's letters, written during Francis' reign, that Calvin was well aware of the difficult situation; indeed, he involved himself politically and pastorally for the good of the Church in his homeland of France. As early as October 1533, the reformer wrote to Francis Daniel about the nascent reformation developing in Paris and the censorship of written works to which the Sorbonne theologians, presumably, had taken offence.[9] By 1537—just twelve months after the original edition of the *Institutes*, with the prefatory letter to Francis I attached—Calvin writes of 'A new outbreak of the cruel rage of the ungodly [that] has burst forth at Nismes, as the place is now called . . . against the unhappy brethren who reside there, scattered up and down.'[10] This, he says, had come as a shock as Calvin had been led to believe, falsely as it happens, that those imprisoned in France on account of their religious convictions were soon to be released. 'We rested secure in this expectation,' he admits, somewhat despondently.[11] Indeed, the situation was worse than he had imagined: two people had already been burned alive, many believers had been imprisoned; many lived 'in jeopardy of their lives'. The reformer's subsequent fear is that those persecuting, having tasted power and 'success' (in their terms), may now not know where to stop; that those 'already drunk with the blood of these two victims, are not otherwise at all likely to set any bounds to their persecuting spirit'.[12]

Calvin was, then, acutely aware of the dire situation that evangelicals faced in France during this precarious time. He certainly kept abreast of the changing fortunes of the Church there, even from an early stage of his career. He speaks of the on-going persecution as 'attempted terrorism' in a letter to William Farel in May, 1540.[13] Later, he describes Reformed believers as 'the brethren who suffer in behalf of the Gospel'[14] and those who persecute them as 'the disciples

---

Thomas A. Brady, Heiko A. Oberman and James D. Tracy (eds), *Handbook of European History 1400-1600. 'Late Middle Ages, Renaissance and Reformation'* (Leiden: Brill, 1995), 385-415. Also, chapter 7 of the present volume.

[9] To Francis Daniel, Paris, October, 1533; Calvin, *Letters*, 1.36-40. For the most part, throughout this present volume I am employing John Calvin, *Letters*, 4 volumes (edited by Jules Bonnet; translated by Marcus R. Gilchrist; Philadelphia: Presbyterian Board, 1858). See, also, John Calvin, *Lettres françaises*, 2 volumes (edited by Jules Bonnet; Paris: Meyrueis, 1854) and *Ioannis Calvini Opera quae supersunt omnia* [CO] (Corpus Reformatorum: Brunswick: Schwetschke et Filium, 1863–1900).

[10] To the Ministers of the Church of Basel, Geneva, November 13, 1537; Calvin, *Letters* 1.58.

[11] Calvin, *Letters*, 1.58-59.

[12] Calvin, *Letters*, 1.59. See, also, Calvin's letter to Farel, Strasbourg, December 31, 1539; Calvin, *Letters*, 1.168-71.

[13] To Farel, Strasbourg, May 1540; Calvin, *Letters*, 1.178-86 (181). See, also, Calvin's letters to Farel, Strasbourg, June 21, 1540; Calvin, *Letters*, 1.190; to Viret, Strasbourg, October 8, 1540; Calvin, *Letters*, 1.202-203.

[14] To Farel, Strasbourg, July 1541; Calvin, *Letters*, 1.273.

of Antichrist'—signalling quite clearly the defining distinctions and demarcation within the situation.[15]

He writes of his intense grief and sorrow as reports of the atrocities reach him. To his friend Peter Viret, for example, he says:

> Your letter was a very sad one to me, and all the more so because I can well imagine that cruel butchery to boil over without measure, as always happens whenever it has once burst forth, and there is no way of putting a stop to it.... Wherefore, unless the Lord open up some new outlet, there is no other way of helping our unhappy brethren than by our prayers and exhortations.... The only remedy which almost alone remains, therefore, seems to be, that we commit their safety to the Lord.[16]

We note, again, the reformer's fear of unbridled discrimination and harassment. Again, sometime later, on hearing reports that several villages in an evangelical area of Provence had been set on fire, the reformer's sadness and inability to change the situation is evident. He says that he has heard

> that most of the old men had been burned to death, that some had been put to the sword, others having been carried off to abide their doom; and that such was the savage cruelty of these persecutors, that neither young girls, nor pregnant women, nor infants, were spared. So great is the atrocious cruelty of this proceeding that I grow bewildered when I reflect upon it.[17]

He closes, 'I write, worn out with sadness, and not without tears, which so burst forth, that every now and then they interrupt my words.'[18] Nine months later, he writes of the 'cruel measures against the godly in France'.[19]

As we may appreciate, the question of how to assist the Church is central to Calvin's thinking at this juncture. At times he declares that the only thing that he can think of to do is to pray, to ask God to intervene, to plead for divine mercy: 'May the Lord stretch forth his arm of might for the safety of the godly,' he pleads in one letter;[20] 'May the Lord have respect for his Church!' in another.[21] However, the reformer recognises that in concrete political terms the situation is largely dependent upon the King of France in relation both to the Emperor, Charles V, and to the Pope.[22] He fears at times that the king will make a treaty with the Emperor which will make the situation even worse for the Reformed in France and, indeed, evangelicals throughout the whole of Eu-

---

[15] To Viret, Geneva, March 15, 1545; Calvin, *Letters*, 1.451.
[16] To Peter Viret, Strasbourg, May 19, 1540; Calvin, *Letters*, 1.187.
[17] To Farel, Geneva, May 4, 1545; Calvin, *Letters*, 1.458.
[18] Calvin, *Letters*, 1.459.
[19] To Farel, Geneva, January 26, 1546; Calvin, *Letters*, 2.27.
[20] Calvin, *Letters*, 1.451.
[21] To Farel, Geneva, February 20, 1546; Calvin, *Letters*, 2.35-36.
[22] For an extremely able account of Calvin's political understanding of the complex situation, generally, see Jon Balserak, *John Calvin as Sixteenth-Century Prophet* (Oxford: Oxford University Press, 2014).

rope. And this fear becomes a refrain through many of his letters of this period.[23]

It is clear from the letters that the reformer and others have attempted to intervene in the situation to improve the circumstances of their evangelical brethren. In September 1539, for instance, he speaks of the Senate of Strasbourg interceding on behalf of the French Protestants.[24] A year later, in October 1540, Calvin informs Farel that he has written to the influential Queen of Navarre on behalf of the faithful persecuted in France, 'that she should not desert us in a time of so great affliction'.[25] There is evidence in the correspondence, too, that Calvin and others attempted during this time directly to persuade the King of France to change his mind and policy towards the evangelicals. In 1545 letters were dispatched urgently to the king to intercede for those persecuted in France.[26] In a letter, written to both Farel and Viret, Calvin suggests that the courts have promised leniency for those imprisoned in France, but, being 'aware of the hollowness of courts,'[27] the reformers need to ask the king himself to set up a commission of inquiry and to nominate extraordinary impartial judges to oversee the situation and to see justice ultimately done.[28] Calvin concludes that 'To aim at anything beyond this would . . . be superfluous.'[29] In an interesting comment, he says that it would be in vain to ask of the King what he ought to do of his own accord.[30]

The significance of these few comments from the reformer's correspondence and their relation to the prefatory letter to Francis I in the 1536 *Institutes* ought to be obvious, of course. The *Institutes* were written and continued to be expanded and published in periods of persecution that beset Calvin's beloved Church in France. And, together with the theological text, the reformer continued to attach his letter to King Francis I of France during his lifetime and long after he had died. This short chapter seeks to explore this fact against the political situation outlined above and in relation to the letter's literary significance as well. What was the purpose of the *Institutes*? Who were its intended readers?

---

[23] 'If they can agree together,' he writes to Farel, 'we may well be apprehensive of their conspiring for our destruction'—to Farel, Strasbourg, February 6, 1540; Calvin, *Letters*, 1.174. See, specifically, his letter to Farel, Strasbourg, May 1540; Calvin, *Letters*, 1.181. Also, Calvin's letters to Farel, Strasbourg, October 1540; Calvin, *Letters*, 1.207; to Oswald Myconius, Geneva, June 24, 1544; Calvin, *Letters*, 1.421-22; to Melanchthon, January 21, 1545; Calvin, *Letters*, 1.439, and to Viret, February 2, 1545; Calvin, *Letters*, 1.447-49.

[24] To Farel, September, 1539; Calvin, *Letters*, 1.150.

[25] Calvin, *Letters*, 1.207. Note the inclusivity in the word 'us'. See, also, Calvin's letter to Viret, Geneva, August 19, 1542; Calvin, *Letters*, 1.340-44.

[26] To Viret, Geneva, May 25, 1545; Calvin, *Letters*, 1.460-61. See, also, Calvin's letter to the Pastors of Schaffhausen, Geneva, July 24, 1545; Calvin, *Letters*, 1.472-73.

[27] To Farel and Viret, Geneva, May 1, 1546; Calvin, *Letters*, 2.58.

[28] Calvin, *Letters*, 2.59.

[29] Calvin, *Letters*, 2.59.

[30] Calvin, *Letters*, 2.59.

How did the letter fit into that purpose? What is the letter's place in Calvin's thinking? Why retain the letter to Francis for years after his death? This is an interesting area of inquiry that deserves more length than this short essay can give. However, this essay forms a beginning, perhaps.

The prefatory letter: recent interpretation

The consensus of opinion appears to be that the original edition of the *Institutes* (1536), 'the primitive core' as Bernard Cottret aptly terms the edition,[31] was modelled on the shape of traditional catechisms (both medieval and contemporary to Calvin) which aimed at teaching those beginning in the Christian faith. This certainly appears to be a reasonable conclusion. Besides translations of Luther's two catechisms—the *Small Catechism* (1522) and the *Large Catechism* (1529)—Calvin would have known William Farel's *Sommaire et briefve declaration dauscuns fort necessaires a ung chascun chrestien pour metre sa confiance en dieu et ayder son prochain* (Basel, 1525) and the *Somme Chrestienne* of Francis Lambert of Avignon (1529).[32]

Catechetical literature generally took the form of simple expositions of the law, the Apostles' Creed, the Lord's Prayer, and so on. Similarly, the first edition of the *Institutes* had six chapters. Chapter 1 expounds the Ten Commandments; chapter 2, the Apostles' Creed; chapter 3, the Lord's Prayer; and chapter 4, the sacraments. The fifth chapter is a lengthy rejection of the Catholic sacraments that Calvin deemed to be unscriptural and, therefore, to be false—confirmation, penance, extreme unction, orders and marriage—whilst it retains the two sacraments acceptable to the evangelicals, the Lord's Supper and baptism. The concluding chapter of the original *Institutes* (chapter 6) contains three related themes—those of Christian freedom, ecclesiastical power and political power.[33]

Battles suggests that Calvin was drawn to the need of a good catechism,[34] but this, as it stands, seems unlikely at this stage of his career, before he had taken on the reins of the church in Geneva and during a time in which he had

---

[31] Cottret, *Calvin*, 310.
[32] See Battles, 'The First Edition,' 92. Farel's *Sommaire* was published on the insistence of Johann Oecolampadius. Battles states that though there is overlap, Calvin owes nothing to Farel's work in style, structure or even content. See, also, John I. Hesselink, *Calvin's First Catechism. A Commentary* (Louisville: Westminster John Knox, 1997), 42; Alister E. McGrath, *A Life of John Calvin. A Study in the Shaping of Western Culture* (Oxford: Blackwell, 1990), 137. However, recently, Michael A. Mullett *John Calvin* (Abingdon: Routledge, 2011), 23, has suggested that the *Institutes* bears close resemblance to the Augsburg Confession (*Confessio Augustana*), drawn up by Philip Melanchthon and submitted to the Emperor Charles V at the German Diet of Augsburg in 1530.
[33] See Battles' excellent, introductory exposition of these chapters, 'The First Edition,' 104-110. See, also, Parker, *Calvin*, 4-10.
[34] Battles, 'The First Edition,' 91.

wished more to be a humanist writer than a pastor of a church or a reformer. William Bouwsma's comment that Calvin, the 'young French Catholic,' was 'still exploring his own position' may have some truth in it.[35] Nevertheless, we might ask who Calvin intended as the readership for the first edition.

I say the first edition because it is important to keep in mind that the readership envisaged for the 1536 edition was somewhat different from subsequent editions of the work. In this context there is a very real distinction between the first and second (and, consequently, subsequent) editions. From 1539 onwards the intention was that students of theology would read the work.[36] From the second edition onwards the catechetical form had been replaced by a more systematic organization of the theological themes. 'The new category,' T.H.L. Parker observes, referring to the 1539 edition, 'implies a change of tone from helping on babes in the Faith to instructing the more mature. . . . If the first edition was the 'catechetical' *Institutio*, the second might be called the 'topical' *Institutio*, the *Institutio* of the *Topoi*, the *loci communes*.'[37] Indeed, Randall Zachman astutely remarks that from the 1539 edition,

> Calvin intended the *Institutes* primarily as a book that would re-educate those who had already received a theological education in the Roman Church, so that they could now become more effective teachers and preachers of the gospel and more clearly distinguish the teaching of the gospel from that of the Church of Rome, as well as from other false teachers of doctrine in his day.[38]

Alister McGrath seems off the point in his remark that, though the readership of the 1536 edition is often thought of as French evangelicals, 'anxious to consolidate their understanding of their faith,' in fact it is rather different: '[T]he book,' he says, 'is primarily intended to prove the utter stupidity of the allegation that the persecution of the *évangéliques* could be justified by comparing them with German Anabaptists.'[39] Nevertheless, as we will see, this ignores Calvin's own comments in the prefatory letter. In fact, McGrath himself says as

---

[35] William J. Bouwsma, *John Calvin. A Sixteenth Century Portrait* (New York: Oxford University Press, 1988), 18, 17, respectively.

[36] See *Inst.* 1.4 (OS 3.40-44) and 1.7 (OS 3.65-71). See D.S. Sytsma, 'The Exegetical Context of Calvin's Loci on the Christian Life,' *Calvin Theological Journal* 45.2 (2010), 243-55.

[37] Parker, *Calvin*, 6, 8, respectively. See, also, Richard A. Muller, *The Unaccommodated Calvin: Studies in the Foundation of a Theological Tradition* (New York: Oxford University Press, 2000), 5, 129-37; William S. Barker, 'The Historical Context of the *Institutes* as a Work in Theology' in Hall and Lillback (eds), *A Theological Guide to Calvin's* Institutes, 9.

[38] Randall C. Zachman, 'What Kind of a Book is Calvin's *Institutes*?' in *John Calvin as Teacher, Pastor, and Theologian. The Shape of his Writings and Thought* (Grand Rapids: Baker, 2006), 83. Wandel, *The Reformation*, 104, states that the *Institutes* was 'an effort to provide the foundation for a common reading [of Scripture] that would, in turn, form the basis for building communities of Christians across Europe and the Americas'. See 103-104.

[39] McGrath, *A Life of John Calvin*, 76, 77, respectively.

much—he qualifies his conclusion with the following remark: 'when all the diplomatic conventions and niceties of the prefatory letter are *discounted*'.[40] Yet he makes no argument for disregarding what the reformer says there, unlike Don Compier, for example, who argues vigorously for a political purpose for the *Institutes* (see below).[41] However, the first edition appears to have been written for religious inquirers, to provide a summary and an apology for the evangelical faith, for those 'hungering and thirsting for Christ,' as Calvin himself puts it.[42]

There are, however, different readings of the 1536 *Institutes* and its prefatory letter, different approaches to the edition that are worth summarising at this point. There are specifically three readings that will be examined briefly, the rather conservative reading of Ford Lewis Battles, the political-rhetorical reading of Don Compier, and the literary-rhetorical reading of Serene Jones.

Ford Lewis Battles: Calvin at face value

In his fine, balanced and somewhat seminal essay, 'The First Edition of the *Institutes of the Christian Religion* (1536),'[43] the great translator of Calvin's work, Ford Lewis Battles, outlines the themes of the first edition and briefly examines the prefatory letter to Francis I.

It is important to notice that Battles takes the following paragraph from the prefatory letter, in which the reformer states his original intention, at face value—he says as much.[44] Calvin says,

> When I first set my hand to this work, nothing was farther from my mind, most glorious King, than to write something that might afterwards be offered to Your Majesty. My purpose was solely to transmit certain rudiments by which those who are touched with any zeal for religion might be shaped to true godliness (*formentur ad veram pietatem*). And I undertook this labor especially for our French countrymen, very many of whom I knew to be hungering and thirsting for Christ; but I saw very few who had been duly imbued with even a slight knowledge of him. The book itself witnesses that this was my intention, adapted as it is to a simple and, you may say, elementary form of teaching.[45]

Here, Calvin states that his sole purpose initially has to do primarily with 'true godliness' or piety. His hope was to teach doctrine that might help transform his fellow Frenchmen, those who were 'hungering and thirsting for Christ'. It is noticeable that he claims that the book itself demonstrates this, having 'a simple . . . elementary form of teaching' (that is, the catechetical form). Also, it is important to note that the reformer says that his dedication of the book and, there-

---

[40] McGrath, *A Life of John Calvin*, 77, emphasis added.
[41] See Don H. Compier, *John Calvin's Rhetorical Doctrine of Sin* (Lewiston: Edwin Mellen, 2001).
[42] Calvin, *Institutes*, Prefatory letter, 9.
[43] Battles, 'The First Edition of the *Institutes of the Christian Religion* (1536)' in Benedetto, *Interpreting John Calvin*, 91-116.
[44] Battles, 'The First Edition,' 93.
[45] Calvin, *Institutes*, prefatory letter, 9.

fore, his prefatory letter to Francis I was incidental: 'nothing was farther from my mind . . . than to write something that might afterwards be offered to Your Majesty,' he writes.

Battles suggests that Calvin must have planned a French version of the 1536 edition because Latin (the *lingua franca*) would have meant nothing to most ordinary Frenchmen of the time. In fact we know that he did plan such a translation. He says in a short letter to Francis Daniel, written in October 1536, that he is working on a French translation of the *Institutes*—'my little book,' as he calls it.[46] It is interesting, as well, that Calvin makes this remark in the context of a short summary, as it were, of the developing Reformation:

> Already, in many places, the idols and altars of Popery have begun to disappear, and I hope it will not be long before all remaining superstition shall be effectually cleared away. The Lord grant that idolatry may be entirely uprooted out of the hearts of all.[47]

However, there is no evidence that the French version was ever published.[48]

In the English translation, the prefatory letter has now been broken into sections, but Calvin's original piece was one. Battles, for his part, suggests 8 sections. We may summarise them briefly in the following way:

1. Circumstances in which the book was first written – asks for a full and fair inquiry into the evangelicals' case.
2. Pleads for the persecuted evangelicals – their scriptural faith and heroic martyrdom.
3. Takes up four basic charges of the Catholics against the Reformed Faith: that it is new, unknown, uncertain, and unsupported by miracles.
4. Calvin disposes the oft-repeated argument that the evangelicals have thrown out the Church Fathers. Full of antitheses:
   a] God doesn't need gold or silver / look at their lavish fasts
   b] Christians may either eat meat or abstain from it / Lenten fasts
   c] monks must work / idle, licentious monks of our day
   d] no images of Christ or saints / churches crawling with images
   e] after burial of the dead let them rest / perpetual concern for the dead
   f] bread and wine remain in the Eucharist / transubstantiation
   g] all present must partake of the Lord's Supper / public and private Masses put grace and merit of Christ up for sale

---

[46] To Francis Daniel, Lausanne, October 13, 1536; Calvin, *Letters*, 1.45. Mullett, *John Calvin*, 22, reminds us that Calvin spoke of the book as a *libellous*, a booklet or pocket-book.
[47] Calvin, *Letters*, 1.46.
[48] See D.F. Wright, 'Calvin's Role in Church History' in Donald K. McKim (ed.), *The Cambridge Companion to John Calvin* (Cambridge: Cambridge University Press, 2004), 279; McGrath, *A Life of John Calvin*, 138.

h] rash verdicts without basis in Scripture disallowed / jungle of constitutions, canons, etc., not based on God's Word

i] marriage affirmed for clergy / celibacy enjoined

j] God's Word to be kept clear of sophistries / look at their speculative theological brawls!

5. Against the Romanists' assertion of custom – numbers don't sanction or excuse things.
6. Where then is the true Church to be found? Not merely in observable form.
7. Renewed preaching of the gospel was destroying peace and bringing in its train tumult and revolution. Postulates a twofold satanic strategy: kept the Church asleep; prompts religious strife.
8. Realistically sizes up the likelihood that his appeal will actually reach the king and, if it does, whether it will sway him in the least. Whether their earthly king listens or not to their plea, really recognizes them as loyal Frenchmen, the evangelicals will ultimately put their faith in the King of kings, whose rule is perfect justice and who will hear their plea.[49]

Battles suggests that at the heart of the *Institutes* (1536) is the contrast between the extremes of the Roman Catholic Church and the Anabaptists (as Calvin perceived them) and that 'We may conclude that the *Institutes* took shape between these two opposing religious tendencies.'[50]

Interestingly, Battles points out the last sections of the *Institutes* (1536) on political power, and particularly the end which is a final plea of obedience to the earthly monarch, and that 'at the very last the ringing assertion that obedience to human authority must not become disobedience to God'.[51] The significance of this is that he suggests that the final chapter of 1536 is really rhetorically the conclusion of the prefatory letter to Francis I. The shape he posits, then, is this:

a) the dedicatory letter to the king,
b) the catechism of chapters 1-5, and
c) the conclusion to the whole (including the prefatory letter) in chapter 6, on ecclesial and temporal authority and power.

The shape, itself, is said to have been designed to assure the king of the evangelicals' political loyalty and of their firm rejection of the political position taken by the Anabaptists, which to Calvin appeared to be disloyal and seditious.[52]

---

[49] Battles, 'The First Edition,' 102.
[50] Battles, 'The First Edition,' 104.
[51] Battles, 'The First Edition,' 103.
[52] Battles, 'The First Edition,' 110-111.

The implications of Battles' essay for our purposes are not difficult to underline. First, Battles insists on taking Calvin's words at face value. This, he says, is an important starting point for any examination of someone else's work. Second, Battles sees the prefatory letter as an integral part of the whole. That is, the letter is not simply attached to the first edition of the *Institutes*, but it is a rhetorical device forming as it does the political introduction to the *Institutes'* conclusion in chapter 6. Battles' conclusion may be inconsistent with taking Calvin's words at face value though, for the reformer claims that the letter itself was incidental and only added to the theological text later. However, Battles' idea is a suggestion taken up by others—notably by Don Compier.

Don Compier: authorial intent

Don Compier's intriguing work, *John Calvin's Rhetorical Doctrine of Sin*, seeks to emphasize the political nature of the reformer's intention in writing the *Institutes*.[53] Though Compier's study looks mostly at the later editions of 1559/1560, he comments on the first edition and the prefatory letter early on in the work. Therefore, it will be useful to our purpose to summarise his argument.

In exploring Calvin's objective, Compier certainly gives some weight to the prefatory letter; after all, as he correctly suggests, whereas the letter to the reader changes with subsequent editions over the years, the prefatory letter to the king remains the same. Despite that fact and his underlining of it, though, in effect he sidesteps the letter in order to give more weight to Calvin's much later comment from the preface to his commentary on the Psalms (written in 1557), a comment that Compier sees as 'the most explicit declaration of authorial intent'.[54] He quotes it at some length:

> While I was hidden unknown at Basel, a great fire of hatred [for France] had been kindled in Germany by the exile of many godly men from France. To quench this fire, wicked and lying rumors were spread, cruelly calling the exiles Anabaptists and seditious men, men who threatened to upset, not only religion, but the whole political order with their perverse madness. I saw that this was a trick of those in [the French] court, not only to cover up with false slanders the shedding of innocent blood of holy martyrs, but also to enable the persecutors to continue with pitiless slaughter. Therefore I felt that I must make a strong statement against such charges; for I could not be silent without treachery. This was why I published the *Institutes*—to defend against unjust slander my brothers whose death was precious in the Lord's sight. A second reason was my desire to rouse the sympathy and concern of people outside, since the same punishment threatened many other poor people.[55]

---

[53] See Don H. Compier, *John Calvin's Rhetorical Doctrine of Sin* (Lewiston: Edwin Mellen, 2001), particularly, chapter 2, 'The political purpose of the *Institutes of the Christian Religion*,' 43-70.

[54] Compier, *John Calvin's Rhetorical Doctrine of Sin*, 43.

[55] Quoted by Compier, *John Calvin's Rhetorical Doctrine of Sin*, 44.

It must be acknowledged, of course, that the reformer is certainly claiming that the reason for publishing the *Institutes* (1536) was a political one. He is adamant that the purpose was to contradict the 'charges' that the French evangelical exiles in Germany were, if truth be told, Anabaptists.[56] Again, he uses the legal phrase, 'to defend against unjust slander'. The second reason he gives is that he wished to awaken sympathy. Compier rests his argument squarely on this paragraph, written considerably later—21 years—than the 1536 prefatory letter to Francis I.[57] According to him, Calvin wrote the *Institutes* primarily for political reasons and, therefore, he argues for the thoroughly political character of the *Institutes*.[58] He suggests, for example,

> that part of the considerable attraction this tome exercised upon contemporary readers derived from its complete and persistent promotion of a single, clearly defined program of transformation. The advancement of a passionately held unitary vision is often a key ingredient explaining *the political success* of a movement.'[59]

However, it appears to me somewhat unconvincing. After all, Calvin suggests the political nature of the *Institutes* (1536) in his prefatory letter to Francis I, but maintains that anything of that nature was incidental, insisting that primarily he wrote the *Institutes* for those 'hungering and thirsting for Christ,' those seeking godliness and true piety. Then as we have seen, in the reformer's view, the catechetical form of the book attests to and underlines *this* intention. It is not surprising that twenty-one years later—given the terrible persecution that ensued and the part played by the *Institutes*, galvanizing the Reformed Church throughout Europe—that the older Calvin would single out the (secondary) political role.

In a fascinating section that follows, 'Calvin's Appeal to the French Monarchy,'[60] Compier examines the reformer's rhetoric, asserting that 'Whenever reading a text which consciously deploys rhetorical art, the beginning and ending of the treatise offer important clues for reconstructing the essential argument.'[61] He distinguishes between the *exordium* and the *peroration*: the former seeks to create a favourable impression at the beginning of the work by giving a brief summary of the argument and Compier claims that the prefatory letter does just this. The latter (the *peroration*) concludes the work and in this case

---

[56] For a good account of Calvin's own conflict with those he termed 'Anabaptists' see Donald D. Smeeton, 'Calvin's Conflict with the Anabaptists,' *Evangelical Quarterly* 54.1 (1982), 46-54. See, also, J.S. Oyer, 'The Reformers Condemn the Anabaptists' in J.D. Roth (ed.), *They Harry the Good People out of the Land* (Goshen: Mennonite Historical Society, 2000), 3-16.
[57] Cottret, *Calvin*, 118, 119, says, 'The view taken by faith is often retrospective.' He continues, 'This intrusion of meaning, this grammar of behaviour, this renewed attention to grace . . .'
[58] Compier, *John Calvin's Rhetorical Doctrine of Sin*, 69.
[59] Compier, *John Calvin's Rhetorical Doctrine of Sin*, 44, emphasis added.
[60] Compier, *John Calvin's Rhetorical Doctrine of Sin*, 56-70.
[61] Compier, *John Calvin's Rhetorical Doctrine of Sin*, 56.

Compier suggests that the section in the *Institutes* on civil government fulfils that purpose. There are clear echoes of Battles' earlier argument here, of course. Compier's conclusion is this: 'Given this fact, I do not see how the political character of the work can be considered anything other than a central feature of Calvin's purpose.'[62] In much the same way as Battles, before him, Compier claims that the concluding section of the *Institutes* (1536) on civil government 'establishes a non-negotiable either/or: when their commands appear to be in conflict, persons must choose between obedience to kings and fidelity to the supreme ruler of heaven and earth. Calvin leaves no room for compromise.'[63] But—given Calvin's view of the temporal kingdom—Compier's comments on the *exordium* and *peroration* need to be examined (see below). It appears to me too artificial a conclusion to draw from the evidence.

Serene Jones: the rhetoric of otherness

A few years before Compier's fine study Serene Jones argued, convincingly, for a 'rhetoric of otherness' in Calvin's prefatory letter.[64] Notice, she argues for the political intention of the letter as it introduces the following catechetical text:

> Calvin explains here that he intended the letter to serve as the opening remarks of an extended defense of the evangelical church against the charges of heresy and sedition. He makes this point at the beginning of the letter when he asserts his intention to tell the king of France the truth about this faithful community and thereby to counter the 'many lying slanders' (*mendaces calumniate*) his opponents have incorrectly attributed to them. Appealing to the king's sense of justice, Calvin claims he has written the *Institutes* so that 'from this you [King Francis] may learn the nature of the doctrine against which those madmen burn with rage who today disturb your realm with fire and sword'. Thus, in contrast to the lying slanders of the opposition, Calvin intends to present the king with a true account of his community's faith, an account that performs the critical task of correcting false reports.[65]

This largely accords with Don Compier's interpretation, of course. However, unlike Compier, Jones emphasizes that the primary intention, the principal agenda, if you like, of the *Institutes* (1536) is pedagogical, *not* political. The primary focus, as Jones sees it, is to teach evangelical believers to respond appropriately to the struggling situation in which the Church finds herself, partic-

---

[62] Compier, *John Calvin's Rhetorical Doctrine of Sin*, 56. See also, 68. Compier also sees Calvin as breaking the link between secular and sacred (60), though he qualifies it somewhat later (61): 'We are still some distance from the later separation of church and state.' Compier follows Battles as well in writing briefly about Calvin's 'cherished device, antithesis'—see 63.

[63] Compier, *John Calvin's Rhetorical Doctrine of Sin*, 69.

[64] Serene Jones, *Calvin and the Rhetoric of Piety* (Louisville: Westminster John Knox, 1995).

[65] Jones, *Calvin*, 54.

ularly in France at this time.[66] Further, she argues that Calvin defends his text from those who might, or perhaps inevitably will, misread it. 'The fact that Calvin refers to these misreadings as "abuses",' she states, 'presupposes the possibility of a correct or respectful reading and the corresponding possibility that his readers are capable of grasping it'.[67] So, the reformer intends that his text is read correctly, not falsely interpreted or distorted by those who oppose his views.

It is Jones' reading of the dedicatory letter's text that mostly interests us here. She explores the letter's content and rhetoric within the overarching concept of the world as interpreted by Calvin.[68] She states that the reformer's writings and teaching, generally, served a critical social function; that is, the

> construction of a narrative framework within which this still-young community of believers could locate themselves and make sense of the chaos surrounding them. ... In this sense, he was called upon to help them construct their identity, to form a name for themselves, in short, to articulate the language of their shifting and emerging subjectivity.

They were, she claims, 'an audience who stood in the middle of a process of becoming a people'. And so, in this context, she speaks of the prefatory letter as 'the most graphic description of Calvin's view of that community's emerging self-understanding'.[69] Jones, therefore, explores the letter as though it was a narrative with its own characters and its own storyline. However, specific details need not detain us at this juncture.

Who are the characters? First, the faithful members of the French community, those abused, afflicted, helpless victims, 'this poor little church'. They are described in Christological images such as sheep to the slaughter, they are moral, righteous, humble, saints, martyrs and so on. Second, those persecuting the church, 'men institutionally aligned with the Roman church'.[70] Later, she says the following: 'In order to identify the faithful in this way, Calvin rhetorically profits from the construction of a polemical foe whose contrasting identity reveals the "purity" and "godliness" of the people he seeks to support, teach, and theologically edify'. However, the phrase 'polemical foe' hardly does justice to the concrete situation of the present persecution of evangelical believers.[71]

What, then, is the narrative storyline? Calvin draws a picture of a fierce struggle in which the humble believers have divine strength: 'Calvin . . . discursively

---

[66] Jones, *Calvin*, 61, 63-64. For the theological significance, see 56-58. For a discussion of the intended readership; see 60-62.
[67] Jones, *Calvin*, 55.
[68] See Jones, *Calvin*, 65-69.
[69] Jones, *Calvin*, 65. See, also, the very useful discussion by Delwin Brown, *Boundaries of Our Habitations: Tradition and Theological Construction* (New York: Sate University of New York, 1994).
[70] Jones, *Calvin*, 67; see 65-67.
[71] Jones, *Calvin*, 176.

positions the faithful as the other, the outsider, the marginal. The territorial space of their identity and faith is the space the ungodly transgress.'[72] Rhetorically, the reformer inverts the order he has established, a new order in which the oppressors contravene the boundaries set by the ancient church and those being persecuted respect them.

> Therefore, when viewed from the perspective of divine truth, the weak and oppressed but faithful French evangelical community actually appears as the more powerful party. Consequently, in this scenario, their oppressors stand on the outside as the exiled, the other, and the marginal with respect to God's providence and power.[73]

Then Calvin introduces a third party: the king. 'Calvin discursively situates him in a position not unlike that of a judge before whom both the accused and the accusers must argue their case.'[74] That is, Calvin positions the king centrally, not on either side. He is neutral. Having defended the harassed evangelicals in France, the reformer essentially puts their opponents on trial. The king has to resolve whether he will side with the old Church or whether he will now throw his weight with the Reformed evangelicals.

Jones goes on to explain that this narrative, rhetorical device continued and sharpened over subsequent editions of the *Institutes*. For example, she says, that 'As evangelist, apologist, and confessional leader of a marginal but growing community of faith in Geneva and France, the task of carving out the character of his community's identity remained a central one for Calvin.'[75] And, of course, this is true for later editions. Yet, there is a problem with Jones' fascinating study at this point, I think, for she appears to allow too much weight on who Calvin was at the time of writing the 1536 edition of the *Institutes*. It is, in fact, probable that Calvin was relatively unknown at that time.[76] He was certainly not a key leader of the Reformation movement (though he was shortly to become that), but neither was he simply defending his own theological position, as Bernard Cottret implies.[77] It is probable that his rhetoric, outlined by Serene Jones, underlines the fact that he genuinely wished to affect the king in favour of the evangelicals—a wish he hadn't given up on as late as 1546 (a year before the king's death), as we have seen from his letters—and that the 1536 catechetical form of the text demonstrates his desire to put down on paper, as it were,

---

[72] Jones, *Calvin*, 68.
[73] Jones, *Calvin*, 68.
[74] Jones, *Calvin*, 68.
[75] Jones, *Calvin*, 175.
[76] See Richard Hörcsik, 'John Calvin in Geneva, 1536-38. Some Questions about Calvin's First Stay at Geneva' in Wilhelm H. Neuser (ed.), *Calvinus Sacrae Scripturae Professor: Calvin as Confessor of Holy Scripture* (Grand Rapids: Eerdmans, 1994), 159-62; Phillip R. Johnson, 'The Writer for the People of God' in Burk Parsons (ed.), *John Calvin. A Heart for Devotion, Doctrine and Doxology* (Orlando: Reformation Trust, 2008), 99.
[77] Cottret, *Calvin*, 112.

his own thinking and to teach and encourage others in their faith under the strains of terrible on-going persecution.

The prefatory letter: the text

As we have previously observed, the first paragraph of the letter is most significant, giving as it does Calvin's reasons for writing to the king. Immediately, the reformer makes the point that dedicating the work (the *Institutes* 1536) to the king was, in fact, an afterthought, incidental to the intention of the work as a whole: 'nothing was farther from my mind . . . ,' he says, 'than to write something that might afterward be offered to Your Majesty'—and with this he refers to the *Institutes*, not the letter, of course! He says a little later that it was as a consequence of what he had observed of the condition of doctrine in France that 'I should be doing something worthwhile if I both gave instruction to them [those hungering and thirsting for Christ] and made confession before you with the same work.'[78] Contrary to Don Compier's conclusion at this point, there seems no compelling argument not to accept these words at face value, whatever Calvin himself later says in hindsight, twenty-one years after the event. In this matter I completely agree with Ford Lewis Battles and T.H.L. Parker, for example. It is significant too, that Calvin clearly distinguishes the intention of the letter from that of the work: on the one hand, the letter makes confession, or is an apology for the king; on the other hand, the work is instruction for French believers.

In Calvin's address to the king and the subsequent introductory comments we see immediately that the reformer wishes to position him as a witness (or perhaps as a judge, as Serene Jones suggests) between the parties as if they stood in a legal trial in a court setting. And, indeed, that is the imagery that he continually employs: 'fraud', 'accusation', 'sit in judgment', 'what crime?' 'their defense' and so on. The strength of his judicial argument is that the reformer takes his opponents' accusations to their logical and exaggerated conclusion to clearly demonstrate their falsity. At one point, for example, Calvin says that

> It is as if this doctrine looked to no other end than to wrest the scepters from the hands of kings, to cast down all courts and judgments, to subvert all orders and civil governments, to disrupt the peace and quiet of the people, to abolish all laws, to scatter all lordships and possessions—in short, to turn everything upside down![79]

Again, he says, invoking the possibility of persecution itself, 'If these were true, the whole world would rightly judge this doctrine and its authors worthy of a thousand fires and crosses.' In this way Calvin invites the king to realise

---

[78] *Inst.*, prefatory letter, 9.
[79] *Inst.*, prefatory letter, 10.

the present situation and to look and to see that this supposed social disruption is not the case in areas of Reformed influence. Having addressed the king as 'most Christian King of the French,' he states, 'You can be our witness, most noble King.'[80] Calvin knows that in reality though, the king, is deeply involved with the situation; yet, diplomatically, he speaks of his involvement in purely passive terms. Speaking of the antagonists, for instance, he says, 'they have filled your ears and mind,' and, later, that 'lying slanders' are being repeated 'in your [the king's] presence'.[81]

Continuing the legal imagery, the reformer now pleads for the persecuted believers in France. He asks the king 'to undertake a full inquiry into this case'. Again, tactfully, he distances the king from the problem which, he states, comes 'more from the tyranny of certain Pharisees than with your approval'.[82] Yet, immediately, he draws the king into the predicament as he sums up the whole situation with one very pointed question that demands to be answered:

> [A] very great question is at stake: how God's glory may be kept safe on earth, how God's truth may retain its place of honor, how Christ's Kingdom may be kept in good repair among us. Worthy indeed is this matter of your hearing, worthy of your cognizance, worthy of your royal throne! Indeed, this consideration makes a true king: *to recognize himself a minister of God in governing his kingdom.*[83]

We notice the rhetorically demonstrative repetition of the word 'how': '*how* God's glory may be kept safe on earth, *how* God's truth may retain its place of honor, *how* Christ's Kingdom may be kept in good repair among us'. This repetition gives the sense of urgency to the situation, followed as it is by the repetition of the word 'worthy': '*worthy* indeed is this matter of your hearing, *worthy* of your cognizance, *worthy* of your royal throne'. Fast on the heels of this urgent point at issue comes the demand, the accusation, if you like, for Calvin then declares that the very definition of true kingship is tied up with the way Francis responds to the question in this context—note the use of the word 'your' throughout: '*your* hearing,' '*your* cognizance,' '*your* royal throne!' Is the king for God's glory, God's truth, Christ's kingdom, or is he against it? To answer negatively would be to insinuate his utter disregard for his divinely-given position in a realm (the *ordinem politicum*) that is equally God's as is the spiritual. To answer negatively would also be to announce his total lack of humility before God (*coram Deo*). To answer negatively would be to demonstrate his false credentials—in effect, he would be a usurper—according to classical

---

[80] See *Inst.*, prefatory letter, 10-11. The phrase 'most Christian King of the French' is drastically limited by Calvin in his final remarks of the prefatory letter in which he prays that the Lord, 'the King of Kings,' may establish Francis' throne— *Inst.*, prefatory address, 31. Francis is a king, of course, but not *the* king! The implication is that he needs to remember his place.

[81] *Inst.*, prefatory letter, 10.

[82] *Inst.*, prefatory letter, 11.

[83] *Inst.*, prefatory letter, 11-12, emphasis added.

Christian definitions of kingship from at least Augustine on. Calvin is adamant and unafraid to give the logical conclusion: 'Now, that king who in ruling over his realm does not serve God's glory exercises not kingly rule but brigandage.'[84]

At this point Calvin sets up a clear distinction between the true Church—'the poor little church'—and its adversaries, much as he will do to good effect in his letter to Cardinal Sadoleto, and later in *Concerning Scandals* (*De Scandalas*) and elsewhere.[85] The Reformed Church is 'completely torn and trampled . . . utterly forlorn . . . wasted with cruel slaughter or banished into exile . . . so overwhelmed by threats and fears that it dare not open its mouth'.[86] The Church is despised by others, 'the off-scouring and refuse of the world' (1 Cor. 4.13). Notice, in the following, Calvin's strong, patent identification with this weak and scorned Church: 'Some of us,' he says; then, 'All of us . . . '

> [S]ome of us are shackled with irons, some beaten with rods, some led about as laughingstocks, some proscribed, some savagely tortured, some forced to flee. All of us are oppressed by poverty, cursed with dire expectations, wounded by slanders, and treated in most shameful ways.[87]

Echoing Luther's theology of the cross (*theologia crucis*)[88] Calvin asks a set of rhetorical questions that demonstrate that the Church's weakness is part and parcel of its being and calling, because only in that state can it know the grace and power of God:

> For what is more consonant with faith than to recognize that we are naked of all virtue, in order to be clothed by God? That we are empty of all good, to be filled by him? That we are slaves of sin, to be freed by him? Blind, to be illumined by him? Lame, to be made straight by him? Weak, to be sustained by him? To take away from us all occasion for glorying, that he alone may stand forth gloriously and we glory in him (1 Cor. 1.31; 2 Cor. 10.17)?[89]

---

[84] '*Nec iam regnum ille sed latrocinium exercet*'—*Inst.*, prefatory letter, 12. Calvin uses the words '*Rex christianissimus, le roi très chrétien*' to remind the king of his *duty* to actively promote Christ's religion—Mullett, *John Calvin*, 24.

[85] See *A Reformation Debate. Sadoleto's Letter to the Genevans and Calvin's Reply* (edited by John C. Olin; New York: Fordham University Press, 2000), particularly, 43-88, and John Calvin, *Concerning Scandals* (Edinburgh: Saint Andrew Press, 1978). See, further, chapter 4 of the present volume, and Bonnie Pattison's illuminating discussion, 'The suffering church in Calvin's *De Scandalis*: an exercise in Luther's *Theologia Crucis*? in Michael Parsons (ed.), *Since we are Justified by Faith. Justification in the Theologies of the Protestant Reformation* (Milton Keynes: Paternoster, 2012), 117-37.

[86] *Inst.*, prefatory letter, 11.

[87] *Inst.*, prefatory letter, 14.

[88] See Pattison, 'The suffering church,' 121-37.

[89] *Inst.*, prefatory letter, 13.

The adversaries of this weak church, however, are labelled as 'wicked persons,' 'madmen,' powerful, violent opponents, 'ungodly'[90]—people concerned only with their own and the Old Church's authority, not with true faith: 'No one,' he states, 'gives the slightest indication of sincere zeal.'[91]

In the next long section that takes the letter to its conclusion, Calvin argues specifically against the antagonists' charges against the Reformed Church. Basically, there are six charges:

1) that it is new or 'of recent birth';
2) that it is doubtful or uncertain;
3) that it has not been confirmed by miracles;
4) that it is in disagreement with the Church Fathers and with custom;
5) that it casts dispersion on the previous Church;
6) that it engenders licentiousness, rebellion and the like.[92]

Calvin rebuts these charges and in doing so he turns the original indictment against his opponents.

1) *that it is new or 'of recent birth'*: Calvin accuses them that they find the 'restored' gospel and even Jesus Christ new because these have been buried for years by 'man's impiety' until their recovery through divine grace at the present time.[93]

2) *that it is doubtful or uncertain*: Calvin questions their accusation of uncertainty by asking whether his opponents would be as willing as the Reformed Church to suffer for *their* religion. How certain are *they*? This questioning brings the subject to the ultimate reckoning.

> But however they may jest about its uncertainty, if they had to seal their doctrine in their own blood, and at the expense of their own life, one could see how much it would mean to them. Quite the opposite is our assurance, which fears neither the terrors of death nor even God's judgment seat.[94]

---

[90] *Inst.*, prefatory letter, 9, 10, 11, respectively.

[91] *Inst.*, prefatory letter, 14.

[92] Calvin lists these at *Inst.*, prefatory letter, 15, and speaks of them from 15-30. Given his introductory paragraph outlining the charges against the Church, Calvin appears to speak of them at *Inst.*, prefatory letter, 15-30; not, as with Battles, at 14-18.

[93] *Inst.*, prefatory letter, 16. Elsewhere, Calvin says that 'it has come to this, that the grace of Jesus Christ was, as it were, buried out of sight to us'—letter to Monsieur le Curé de Cernex; Calvin, *Letters*, 1.364-73 (369).

[94] *Inst.*, prefatory letter, 16. Note, too, on another level, Calvin's realistic comment on this: 'When we inculcate that faith ought to be certain and secure, we conceive not of a certainty attended with no doubt or of a security interrupted with no anxiety; but we rather affirm that believers have a perpetual conflict with their own distrust and are far from placing their consciences in a placid calm, never interrupted by any disturbance,' *Inst.* 3.2.17 (OS 4.27). On this important topic, generally, see Susan E. Schreiner, '"The Spiritual Man Judges all Things": Calvin and the Exegetical De-

Even 'the terrors of death' and the ultimate scrutiny of God, the Judge, cannot shake the evangelicals from their assurance because they know and hold to the truth of what they believe.

3) *that it has not been confirmed by miracles*: Calvin reassures them that gospel truth rests on the miraculous. However, the miracles that Calvin rests upon to confirm Reformed doctrine are those recorded in the New Testament, those performed by Jesus Christ and his apostles. The very purpose of miracles then was to confirm truth; they were the seal of the gospel, not of falsehood. Citing numerous scripture passages—Mk 16.20, Acts 14.3, Heb. 2.4, John 7.18, 8.50, Deut. 13.2, 2 Thess. 2.9-10, Matt. 24.24, 2 Cor. 11.14, 2 Thess. 2.11—the reformer, by implication, accuses the antagonists of being false prophets and, explicitly, that their miracles (principally, at the Eucharist) are 'sheer delusions of Satan'. In an intriguing contemporary allusion, Calvin says, '[W]e are not entirely lacking in miracles, and these very certain and not subject to mockery.' However, he makes no effort here to clarify the remark. Is he speaking about the effects of Reformed preaching, about the spiritual formation of those submitted to the gospel, or about the courage of those being persecuted? Of course, we do not know.[95]

4) *that it is in disagreement with the Church Fathers and custom*: In a brazen rebuttal of the accusation that the Reformed Church opposes the Church Fathers Calvin asserts the fact that the Church Fathers were not always right, that the evangelicals follow them only when they agree with Scripture and that the Roman Church appears to follow them even in their mistakes! As Serene Jones puts it, Calvin uses 'voices from the past' not because of their weight, but rather because they agree with his theological position.[96] Notice how the reformer uses Scripture to judge the Fathers' position and to make sure that it is clear that the one they should obey is Christ, not the Fathers:

> [W]e are so versed in their writings as to remember always that all things are ours [1 Cor. 3.21-22], to serve us, not to lord it over us [Lk. 22.24-25], and that we all belong to the one Christ [1 Cor. 3.23], whom we must obey in all things without exception [cf. Col. 3.20].[97]

The implications for the members of the Roman Church are clear; but, Calvin does not miss the chance to apply this 'rule' to the practices of the Church, indicating in example after example that its priests transgress even the limits (the

---

bates about Certainty in the Reformation' in R.A. Muller and J.L. Thompson (eds), *Biblical Interpretation in the Era of the Reformation* (Grand Rapids: Eerdmans, 1996), 189-215.

[95] *Inst.*, prefatory letter, 16-17. See Peter F. Jensen, 'Calvin, Charismatics and Miracles,' *Evangelical Quarterly* 51.3 (1979), particularly, 136-44. See, also, Calvin, *Comm. Gen.* 7.1.

[96] Jones, *Calvin and the Rhetoric of Piety*, 33-34.

[97] *Inst.*, prefatory letter, 18-19.

boundaries) set by the Fathers.[98] They cannot even be obedient to those they have established to guide the Church; they 'reject the yoke of the fathers,' as Calvin later puts it.[99] The reformer underlines the irony:

> It was a father who deemed that one must listen to Christ alone, for Scripture says, 'Hear him' [Matt. 17.5]; and that we need not be concerned about what others before us either said or did, but only about what Christ, who is the first of all, commanded. . . . It was a father who contended that the church ought not to set itself above Christ.[100]

Importantly, Calvin employs the word 'boundary': the adversaries accuse the evangelicals of going beyond boundaries, when, in fact, Calvin claims that it is the Roman Church that disregards the boundaries established by Christ and, later, by some of the Fathers.

Against the supposed authority of custom, Calvin claims that custom derives from things upon which the majority agrees or practises, which, given the sinfulness of humanity, cannot be a good foundation. Instead, characteristically, he asserts the significance of divine truth: '[I]n the Kingdom of God,' he says, 'his eternal truth must alone be listened to and observed, a truth that cannot be dictated to by length of time, by long-standing custom, or by conspiracy of men.' Citing the biblical account of the Flood of Genesis 6–9 (underlining the significance of the minority in that event), he concludes: 'To sum up, evil custom is nothing but a kind of public pestilence in which men do not perish the less though they fall with the multitude.'[101]

5) *that it casts dispersion on the previous Church*: Against the charge that evangelical believers disparage the centuries-old Church, Calvin seeks to define the Church over against the opponents' definition which necessarily includes visible appearance, hierarchy and grandeur:

> Surely the church of Christ has lived and will live so long as Christ reigns at the right hand of his Father. It is sustained by his hand; defended by his protection; and is safe through his power. . . . Against this church we now have no quarrel. For, of one accord with *all believing* folk, we worship and adore one God, and Christ the Lord [1 Cor. 8.6], as he has always been adored by *all godly* men.[102]

Note how the italicised words appear to question the spiritual credentials of the adversaries and, at the same time, emphasize the relational nature of Church. The biblical records, says Calvin, show that God sometimes extinguishes the *outward appearance* of the true church as punishment for humanity's ingratitude. The reformer now delineates his view that the church has a couple of le-

---

[98] For details, see *Inst.*, prefatory letter, 19-23.
[99] *Inst.*, prefatory letter, 22.
[100] *Inst.*, prefatory letter, 22. The editor suggests that Calvin is referring to Cyprian and Augustine, respectively—see 22.ns 34 and 35.
[101] *Inst.*, prefatory letter, 23.
[102] *Inst.*, prefatory letter, 24, emphasis added.

gitimate marks or characteristics: the pure preaching of the Word of God and the lawful administration of the sacraments—just two, baptism and the Lord's Supper.

Having argued at length against 'such pomp,' 'this outward mask,'[103] that the adversaries propose, Calvin concludes with harsh words, that if King Francis devoted a little time to reading the prefatory letter he would recognise that 'this doctrine itself whereby they claim to be the church, is a deadly butchery of souls, a firebrand, a ruin, and a destruction of the church'.[104] We notice, too, that this quotation seems to emphasize the purpose of the prefatory letter as spiritual.

6) *that it engenders licentiousness, rebellion and the like*: Calvin states the final charge levelled against the evangelical church: that it is the cause of sedition and licentiousness—a charge that the reformer strenuously refutes. His adamant conclusion is simply that the charge is levelled in the wrong direction, that the culprit is, in fact, Satan himself: 'Here is, as it were, a certain characteristic of the divine Word, that it never comes forth while Satan is at rest and sleeping.'[105] This, he says, is 'the surest and most trustworthy mark to distinguish it from lying doctrines'. For centuries, he says, Satan 'lay idle and luxuriated in deep repose . . . in tranquil and peaceable possession of his kingdom'.[106] The devil's strategies have become clear: at first he caused men and women violently to oppose the truth; he aroused disagreements through the Anabaptists ('and other monstrous rascals'), to obscure the truth; and now he seeks to uproot the truth through brutal persecution. The reformer notes that this was the same charge laid against Elijah in the Old Testament (1 Kgs 18.17, 18), against Jesus in the Gospels (Luke 23.5; John 19.7), and against the apostles, themselves (Acts 24.5).[107] And, again, he offers a long list of biblical allusions to prove the point.[108] Against this turbulence Calvin reminds the king of the eternal and life-giving nature of the true gospel.

Following the rebuttal of charges brought against the reforming church Calvin brings the letter to a close. He is, at least, rhetorically aware that the king may

---

[103] *Inst.*, prefatory letter, 26.

[104] *Inst.*, prefatory letter, 27. In this manner, as David Steinmetz, 'The Intellectual Appeal of the Reformation,' *Theology Today* 57.4 (2001), 461, argues, 'The Christian past was not so much rejected by the Protestant reformers as refashioned in the light of a different and competing vision of its development and continuing significance.' Steinmetz rightly says that 'the angle of vision' was different. See 461-64.

[105] *Inst.*, prefatory letter, 27-28.

[106] *Inst.*, prefatory letter, 28.

[107] *Inst.*, prefatory letter, 28. 'The apostles in their day,' he says, 'experienced the same things that are now happening to us' (29).

[108] The many biblical allusions include the following: 2 Pet. 3.16; Rom. 6.1, 6.15; 1 Cor. 1.10f.; 2 Cor. 11.3f.; Gal. 1.6f.; Phil. 1.15, 17, 2.21; 2 Pet. 2.22, 2.18-19; 2 Cor. 11.3f.; Acts 6, 11, 15; Rom. 9.33; 1 Pet. 2.8; Isa. 8.14, and so on.

not be listening to such error. It is at this point that the reformer defends himself, as well, for again he includes himself amongst the evangelicals, wrongly charged:[109]

> And we have not, by God's grace, profited so little by the gospel that our life may not be for these disparagers an example of chastity, generosity, mercy, continence, patience, modesty, and all other virtues. It is perfectly clear that we fear and worship God in very truth since we seek, not only in our life but in our death, that his name be hallowed.[110]

He recognizes that there may be people who cause sedition in France, but states that the king should not simply equate them with the evangelical cause, which in itself bears witness to 'innocence and civil uprightness'. He expresses regret for the length of the apology (that is, the prefatory letter); but trusts that the evangelicals can gain the king's favour, 'if in a quiet and composed mood you [the king] will once read this our confession'. Nevertheless, the reformer's last word is one of implied prophetic threat, for if the king does not change the course of things the Church awaits 'the strong hand of the Lord, which will surely appear in due season, coming forth armed to deliver the poor from their affliction and *also to punish their despisers*, who now exult with such great assurance'.[111]

Reflections

Taking the prefatory letter at face value at the point at which the reformer states his intention for the *Institutes* (1536)—which I think we must, as there appear to be no compelling reasons for doing otherwise—it is clear that the young Calvin delineates the sequence of events as follows. First, he responds to the paucity of spiritual and doctrinal understanding amongst the persecuted French evangelicals by writing the theological text in a catechetical form in order to teach and to help shape true piety in those 'hungering and thirsting after Christ'. This task is far from theoretical, given the situation that the Protestants faced at that time. They needed a robust and confident (or 'certain') faith with which to face maltreatment, terrible oppression and even death. Second, towards the end of writing the text of the *Institutes* Calvin realised that he might dedicate the work to the King of France, Francis I, thereby allowing that work to become apologetic in a secondary manner. The letter thereby seeks to persuade the king to step in to defend the true but troubled Church in his realm. Third, the reformer writes the prefatory letter, which had, as he says, not been in his original planning: '[N]othing was farther from my mind.'[112] Though this

---

[109] Calvin appears to defend himself only in so far as he identifies with the French evangelicals; contra, for example, Cottret, *Calvin*, 112, and Barker, 'The Historical Context,' 4.

[110] *Inst.*, prefatory letter, 30.

[111] *Inst.*, prefatory letter, 31, emphasis added.

[112] *Inst.*, prefatory letter, 9.

account does not accord with Don Compier's retelling, for example, it finds full agreement in T.H.L. Parker's well-argued insistence that the form of the work reflects Calvin's intention.[113]

Of course, the scholarly prefatory letter *is* politically motivated. There can be no argument with that conclusion. Its forensic style is entirely appropriate to an apology of its kind. Its initial intention was a plea for clemency and consideration, but the question remains as to why Calvin retained the letter long after the king's death. Perhaps, as Compier claims, the letter continued with the same intention.[114] But this, as it stands, seems too straightforward and unlikely as the letter's intention clearly includes reference to Francis I. Why would Calvin insist on the same letter with every new edition of the *Institutes*, but not change the letter's recipient to Francis' successor, Henry II? Of course, we do not know. But it may be that in retaining Francis' name at the head of the letter, Calvin is underlining the implication of much of the thrust of the letter: that the kingdom of Christ (represented in France by the weak and persecuted evangelical Church) perseveres and lasts through divine power and grace, whereas godless individuals—even kings—do not! Initially, the reformer looked for help and mercy from the French king, Francis I; but, sadly, it was not forthcoming. The king is now dead. The Church is living. The Church, though struggling, though suffering still, continues to show the power and, importantly, the life of God. '[W]e are not entirely lacking in miracles, and these very certain and not subject to mockery.'[115]

---

[113] Parker, *Calvin*, 5.
[114] Compier, *John Calvin's Rhetorical Doctrine of Sin*, 52.
[115] *Inst.*, prefatory letter, 17.

CHAPTER 4

'Such is our consciousness of the truth.'[1]
Calvin's letter to Cardinal Sadoleto

In April 1538 the city's two Protestant reformers, William Farel and John Calvin, were banished from Geneva, ostensibly for refusing to offer the Eucharist on Easter Sunday. They were summarily dismissed from their office by the Council of Two Hundred on April 22, a decision confirmed by both the General Council and the Little Council the following day. The history of the event is well enough known. However, this dismissal and the departure of the two men naturally left a very unsettled state of affairs in Geneva.[2] As we know, the city had rather loosely adopted the Reformation as early as 1532,[3] but, in reality, Catholic citizens were still numerous and Protestants probably remained very much in the minority at this juncture.[4] Almost a year after the reformers' removal from Geneva (March 18, 1539) Cardinal Jacopo Sadoleto (1477-1547), bishop of Carpentras in Southern France, wrote a short unsolicited letter to the Genevans suggesting to them that they should return to the fold of the Catholic Church (the *ecclesia Catholica*)—though the letter was delivered a full two weeks later.[5]

John Olin, the recent editor of the debate, suggests that the open letter might have been the Cardinal's own idea, though it may also have originated with a

---

[1] From Calvin's reply to Sadoleto from *A Reformation Debate. Sadoleto's Letter to the Genevans and Calvin's Reply* (edited by John C. Olin; New York: Fordham University Press, 2000), 75; hereafter, Calvin, 'Reply'. For historical and contextual details see Olin's introduction, hereafter, Olin, 'Introduction'. Amongst other texts, I have used Olin extensively in this brief introduction to chapter 4.

[2] 'Schism and collapse now threatened the young church'—Olin, 'Introduction,' 12.

[3] Of course, reform in Geneva had begun with the preaching and pastoral endeavours of William Farel and Peter Viret, before John Calvin's arrival in 1536. See, generally, William J. Bouwsma, 'The Peculiarity of the Reformation in Geneva' in Steven Ozment (ed.), *Religion and Culture in the Renaissance and Reformation* (16th Century Publications, 1989), 65-76.

[4] See the excellent essay, Karen E. Spierling, 'Friend or Foe. Reformed Genevans and Catholic Neighbors in the Time of Calvin' in R.C. Zackman (ed.), *John Calvin and Roman Catholicism. Critique and Engagement. Then and Now* (Grand Rapids: Baker, 2008), 79-98

[5] This letter was written in Latin and accordingly would not have achieved a very wide circulation—Olin, 'Introduction,' 18.

conference of Catholic prelates who met at Lyons in the previous December (1538). Significantly, the conference included Bishop Peter de la Baume, the ousted bishop of Geneva.[6] Certainly, Sadoleto was an appropriate person to have penned the letter. Olin suggests that he was 'one of the most eminent and respected members of the Sacred College of Cardinals'.[7] The Cardinal was well respected, learned, an accomplished scholar—a disciple and friend of Erasmus.[8] Alexandre Ganoczy speaks of him as 'an irreproachable reformer' in his own right.[9] He was genuinely concerned with reconciliation with the Protestant faction, professing friendship with (certainly, admiration of) John Sturm, Philip Melanchthon and even Martin Bucer.[10] Calvin's biographer, Bernard Cottret, reminds us of the Cardinal's compassion and moderation, quoting a letter that he wrote to Cardinal Farnese:

> The weapons I prefer . . . the truth itself, it is extreme clemency that will make them [Protestants] admit their errors not with the mouth only [as torture might], but in the heart.[11]

A significant member of the Oratories of Divine Love,[12] Sadoleto collaborated in drafting the *Consilium de emendada ecclesia*—according to Olin, 'one of the great documents of Catholic reform'—and, later, in 1542, returned to Rome to

---

[6] Olin, 'Introduction,' 6.

[7] Olin, 'Introduction,' 2.

[8] See N.R. Needham, *2000 Years of Christ's Power*. Part 3 'Renaissance and Reformation' (London: Grace Publications Trust, 2004), 451-52.

[9] Alexandre Ganoczy, 'Calvin's Life' in Donald K. McKim (ed.), *The Cambridge Companion to John Calvin* (Cambridge: Cambridge University Press, 2004), 3-24 (12). See, also, Herman J. Selderhuis, *John Calvin. A Pilgrim's Life* (Downers Grove: IVP Academic, 2009), 100.

[10] Olin, 'Introduction,' 5. Apparently, Sadoleto wrote to Melanchthon in 1537, but without success. See, also, Elizabeth G. Gleason, 'Catholic Reformation, Counter Reformation and Papal Reform in the Sixteenth Century' in T.A. Brady, H.A. Oberman and J.D. Tracy (eds), *Handbook of European History 1400-1600, Late Middle Ages, Renaissance and Reformation*, volume 2, 'Visions, Programs and Outcomes' (Leiden: Brill, 1995), 317-45 (328).

[11] Letter to Cardinal Farnese, July 28, 1539; quoted by Bernard Cottret, *John Calvin. A Biography* (Grand Rapids: Eerdmans / Edinburgh: T&T Clark, 2000), 152. This attitude is seen clearly late in his letter to the Genevans where he says,

> I will not, indeed, pray against them that the Lord would destroy all deceitful lips and high-sounding tongues; nor, likewise, that He would add iniquity to their iniquity, but that He would convert them, and bring them to a right mind, I will earnestly entreat of the Lord, my God, as I do now (Sadoleto, 'Letter,' 41).

[12] See Rudolph W. Heinze, *Reform and Conflict. From the Medieval World to the Wars of Religion, AD 1350-1648* (Grand Rapids: Baker, 2005), 258-59.

help plan the massively important Council of Trent,[13] though, apparently, he did not attend.

In his well-penned epistle the Cardinal appeals for reunion between the Genevans and the Catholic Church. As a consequence, in March 1539 the Little Council decided that a response should be made, but could not specify by whom it should be written. A full two months later the city magistrates sent Sadoleto's letter to the leaders of the city of Bern to see if they would sponsor a reply. In July of that year Peter Kuntz suggested to the Council of Bern that they should ask the deposed reformer John Calvin, who at the time resided in Strasbourg, which they did. By mid-August the reformer had replied with what has been acknowledged by many as one of his most masterful, polemical writings.[14] Timothy George, for example, speaks positively of it as 'a literary tour de force, perhaps the best apology for the Reformed faith written in the sixteenth century'.[15]

Surprisingly, Calvin's response (*Responsio ad Sadoletum*) was written at some speed, apparently in just six days. He speaks of this to his friend and exiled colleague, William Farel:

> Sulzer [the minister of the church in Bern] had brought hither the epistle of Sadolet. I was not very much concerned about an answer to it, but our friends have at length compelled me. At the present moment I am entirely occupied upon it. It will be a six days' work.[16]

The response was published, together with Cardinal Sadoleto's letter, by Wendelin Rihel in Strasbourg in September 1539; then Calvin's French translation of both letters was published by Michel du Bois in Geneva the following year

---

[13] Olin, 'Introduction,' 4. Amongst other things, this document criticized papal power and called for thoroughgoing church reform.

[14] Calvin's letter to Sadoleto is 'one of his most attractive and skilful writings'—David F. Wright, 'Calvin's Role in Church History' in Donald K. McKim (ed.), *The Cambridge Companion to John Calvin* (Cambridge: Cambridge University Press, 2004), 277-88 (283).

[15] Timothy George, *Theology of the Reformers* (Nashville: Broadman, 1988), 182. See also, Richard C. Gamble, 'Calvin's Controversies' in Donald K. McKim (ed.), *The Cambridge Companion to John Calvin* (Cambridge: Cambridge University Press, 2004), 188-203 (190-91); Yosep Kim, *The Identity and the Life of the Church. John Calvin's Ecclesiology in the Perspective of his Anthropology* (Eugene: Pickwick, 2014), 108-109; Needham, *2000 Years*, 220; Heinze, *Reform and Conflict*, 180.

[16] To Farel, September 1539; Calvin, *Letters*, 1.150-151 (151). For the most part, throughout this present volume I am employing John Calvin, *Letters*, 4 volumes (edited by Jules Bonnet; translated by Marcus R. Gilchrist; Philadelphia: Presbyterian Board, 1858). See, also, John Calvin, *Lettres françaises*, 2 volumes (edited by Jules Bonnet; Paris: Meyrueis, 1854) and *Ioannis Calvini Opera quae supersunt omnia* [CO] (Corpus Reformatorum: Brunswick: Schwetschke et Filium, 1863–1900). Against this, Michael Mullett's comment that 'Calvin took it upon himself to respond' seems at odds, perhaps, with the history; see Michael A. Mullett, *John Calvin* (Abingdon: Routledge, 2011), 16.

(1540). The French title on this later edition is significant; it reads, 'Letter of Jacques Sadolet, Cardinal, . . . by which he seeks to reduce them [the people of Geneva] under the power of the Bishop of Rome (*par laquelle il tâche les réduire sous la puissance de l'évêque de Rome*).'[17] The phrase 'reduce them under the power of Rome,' with its clear contrast between the powerlessness of the one (the Reformed inhabitants of Geneva) and the dominance of the other (the Catholic Church, represented by the Cardinal), is extremely important in giving us a key into the reformer's understanding of the situation. We will have cause to return to this below.

Critical interpretation of the letters

The consensus

It is helpful for us at this stage to have a brief overview of how these two letters—Sadoleto's initial, unsolicited letter and Calvin's response—have generally been viewed by Reformation scholars. This is particularly so because of a recent and unexpected change in direction together with criticism of what I perceive to be the consensus on the matter.[18]

The consensus, then, appears to be that the two letters are written with a somewhat elevated, rhetorical style[19] and are substantially argued on both sides. However, the polemic of each letter is real, not apparent, and therefore there is a clear and, perhaps, an unbridgeable difference in understanding between the two theologians—understanding of the nature and authority of the Church, of salvation, of faith, of justification by faith, and so on.

As most commentators read the letters they come to similar, though differently nuanced, conclusions about the important themes in them. John Olin, for example, suggests that 'without question, the main issue raised by this exchange . . . is the issue of whether Holy Church or Holy Scripture constitutes the ultimate authority', though he singles out the authority of the Church and justification by faith as significant themes earlier in his introduction.[20] Bernard Cottret, on the other hand, says that the central question of the debate is that of 'Christian authenticity. How to recognize the true church?'[21] And the Luther scholar, Heiko Oberman, concurs,[22] pointing out further the fact that Calvin's theological vision of the Church prevented him from compromise: 'But Calvin's vision,' he says, 'blocks that kind of cheap ecumenism which transcends and escapes the hardships of urgent Church reform by reference to the invisible

---

[17] Quoted by Cottrett, *Calvin*, 153.
[18] See the next section.
[19] Though Cottrett, *Calvin*, 154, points out Sadoleto's use of fear to bring back the Genevans, and speaks of the reformer's letter as 'hyperbolical and flattering'.
[20] Olin, 'Introduction,' 15, 13, respectively.
[21] Cottrett, *Calvin*, 155.
[22] Heiko A. Oberman, *The Dawn of the Reformation* (Grand Rapids: Eerdmans, 1992), 263.

Church-universal,' by which latter phrase he refers to Sadoleto's ecclesiastical vision, of course.[23] Cottret, in characteristic fashion, is adamant on this very point, speaking in the following way of the Protestant reformer's response: 'It was the defiance of the strong by the weak, of the man of the church by the prophet.'[24] Calvin's reason for so defending the Reformation doctrines of the Church, faith, justification and so on, is that he sees the Cardinal's interference into Genevan affairs as a potential threat to the city to which, though absent, he still felt called by God.[25]

The Catholic theologian, Alexandre Ganoczy, in his early seminal work on the young Calvin, speaks of the reformer's letter as follows:

> It is at the same time a brilliant defense of the exiled minister, a justification of the call to the evangelical ministry, a summary of a genuine ecclesiology, and a forceful rebuttal of the Roman Catholic notion concerning the schismatic character of the reform.[26]

Together with this positive evaluation of Calvin's letter, he points out the mistakes—'blunders,' as he terms them—of which Sadoleto is guilty. Aside from the doctrinal ones (defining Church by 'consensus', for example), the Cardinal, he admits, is 'misinformed and awkward', he 'hurls' accusations at Calvin and his colleagues, his knowledge is not first-hand, but only from hearsay. Together with these, Sadoleto makes the mistake of inviting the citizens of Geneva to return to the Roman Church, apparently forgetting or ignoring the fact that in their attempts to reform they had only relatively recently expelled the Catholic bishop from their midst. According to Calvin, Ganoczy remarks, Sadoleto's argument is simply inadequate.[27] Herman Selderhuis adds that Sadoleto 'made one mistake in his plea. His accusation that Calvin acted out of self-interest was like a red cape to a raging bull.'[28]

So, in summary, the general consensus appears to be that the two theologians were writing from entirely different poles of dogmatic understanding; not necessarily opposite poles, but significantly dissimilar. The historical situation would seem to suggest this, of course. On the one hand, Sadoleto is seeking to win back a deliberately disengaged people into the fold of the Catholic Church. On the other hand, Calvin is attempting to retain those same people in the Reformed faith and Church. The former writer does not know them at all; the latter knows them only too well. The former writes from a distance (both geographical and pastoral); true, the latter writes from Strasbourg, but with a pasto-

---

[23] Oberman, *The Dawn of the Reformation*, 263.
[24] Cottret, *Calvin*, 154.
[25] Alister E. McGrath, *A Life of John Calvin* (Oxford: Blackwell, 1990), 101.
[26] Alexandre Ganoczy, *The Young Calvin* (translated by David Foxgrover and Wade Provo; Edinburgh: T&T Clark, 1987), 126.
[27] Ganoczy, 'Calvin's Life,' 14.
[28] Ganoczy, *The Young Calvin*, 279, Selderhuis, *John Calvin*, 100, respectively.

ral heart for the city to which he has and maintains his divine calling.[29] The Cardinal writes *to* the people of Geneva, Calvin writes *for* them, seeking to identify with them as a good pastor of the flock.[30] Similarly, in doctrinal understanding, the two men are at loggerheads—a subject to which we must return below. Generally, then, the consensus conclusion appears to be that Calvin answered Cardinal Sadoleto well; that his arguments were enough to see off the Cardinal, as it were, and, together with him, the discerned 'threat' of the Catholic Church.

Trajectories for ecumenical engagement?

This much would have been reasonably commonplace amongst Reformation scholars until recently, but things have been questioned by those specifically concerned with present-day ecumenism and the possible use of the reformer, John Calvin, to further that interest. I am thinking here, specifically, of Gerard Mannion and his fascinating essay, 'Calvin and the Church: Trajectories for Ecumenical Engagement Today—Volume Introduction.' The volume in question is a thoroughly original and well worthwhile engagement with Calvin for today's Church, namely, *John Calvin's Ecclesiology. Ecumenical Perspectives* (2011), of which Mannion is one of the two editors, along with Eduardus Van der Borght.[31]

In his interesting short introductory essay Mannion lists the seven themes he discerns in the correspondence between the two men, themes that he sees as central to the argument:

1) the nature and authority of the Church,
2) reflections on the Christian life,
3) reflections on church governance, authority and ministry,
4) justification by faith,
5) the nature of faith itself,
6) Christian action inspired by love,
7) an understanding of salvation.

In further reducing the argument to two points of focus, he lists simply justification by faith and the theology of the Word. However, somewhat confusingly—the image of Russian dolls comes to mind here, with each suggestion becoming more concentrated and somehow nearer the nucleus—he insists that the

---

[29] See chapter 1, on Calvin's calling and return to Geneva.

[30] It may be obvious, but we should remember that Sadoleto is not writing to Calvin, but to the people of Geneva. Calvin's response is aimed directly at the Cardinal, with the people of Geneva in view. Clearly, his words are intended for the Genevans, too.

[31] Gerard Mannion, 'Calvin and the Church: Trajectories for Ecumenical Engagement Today – Volume Introduction' in Gerard Mannion and Eduardus Van der Borght (eds), *John Calvin's Ecclesiology. Ecumenical Perspectives* (London: T&T Clark, 2011), 1-30. See my very brief review, 'Review of G. Mannion & E. Van der Bought, *John Calvin's Ecclesiology* (Edinburgh: T&T Clark, 2011)' in *The Baptist Quarterly* 44 (2012), 442-43.

'*real* core focus of both letters is the understanding of the church that each theologian subscribes to'. This, he says, 'dominates the exchanges,' both implicitly and explicitly.[32]

Mannion concludes that Calvin's letter is not the 'unanswerable riposte' that so many scholars have previously suggested, that it is 'brisk, and it must be said aggressive in tone'. He complains that Calvin takes things too personally and responds too aggressively; that it's not too long 'before the gloves are off'.[33] According to the writer, the reformer is too proud, 'somewhat lacking the humility for his own perspective'.[34] Whilst understandably deficient in detailed analysis of the two epistles, Mannion makes suggestions that betray too ecumenical a reading of both Sadoleto's letter and Calvin's response to it. It seems to me that, in seeking more common ground upon which to build an argument for using John Calvin as a conversation partner in ecumenical debate, Mannion is tempted to draw the two protagonists too closely together.[35] A few examples will suffice here.

First, he argues that it is actually in their style, not so much their substance, that the two letters show their disagreement.

> It would appear that theological nuance and ecclesiastical priorities and characteristics lead to both Calvin and Sadoleto employing language that seemingly accentuates differences between them when, in actual fact, *their positions might not be so far apart* as their respective rhetorical flourishes suggest to some interpreters.[36]

As we will see, both men use language ('rhetorical flourish,' if you like) in order to demonstrate their theological understanding: rhetoric in the employment of theology, style to convey meaning, language in the service of persuasion. Rhetoric must never be divorced from actual meaning.

Second, Mannion suggests that the local historical situation, including the very task of writing letters at a distance from each other,[37] made their argument more contrary than it ought to have been.

> If only they could have found a somewhat different forum more conducive to dialogue and to debating the finer points that was less emotionally charged than that distanced fashion in which their ideas did come into contact, what additional benefits to the cause of Christian harmony might have followed? It is not as if this was an either / or, a zero-sum ecclesiological situation.[38]

It is questionable whether this does justice to the concrete historical situation in which Calvin found himself. After all, Sadoleto chose to write an epistle to the

---

[32] Mannion, 'Calvin and the Church,' 1, emphasis added.
[33] Mannion, 'Calvin and the Church,' 3, 6, 7, respectively.
[34] Mannion, 'Calvin and the Church,' 18.
[35] 'Calvin offers a *supposedly* different fundamental ecclesiology,' Mannion, 'Calvin and the Church,' 8, emphasis added.
[36] Mannion, 'Calvin and the Church,' 9, emphasis added.
[37] See footnote 28.
[38] Mannion, 'Calvin and the Church,' 10.

Genevans, knowing of the departure of the reformers, Calvin and Farel, in such adverse circumstances. Calvin appropriately followed suit, replying in kind. Their purpose was not 'dialogue' and debate, but contention against the persuasive approach of the other. Indeed, we will see below that the argument *was* 'an either / or . . . situation'; the stakes were as high as they could possibly be. The 'forum' (letter writing) corresponded to the circumstances—distant, singular, vital and adamant.

Third, Mannion suggests that the centre of the problem is not ontological or even theological but 'emphasis, language and questions of authority and governance'.

> I would suggest perhaps the deepest actual differences lie in terms of emphasis, language and questions of authority and governance, rather than what lies at the theological and ontological core of both scholars' ecclesiologies, between which there is actually much common ground.[39]

Again, we will see that 'questions of authority and governance' *are* matters of theology, ontological to the core, for both men. Both of them believe that our understanding of authority and governance are grounded in what we think the Church is by definition (that is, ontologically), and what its divinely-given task or mission is.

Sadoleto's letter to the Genevan authorities

Sadoleto writes to the Genevans, as he himself puts it, 'as a brother to brethren, and friend to friends'.[40] Although he admits that he does not know them personally (apparently, he has never met them), he calls them 'Very dear brethren in Christ' and speaks of his divine vocation as including and prompting his love for 'a people [the letter's recipients] who will always remain seated in my inmost heart'.[41] His opening salutation, then, is full of (patronizing) flattery, which causes Bernard Cottret to say that he flatters 'with all the condescension of a prince addressing himself to provincials'.[42] He speaks of residing in Carpentras (but being ready to return to Rome if the Pope so wishes it) and it is from there that he has heard of their plight which has caused him both grief and, he admits, a little hope. Employing the well-worn patristic personification of the Catholic Church as mother, he speaks of her 'weeping and lamenting at being deprived at once of so many and so dear children'.[43]

---

[39] Mannion, 'Calvin and the Church,' 12.
[40] Sadoleto, 'Letter,' 25. See, also, 39.
[41] Sadoleto, 'Letter,' 23.
[42] Cottret, *Calvin*, 100. Sadoleto says, for example, that he has learned to 'love your noble city, the order and form of your republic, the worth of its citizens, your hospitality to strangers and foreigners' and so on (24).
[43] Sadoleto, 'Letter,' 25.

Rhetoric of fear

Sadoleto's rather short letter to Geneva's authorities, and through them to its citizens, has understandably been labelled 'an essay in humanist rhetoric'[44] and nowhere is this more clearly seen than in the underlying call to individual self-interest against the back-drop of the fear of damnation and eternal death that pervades the letter. 'The point in question,' he states dogmatically, 'is jeopardy to our salvation.'[45] More fully, the Cardinal expresses it in these terms:

> We all, therefore, (as I said) believe in Christ *in order* that we find salvation for our souls, i.e., life for ourselves: than this there can be nothing more earnestly to be desired, no blessing more internal, more close and familiar to us. For in proportion to the love which each man bears to himself is his salvation dear to him; if it be neglected and cast away, what prize, pray, of equal value can possibly be acquired? ... This possession, therefore, so large, so dear, so precious to every man as is his soul, we must use every effort to retain.[46]

The italicised words infer the reason behind belief or faith—eternal life, salvation[47]—the final words imply the weight of threat if that most essential possession, the soul, is lost.[48] And, as we would expect, perhaps, Sadoleto quotes the well-known question of Christ, concerning the profit gained by losing the soul or by exchanging it for the whole world (see Matt. 16.26). In this, Sadoleto points out that the Reformation question of religious allegiance inherently brings with it the highest of stakes, nothing less than a person's eternal wellbeing. That is what is in the balance. It is not a theoretical or speculative question of theology and such like, but a pragmatic one of infinite, personal and existential significance. And so he emphasises the fear of the situation; and this emphasis on fear continues throughout the work. A little later, for example, he says the following:

> I ask, with what care and anxiety of mind, ought we to guard against exposing our life and salvation to this great danger? You will surely grant and concede to me, that nothing more pernicious and fearful can happen to anyone than the loss of his soul.[49]

Before the rhetorical use of the well-known judicial scene later in the letter, to which we return below, he states that 'the salvation of every man's soul, the pledges of future life, are at stake—whether it is our lot to be one of eternal felicity, or of infinite misery?'[50] And again, '[T]he salvation of every man's

---

[44] Michael A. Mullett, *John Calvin* (London: Routledge, 2011), 16; on this, see, generally, 71-74.
[45] Sadoleto, 'Letter,' 34.
[46] Sadoleto, 'Letter,' 28-29, italics added.
[47] People put their faith in Christ, he says, for one reason, 'that they may obtain salvation for themselves and their souls'—Sadoleto, 'Letter,' 26.
[48] '[O]ur soul is our whole selves'— Sadoleto, 'Letter,' 30.
[49] Sadoleto, 'Letter,' 32.
[50] Sadoleto, 'Letter,' 36.

soul, the pledges of future life, are at stake.'[51] Indeed, it is the reformer and, by implication, those who follow him, who will 'be cast into outer darkness ... where he will forever lament his miseries ... because when it was in his power, if he had chosen, to avoid that most dreadful calamity, he had neglected to do so?' Cardinal Sadoleto continually puts this grim and weighty responsibility onto the shoulders of those to whom he writes. So, this quotation continues,

> *Every person can understand for himself* what wretched and dismal companions grief and fury are to pass one's life with, especially when there will never be any end or any limit of the fatal loss—when weeping and wrath shall never cease.[52]

In this negative, somewhat passively threatening context, he affirms that he is desirous of their salvation, that he is not after his own good or advantage[53]— '[O]ur eager desire,' he states, '[is] for your salvation.' Again, he speaks of himself at the conclusion of the letter as 'a constant suppliant to God' on their behalf.[54] Together with the letter's opening flattery, this rhetoric seems to put him squarely on their side, of course. And, conversely, it tends to put Calvin, the reformer, and his colleagues in a position which appears to be against their good; that is, against their eternal wellbeing and salvation.

Cardinal Sadoleto underlines this by commenting directly and indirectly on the reformers, themselves. For example, early in his letter, without naming them, he speaks of them as 'certain crafty men, enemies of Christian unity and peace,' and as 'those who seek new power and new honors for themselves'.[55] According to him, they are innovators, deceivers, proud boasters, fraudulent, malicious, sectarians, 'professed adversaries,' 'authors of dissension,' and damned![56] He argues for the perspicuity of Scripture and a humble reading against these men who have boasted over 'hidden interpretations of Scripture'—representing it, according to him, by the misnomers of 'learning and wisdom'.[57] In a move that Herman Selderhuis specifies as Sadoleto's 'one mistake' he makes a personal slight of Calvin himself, speaking of his 'ambition, avarice, love of popular applause, inward fraud and malice' of which, according to the Cardinal, he is perfectly aware.[58] It is surely against this background of antagonism that we need to read some of the letter's themes, the centrality of Christ, salvation, faith, the importance of the Church, and so on. It is this deeply-felt enmity that determines whether there was any possibility of ecumenical

---

[51] Sadoleto, 'Letter,' 36.
[52] Sadoleto, 'Letter,' 40, emphasis added.
[53] Sadoleto, 'Letter,' 25.
[54] Sadoleto, 'Letter,' 42.
[55] Sadoleto, 'Letter,' 24, 25, respectively.
[56] Sadoleto, 'Letter,' 24, 25, 34, 38, 41, respectively.
[57] Sadoleto, 'Letter,' 26, 25, respectively.
[58] Sadoleto, 'Letter,' 39. Selderhuis, *John Calvin*, 100, states that 'Bishop Sadoleto made one mistake in his plea. His accusation that Calvin acted out of self-interest was like a red cape to a raging bull'—although quoted earlier in this essay it is worth noting it again, I think.

discussion, not the themes, which, themselves, are acutely embedded in such opposition.

Jesus Christ, faith and salvation

Structurally, in the pursuit of salvation, as it were, Sadoleto naturally places Christ as central for those who have faith, as we have already seen in the longer quotation above.[59] In relation to God, he speaks of Christ as 'the herald of the true God'. In relation to his followers, Christ is 'adored and worshipped by us, and truly acknowledged to be God, and the Son of the true God'.[60] When the world was 'doomed' and given over to death and destruction, the Cardinal asserts that 'He [Christ] *alone* . . . awoke them from the dead.'[61] Therefore, he insists that our hope for life and resurrection, salvation and eternal wellbeing, is in Jesus Christ alone. God saves us only in and through Christ, his Son. Indeed, Christ chooses to be our 'salvation and deliverance and truth'.[62] There is certainly no question of this important clear emphasis in Sadoleto's argument: Christ is central to salvation from both the divine and the human perspectives, as it were.

This, however, introduces the strongly contested topic of faith: '[W]e obtain this blessing of complete and perpetual salvation by faith alone in God and in Jesus Christ,' the Cardinal declares. As a theological statement, this could have been written by any writer from the sixteenth century Reformed Church in which Christ was seen as central to our redemption. However, Sadoleto argues against 'those inventors of novelties,' who, he says, define faith as 'a mere credulity and confidence in God'. Whilst agreeing that this is the necessary beginning of Christian life (or 'access . . . to God'), he asserts that 'it is not enough': 'we must also bring a mind full of piety toward Almighty God . . . and desirous of performing whatever is agreeable to Him'. He continues, 'This mind, though sometimes it proceeds not to external acts, is, however, inwardly prepared *of itself* for well-doing.'[63] Notice here two things, briefly.

First, he speaks of our 'bringing' 'a mind full of piety' toward God, which implies an active participation on the part of human beings. Indeed, the italicised words make it certain that Sadoleto is stating that we have this preparedness in ourselves; it is something we inherently have and that we bring to God. This demonstrates the Cardinal's optimism about human nature, which, he claims, has the capacity to assist in its own salvation. He seeks to safeguard human freedom and our ability to cooperate in the salvific process of justifica-

---

[59] See the top of page 82, above.
[60] Sadoleto, 'Letter,' 27.
[61] Sadoleto, 'Letter,' 27. Note the emphasis (added here): 'He *alone*.' See, also, 28.
[62] Sadoleto, 'Letter,' 27. See also, 28.
[63] Sadoleto, 'Letter,' 29, emphasis added.

tion.[64] This Pelagian or semi-Pelagian theology was anathema to Calvin, of course.[65]

Second, Sadoleto speaks of the necessity of this in our salvific approach to God. With this assertion he refers to 'good works' as being necessary to salvation. At some length, he says,

> If, then, Christ was sent that we, by well-doing, may, through Him, be accepted of God, and that we may be built up in Him unto good works; surely the faith which we have in God through Jesus Christ not only enjoins and commands us to confide in Christ but to confide, working or resolved to work well in Him. For faith is a term of full and ample signification, and not only includes in it credulity and confidence, but also the hope and desire of obeying God, together with love.[66]

Notice, again, the centrality of Jesus Christ in this: he was sent in order that we would be accepted by God, that we would receive faith, that we would live a life of good works (basically, of sanctification). In arguing in this comprehensive way, Sadoleto makes sure that he agrees with the reformers' theology of faith—in that faith includes credulity and confidence—but, in addition, for him, faith necessarily includes good works. He is adamant that this is inherent in *saving* faith:

> When we say, then, that we can be saved by faith alone in God and Jesus Christ, we hold that in this very faith love is essentially comprehended as the chief and primary *cause* of our salvation.[67]

So, it appears that Sadoleto sees Christ as clearly central to salvation, but perhaps not, in himself alone, sufficient. And, of course, these are the very points that Calvin will later insist on attacking in his rigorous response.

The significance of the Church in salvation

At this juncture, it is important to fully recognise that Sadoleto's argument appears to revolve around a genuine and heart-felt concern for the Genevans' eternal salvation. I have been at pains to underline this above. This, the question of their salvation, it seems to me, is the core of the Cardinal's unease. It would be quite wrong, and terribly superficial, to suggest that he simply wants the Genevan citizens to return to the Catholic, the mother, Church, as if that was somehow enough in and of itself, the goal of his endeavours. Though one would have to say that for Sadoleto entrance into the mother Church is the equivalence of entrance to eternal salvation, it seems to me that any attempt simply to centralise the definition of the true church as the letter's substance or

---

[64] See Olin, 'Introduction,' 17. See Michael Parsons, (ed.), *Since we are Justified by Faith. Justification in the Theologies of the Protestant Reformation* (Milton Keynes: Paternoster, 2012), for something of the diversity of Protestant theologies of justification in the sixteenth century.
[65] See Mullett, *John Calvin*, 72-73.
[66] Sadoleto, 'Letter,' 30.
[67] Sadoleto, 'Letter,' 30, emphasis added. See Olin, 'Introduction,' 17.

focal message must be qualified by a more careful, nuanced reading of the work.

Having asserted that, however, the argument about the individual's salvation does begin to revolve around the definition of the true Church and its central role in the process, as against the Reformed, schismatic church of John Calvin and the others. The most overt reference to the true Church in this salvific aspect comes early in the letter:

> *This Church hath regenerated us to God in Christ*, hath nourished and confirmed us, instructed us what to think, what to believe, wherein to place our hope, and also taught us *by what way we must tend toward heaven*. We walk in this common faith of the Church, we retain her laws and precepts.[68]

The two italicised phrases are significant for they show Sadoleto's underlying argument: it is through the Catholic Church *alone* that we are saved to Christ; and, it is through that Church *alone* that we continue the salvific journey to eternal life itself. The Catholic Church is extensively and intimately involved in the whole of the salvation process—from its beginning to its culmination. And, therefore, because this is so, the Cardinal needs to maintain the Roman Church's credentials in an age of dissent and fraction. This he does in several ways over against the alternative, heretical 'church' that the Protestant reformers were advocating; but he does so always against the backdrop of the fear of losing one's soul. And this culminates in the imagined scene of divine judgement towards the end of the letter. There are other things going on in his complex letter, but to simplify this we need to notice the way Sadoleto goes about this.

First, he draws attention to the 'disturbances' and 'dissensions' caused by the innovations of the reformers that are, notice, 'pestiferous to the souls of men' and 'pernicious . . . to private and public affairs'. Later, somewhat remarkably, perhaps, he will speak of the Catholic Church as one in which no dissensions can exist because of its unity in Christ.[69] He insists that the Genevans have recently had the means of learning about the discord and conflict generated by the new schismatic 'church'—a reference, no doubt, to the expulsion of Farel and Calvin and the quickly ensuing problems thereafter. In this context, Sadoleto says that he is concerned for the Genevans' 'losses and dangers'.[70]

Second, the Cardinal contrasts the truth taught and practised by the Roman Church and the falsity, 'the fraud' and 'fallacy' of the new church's teaching.[71] These men (referring to Calvin and Farel) have misled the people of Geneva 'in

---

[68] Sadoleto, 'Letter,' 31, emphasis added.
[69] Sadoleto, 'Letter,' 25, 35, respectively. Later in his letter, the Cardinal claims a monolithic Church, the same throughout 'the whole world' and for more than 1500 years – as against the new sectarian church of only 25 years (34).
[70] Sadoleto, 'Letter,' 25.
[71] Sadoleto, 'Letter,' 26.

the name of learning and wisdom'.[72] In stark contrast to this, he claims that the Roman Church has always taught the truth, a truth that all people can know because through the Church God reveals it to those who listen.[73] In no space at all, Sadoleto then speaks of obtaining salvation 'for themselves and for their souls'—and he qualifies this as follows, 'not a salvation which is mortal, and will quickly perish, but one which is ever-during and immortal, which is truly attainable only in heaven, and by no means on earth'.[74]

Third, Sadoleto remarks on the longevity and authority of the Roman Church *in relation to salvation*. Its history speaks of 'so many glorious martyrs of Christ in former times,' of 'so many most holy doctors'.[75] Though he moderates this comment a little later with the words 'always by the grace and mercy of God',[76] the Cardinal shows that this Church is the place from which we receive pardon, that its penances (*poenitentiae et satisfactions*) and expiations work, and that if people fall into sin, they can 'rise again in the same faith of the Church'.[77] In application to the Genevans, the contrast drawn, then, is that between the pride of following new ideas and the humility in continuing to follow the Church's traditions and in being obedient to its authority. And, notice, that humility is defined as 'the chief help to our eternal salvation', whereas pride is named as that 'horrid and dreadful sin'.[78] The recipients must 'guard against exposing [their] life and salvation to . . . great danger'. He fears that in following the reformers the Genevans 'no longer leave [themselves] either God or anchor'.[79] Notice, again, how forcefully the Cardinal puts this:

> Let us see then in which party, and in which sect, there is the greatest danger of removing farther from God, and moving nearer to endless destruction.[80]

So it is clearly in this salvific context that Sadoleto defines the Roman Church over against the reformers' 'church'.

> For, to define it briefly, the Catholic Church is that which in all parts, as well as at the present time in every region of the world, united and consenting in Christ, has been always and everywhere directed by the one Spirit of Christ; in which Church no dissension can exist; for all its are connected with each other, and breathe together. But should any dissension and strife arise, the great body of the Church indeed remains the same, but an abscess is formed by which some corrupted flesh,

---

[72] Sadoleto, 'Letter,' 25.
[73] Sadoleto, 'Letter,' 26.
[74] Sadoleto, 'Letter,' 26.
[75] Sadoleto, 'Letter,' 30.
[76] Sadoleto, 'Letter,' 31.
[77] Sadoleto, 'Letter,' 31.
[78] Sadoleto, 'Letter,' 31, 32, respectively.
[79] Sadoleto, 'Letter,' 32, 33, respectively. The Cardinal seeks to show them where the 'greatest hope and security appear' (34).
[80] Sadoleto, 'Letter,' 34.

being torn off, is separated from the spirit which animates the body, and no longer belongs in substance to the body ecclesiastic.[81]

What is noticeable here is the Cardinal's rhetorical use of imagery to draw the contrast in such stark terms. The Catholic Church is described in rich images of life and growth—the use of the biblical image of the body of Christ in which all its parts 'breathe together', its living and essential connection to the Holy Spirit. The reformed sect, on the other hand, is nothing but 'an abscess', 'corrupted flesh', 'torn off', separated from the enlivening, stimulating Spirit. These powerful images move the reader to the direction that comes a little lower: 'Let us inquire and see which is better in itself, and better fitted to obtain the favour of Almighty God.' And he reminds them yet again, that 'the salvation of every man's soul, the pledges of future life, are at stake'.[82]

Fourth, Sadoleto brings his argument to its climax with a vision of the judgement seat of God—'the dread tribunal of the sovereign Judge,' as he puts it;[83] a climax towards which his whole line of reasoning has been heading. This is important to grasp, I think. What I have been arguing is that Sadoleto's central contention is that to leave the Catholic Church is to irreparably endanger one's soul and eternal wellbeing. As we have seen, everything he says lends weight to this opinion.

In brief: the Cardinal pictures two men standing at the end of their lives before God, their Judge: both confess to being Christian; both say they believe in Jesus Christ—but the interrogation continues to its critical conclusion.[84] The first man confirms that he has remained in the Catholic Church, that he reveres it, that he has been obedient to it and that, though others have maliciously sought to lure him away from it, he has remained faithful. He stands before the tribunal 'imploring not strict justice . . . but rather [God's] mercy and readiness to forgive'.[85] The other man (clearly caricaturing a reformer, maybe John Calvin, himself) admits that he has been motivated by envy—his learning had not gained him the position that others had taken—that he was forced to condemn the Church in order to attack them, that he had taught people to trust in faith to the exclusion of works, and that failing to gain anything by learning he had become 'the author of seditions and schisms'.[86] This second speaker, according to Sadoleto, is presumptuous, lacking any humble pleading for divine benevolence. The Cardinal allows himself the aside (almost stage directions) that '[the speaker] has kept back much concerning his ambition, avarice, love of popular

---

[81] Sadoleto, 'Letter,' 35.
[82] Sadoleto, 'Letter,' 36.
[83] Sadoleto, 'Letter,' 36. See Cottret, *Calvin*, 154.
[84] For the whole image, see Sadoleto, 'Letter,' 36-40.
[85] Sadoleto, 'Letter,' 37.
[86] Sadoleto, 'Letter,' 38-39 (39).

applause, inward fraud and malice, of which,' he adds, 'he is perfectly conscious'.[87]

Sadoleto asks his readers to consider which of the two men described would be judged guilty before God (*coram Deo*). It is a foregone conclusion, of course. Sadoleto, as narrator, has seen to that. The former, who obediently followed the Church, will not be judged. The latter, 'trusting in his own head,' will be cast into outer darkness, loss and limitless wrath. How could it be otherwise? The Cardinal states that 'The Truth is always one, while falsehood is varied and multiform.'[88] The resultant invective comes in the form of the following questions (and more):

> Can anyone who acknowledges and confesses Christ, and into whose heart and mind the Holy Spirit hath shone, fail to perceive that such rending, such tearing of the holy Church, is the proper work of Satan, and not of God? What does God demand of us? What does Christ enjoin? That we be all one in Him.[89]

And, so, the Cardinal exhorts his readers to be pleased to return to the Church and 'to worship God with us in one spirit'.[90] He reiterates his earnest desire for their salvation and assures them of his continuing prayer. Before making any general comments about the Cardinal's letter to the Genevans, we turn to a brief engagement with John Calvin's response.

John Calvin's reply to Sadoleto[91]

It must have been a surprise for Sadoleto to discover that it was none other than the reformer, Geneva's ousted minister and presently exiled refugee, John Calvin, who was commissioned to write a response to his letter to the Genevans. Calvin, however, makes sure that the Cardinal and, importantly, the Genevan officials, know that he does so because he is actually obligated to respond by the divine calling that he has received.[92] 'I had a legitimate vocation,' he states. He speaks of his ministry as 'supported and sanctioned by a call from God' and, though at present he is relieved of that specific responsibility, God has 'bound him to be faithful to it forever'. He states, 'I cannot cast off that charge anymore than that of my own soul' and that 'knowing it to be from Christ, I am bound if need be, to maintain with my blood'.[93] This, he says, is a far stronger

---

[87] Sadoleto, 'Letter,' 39.
[88] Sadoleto, 'Letter,' 39-40 (40).
[89] Sadoleto, 'Letter,' 40.
[90] Sadoleto, 'Letter,' 42.
[91] There is no attempt here to outline the whole of the reformer's argument. I have outlined sufficient to give an impression of his answer to Sadoleto's letter—enough for our purposes in this chapter.
[92] See Cottret, *Calvin*, 152.
[93] Calvin, 'Reply,' 44, 45, respectively. In chapter 1 we noted that Calvin spoke clearly of his calling to the ministry of the Genevan church. He states that his own conscience before God is clear on the matter: '[I]t has been by him [God] that we have

obligation than Sadoleto's pretended and flattering love; a love he has never previously intimated.

Calvin is under no illusion, he says; the purport of the Cardinal's argument is that he seeks their return to the power of the Pope. But, early on in his response, the reformer recognises that Sadoleto attempts to soften the Genevans by commenting on the supposed danger to their eternal wellbeing—something which we have noted above. And it is this to which the reformer returns again and again in his letter, as we will see.

First, he structures his response in a way that centres the importance of God and of Jesus Christ as primary, *not* the salvation of Christian believers—though Sadoleto appeared to centre the Church.

> When the Genevese, instructed by our preaching, escaped from the gulf of error in which they were immersed, and betook themselves to a purer teaching of the gospel, you call it defection from the truth of God; when they threw off the tyranny of the Roman Pontiff, in order that they might establish among themselves a better form of Church, you call it desertion from the Church.[94]

Calvin states what he appears to consider to be the foundational principle in this argument: 'We are born,' he says, 'first of all for God and not for ourselves.'[95] Therefore, we are to centre our thoughts and lives on God's glory, not our own salvation and eternity. Genuine piety is to 'ascend higher', not simply to secure our own salvation. We are created and reborn by grace in order to worship the living God. That is true piety, says Calvin.[96]

Second, therefore, he defines the Church in relation to this principle. In it the Word of God and the Holy Spirit are inseparably linked; that is, the Church is ruled by the Holy Spirit, 'annexed to the Word'.[97] According to Calvin, the true Church is

> the society of all the saints, a society which, spread over the whole world, and existing in all ages, yet bound together by the one doctrine and the one Spirit of Christ, cultivates and observes unity of faith and brotherly concord.[98]

Noticeably, the reformer defines the Church as universal and existing over all time—as the Cardinal had previously done[99]—but insists that it exists only

---

been called to the fellowship of this ministry among you. . . . For which reason it cannot be in the power of men to break asunder such a tie'—letter to the Church of Geneva, Strasbourg, October 1, 1538, Calvin, *Letters*, 1.83. On his robust understanding of vocation see pages 13-15 of the present volume.

[94] Calvin, 'Reply,' 51.
[95] Calvin, 'Reply,' 52.
[96] See Calvin, 'Reply,' 52-53.
[97] Calvin, 'Reply,' 54. 'It is no less unreasonable to boast of the Spirit without the Word [the Anabaptists, according to Calvin] than it would be absurd to bring forward the Word itself without the Spirit [the Catholic Church]' (55).
[98] Calvin, 'Reply,' 56.
[99] See 86n.69 of the present volume.

when the evangelical doctrine (the 'gospel') and the Holy Spirit forms it, binding it together in faith and love. This, he continues, has largely perished in the Catholic Church, 'violently driven away by fire and sword'[100]—a clear reference to the contemporary, ongoing persecution that the evangelical Church was suffering.[101]

Third, the reformer underlines the shape of the gospel by stressing the importance of justification by faith through grace alone.[102] The importance of this doctrine within the Reformation generally cannot be exaggerated; so, too, for Calvin's understanding. He says, 'Wherever the knowledge of it is taken away [as in the Catholic Church], the glory of Christ is extinguished, religion abolished, the Church destroyed, and *the hope of salvation utterly overthrown.*'[103] The italicised words are significant, of course. Sadoleto had repeatedly argued that the Genevans' salvation was at stake, their eternal well-being was suspect, but Calvin insists in return that without this evangelical understanding of the gospel message they were truly lost—and he accuses the Catholic preachers of not preaching it and of their gross ignorance of the truth of this doctrine. In a lengthy passage, Calvin then outlines the evangelical gospel, thereby claiming the vital importance of Christ, faith, justification and righteousness to every true believer's experience:

> First, we bid a man [sic] begin by examining himself . . . before the tribunal of God, and when sufficiently convinced of his iniquity, to reflect on the strictness of the sentence pronounced upon all sinners. Thus . . . he is prostrated and humbled before God; and, casting away all self-confidence, groans as if given up to final perdition. Then we show that the only haven of safety is in the mercy of God, as manifested in Christ, in whom every part of our salvation is complete. As all mankind are, in the sight of God, lost sinners, we hold that Christ is their only righteousness, since, by His obedience, He has wiped off our transgressions; by His sacrifice, appeased the divine anger; by His blood, washed away our sins; by His cross, borne our curse; and by His death, made satisfaction for us. We maintain that in this way man is reconciled in Christ to God the Father, by no merit of his own, by no value of works, but by gratuitous mercy.[104]

We might underline several important things in this lengthy passage. First, the rhetorical shape of the passage suggests that this is the preaching pattern of reformed evangelicals, or their actual pastoral approach to those seeking God: 'we bid a man,' 'then we show . . .' he says. Second, we have the sense here that people are brought to realise that there is no good at all in themselves—none of the ability to respond to the divine advance that we observed in the Cardinal's theology, for example. Each person is brought to realise their sin and

---

[100] Calvin, 'Reply,' 57.
[101] See chapter 7 of the present volume for more on this.
[102] On this universal, though nuanced, Reformation doctrine, see Parsons, (ed.), *Since we are Justified by Faith.*
[103] Calvin, 'Reply,' 60, emphasis added.
[104] Calvin, 'Reply,' 60-61.

inadequacy, 'casting away all self-confidence'. This allows the reformer to highlight the mercy of God and the centrality and sufficiency of Jesus Christ in salvation: the mercy of God is 'manifested in Christ, in whom *every* part of our salvation is complete'—*his* righteousness, *his* obedience, *his* sacrifice, *his* blood, *his* cross, *his* death. Finally, Calvin emphasises that we bring nothing at all to merit our own salvation. The reformer's conclusion is clear:

> When we embrace Christ by faith, and come, as it were, into communion with Him, this we term, after the manner of Scripture, *the righteousness of faith*.[105]

In other words, he affirms that faith in Christ (embracing Christ by faith) is absolutely indispensable to salvation and in this way he counters Sadoleto's argument against justification by faith as 'a mere credulity and confidence in God' because he shows that faith rests in a relational acceptance of Christ's person and work for us before God.[106]

Calvin leaves no place for works in our response to God's love towards us. Our only hope, he insists, is 'the mere goodness of God, by which sin is pardoned, and righteousness imputed to us'—Christ's righteousness, that is, not our own.[107]

Fourth, on the back of this succinct exposition of justification (the *summum* or heart of religion), Calvin indicates the necessity of the reformation: 'The necessity was that the light of divine truth had been extinguished, the Word of God buried, the virtue of Christ left in profound oblivion, and the pastoral office subverted.' Therefore, he says, it is the evangelical Church that humbly venerates the Word of God, submitting to its authority.[108] Against this, he complains that Sadoleto is arguing for blind obedience to the Church, 'What they tell you, do.' 'All that you leave to the faithful,' he says elsewhere, 'is to shut their own eyes, and to submit implicitly to their teachers.'[109]

Notice, again, how Calvin turns this against Sadoleto's argument that leaving the Catholic Church is to jeopardise eternal salvation (and note Satan's position in this, too): 'Every soul which depends not on God alone is enslaved to Satan', and, again, 'A soul, therefore, when deprived of the Word of God, is given up unarmed to the devil for destruction.'[110] Or, at length:

---

[105] Calvin, 'Reply,' 61, emphasis original.

[106] See, for example, *Comm. Acts* 10.33 (CO 48.241), *Comm. Rom.* 10.15 (CO 49.205), *Comm. Gal.* 1.8 (CO 50.173), *Comm. Titus* 1.1 (CO 52.404), *Inst* 3.2.2 (OS 4.10), 3.2.7 (OS 4.16). See Gwyn Walters, *The Sovereign Spirit. The Doctrine of the Holy Spirit in the Writings of John Calvin* (Edinburgh: Rutherford House, 2009), 38, 66, 74. Interestingly, elsewhere, Calvin affirms that the Church is indispensible to salvation too: see, for example *Comm. Gal.* 4.26 (CO 50.239), *Comm. Acts* 2.47 (CO 48.61), *Inst* 4.1.4 (OS 5.7).

[107] Calvin, 'Reply,' 61.

[108] Calvin, 'Reply,' 69.

[109] Calvin, 'Reply,' 70, 71, respectively.

[110] Calvin, 'Reply,' 72.

> Christian faith must not be founded on human testimony, not propped up by doubtful opinion, nor reclined on human authority, but *engraven on our hearts by the finger of the living God*, so as not to be obliterated by a coloring of error. . . . it is God alone who enlightens our minds to perceive the truth, who by His Holy Spirit seals it on our hearts, and by His sure attestation to it confirms our conscience.[111]

Clearly, Calvin believes that just as salvation itself is all of God, so too is the reception of biblical truth all of God. The italicised words recall the divine work of giving the Ten Commandments to Moses and the people of Israel.[112] Just so, in a remarkable manner, the Word of God is always imprinted or impressed upon our hearts by the living God, the Holy Spirit, who also seals it there and confirms its truth to us, his people. Again, that reminder: if the Word of God is not in this way accepted, then people will be 'led away to destruction'.[113]

Fifth, Calvin uses the tribunal scene, first offered by Sadoleto, against him.[114] Against the Cardinal's assertion that those who leave the Church would be terrified at the Lord's scrutiny, Calvin comments that 'such is our consciousness of the truth of our doctrine that it has no dread of the heavenly Judge, from whom, we doubt not, that it proceeded'. Rather, this would be 'a day to be desired by the faithful'.[115] In order to strengthen the sense of confidence and assurance the reformer emphasises just who the Judge is:

> Let us direct our thoughts and minds to that Judge who, by the mere brightness of His countenance, will disclose whatever lurks in darkness, lay open all the secrets of the human heart, and crush all the wicked by the mere breath of His mouth.[116]

And with that he turns the scene upon the Cardinal and his Church: 'Consider, now, what serious answer you are to make for yourself and your party.' Calvin's confidence stands with the truthfulness of his ministry. And, 'I know,' he says to God, the Judge, 'that in thy judgment truth always reigns.'[117]

Unlike Sadoleto who offered two characters at the divine tribunal, one representing the confidence of the Catholic Church, the other supposedly representing the fearful dread of the evangelical party, Calvin offers two persons, both from the Reformed Church; one, a preacher of the Word, the other, a faithful believer. Both approach the throne of God with confidence in God's work and grace through Jesus Christ.

The former speaks to God about the two crimes that he is accused of by the Catholic party: heresy and schism. He speaks confidently of truth 'heard from

---

[111] Calvin, 'Reply,' 72-73, emphasis added.
[112] See Exod. 31.18, 'the tablets of stone, inscribed by the finger of God'.
[113] Calvin, 'Reply,' 73.
[114] For the tribunal scene, see Calvin, 'Reply,' 75-84.
[115] Calvin, 'Reply,' 75.
[116] Calvin, 'Reply,' 75.
[117] Calvin, 'Reply,' 76.

God's mouth'. He contrasts this with the way the Catholic Church had transferred glory from God (though they called God the only God) to their 'many gods' (the saints) and the way in which Christ 'passed unnoticed among the crowd of saints, like one of the meanest of them'. He concludes that 'That confident hope of salvation which is enjoined by [God's] Word, and founded upon it, had almost vanished.'[118]

Against the charge of schism the preacher suggests that the church had already scattered and that it was eager for unity: 'Mine, however, was a unity of the Church which should begin with Thee and end in Thee.'[119] He speaks of false leaders and likens himself to a biblical prophet who yearns to revive true religion amongst the people.[120]

> But what did our opponents? Did they not instantly, and like madmen, fly to fires, swords, and gibbets? Did they not decide that their only security was in arms and cruelty? Did they not instigate all ranks to the same fury? Did they not spurn at all methods of pacification?[121]

The import of Calvin's words here is clear. The ministers, accused as they are of heresy and schism, have absolute confidence at the divine tribunal simply because their preaching and the gospel involved come from God and resound to Christ's glory and honour, not their own. They uphold the centrality of Christ and his cross. Their teaching leads to true worship and genuine piety. This is what counts at the Judgement seat of God for those who preach; so much so that this first person states that, 'amidst the great confusion, . . . I am freed from all fear, now that we stand at thy tribunal, where equity, combined with truth, cannot but decide in favor of innocence.'[122]

What counts for the confidence of those who hear the preaching? Calvin's second character is one who has responded to the evangelical gospel. They are ready with their defence. We are not surprised that this resembles a religious testimony of one who has, through the preaching of Reformation truth, discovered the gospel of Jesus Christ and has joined the Reformed community, escaping the error of the Catholic Church.

He speaks of mindless obedience expected by that Church. The small amount that had been taught was not enough to encourage true worship, nor enough to instil 'a sure hope of salvation', nor sufficient to train in righteous, Christian living. He admits that he had been taught that his redemption was through Jesus Christ alone, but denies that it made a difference to his life here and now—salvation's 'virtue could reach me,' he says. The future resurrection

---

[118] See Calvin, 'Reply,' 76-77. Later, he asserts, 'Whatever I felt assured that I had learned from thy mouth, I desired to dispense faithfully to the church' (78).
[119] Calvin, 'Reply,' 79.
[120] Calvin, 'Reply,' 79-80. He cites Matt. 7.15, Acts 20.29, 2 Pet. 2.1 and 1 Jn 2.18.
[121] Calvin, 'Reply,' 80.
[122] Calvin, 'Reply,' 81.

was simply something too dreadful to think upon.[123] The key problem, however, appears to have been the previous depiction of God himself—'a stern judge and strict avenger of iniquity . . . they showed how dreadful thy presence must be'.[124] This resulted in a guilt-ridden conscience and self-delusion to avoid the fear.

This, then, argues from personal experience against the Catholic doctrines espoused by the Cardinal. But what does the reformer say happened to arrest this situation? This appears to be a retelling of Calvin's own experience.[125] He speaks of his first contact with Reformation ideas:

> Offended by the novelty, I lent an unwilling ear, and at first, I confess, strenuously and passionately resisted; for . . . it was with the greatest difficulty I was induced to confess that I had all my life long been in ignorance and error. . . . But [then] . . . I allowed myself to be taught.[126]

A sense of docility (*docilitas* – being teachable) is apparent in this account. Those teaching him convinced him by the word of God that the Catholic Church was not the true church, neither was the Pope the true head of the church (but an antichrist) and that those teaching in the church were the blind leading the blind (Matt. 15.14).[127] This brings him to repentance of his former life:

> My mind being now prepared for serious attention, I at length perceived, as if light had broken in upon me, in what style of error I had wallowed, and how much pollution and impurity I had thereby contracted. Being exceedingly alarmed at the misery into which I had fallen, and much more at that which threatened me in the view of eternal death, I . . . made it my first business to betake myself to thy way, condemning my past life, not without groans and tears.[128]

What a telling paragraph this is! We notice, first, the image of light and darkness: the light of the gospel, as opposed to and in contrast to the darkness of Catholic teaching and practice—a common image amongst the reformers. Light breaks in upon the man; it is active, energetic, alive, transforming. His former life was simply 'error'. Second, note the misery he claims for his former life; and, more, that which threatens him at Judgement. This underlines the central

---

[123] Calvin, 'Reply,' 81.
[124] Calvin, 'Reply,' 82. This, apparently, was why they were driven to the saints for their intercession!
[125] This has been noted for some time. See J.T. McNeill, *The History and Character of Calvinism* (New York, OUP, 1954), 116-18; W. Walker, *John Calvin* (New York, Putnam, 1906), 73-75; F. Wendel, *Calvin* (New York, Harper and Row, 1963), 38-39; cited by Olin, 'Introduction,' 1n.1. More recently, see, C. Lindberg, *The European Reformations* (Oxford: Blackwell, 1996), 252, who notes that Calvin describes his conversion 'in terms similar to Luther's experience of liberation by the mercy of God from the burdens of the confessional and a piety of achievement'.
[126] Calvin, 'Reply,' 82.
[127] Calvin, 'Reply,' 83-84.
[128] Calvin, 'Reply,' 84.

argument that Calvin is having with Sadoleto. Confidence at the divine tribunal comes only through grasping Reformed truth; or, better, grasping God in Christ through that truth. Third, we see the distress that confession and repentance brings—'not without groans and tears,' he says. With this, he confesses that God himself has delivered him. And indeed, God, not men and women, not the Church, but God is central to all of this. The crux of Calvin's main argument with Sadoleto is summed up by the reformer in the words that people 'will stand or fall by the decision of God himself . . . by His own inflexible justice'.[129]

Herman Selderhuis' argument that the letter says 'much not only about Calvin's view of Rome but also reveals a man so deeply hurt by this reproach [Sadoleto's letter] that he appealed to God's courts' appears to be misplaced.[130] In fact, the reformer follows the Cardinal's lead, turning the tribunal that he introduced against him in a remarkably pointed way. If Sadoleto can claim confidence before God, then the reformer can claim more certain confidence!

The reformer's final prayer asks that Sadoleto and the Catholic Church may perceive that true unity would exist *only* if God reconciled the two factions, in fellowship, joining them together with one heart and soul 'through His one Word and Spirit'[131]—rhetoric that indicates, perhaps, that only a miracle of divine grace would see these two adversaries and their parties, the Catholic Church (*ecclesia catholica*) and the Church of Christ (*ecclesia Christi*), united as one.

Reflections

A few closing reflections will suffice at this point. We saw earlier that Gerard Mannion suggests the following seven themes in the correspondence between Sadoleto and Calvin.

1) the nature and authority of the Church,
2) reflections on the Christian life,
3) reflections on church governance, authority and ministry,
4) justification by faith,
5) the nature of faith itself,
6) Christian action inspired by love,
7) an understanding of salvation.[132]

However, Mannion concentrates on one theme as the 'real core focus' of the letter and that is number 7, the understanding of the church.[133] We noted, too,

---

[129] Calvin, 'Reply,' 85.
[130] See Selderhuis, *John Calvin*, 100.
[131] Calvin, 'Reply,' 88.
[132] Mannion, 'Calvin and the Church,' 1-30.
[133] Mannion, 'Calvin and the Church,' 1.

that he claims that in the disagreement between the two men the argument is *not* 'an either / or, a zero-sum ecclesiastical situation'.[134]

I think that the major over-arching problem with Mannion's reading of these letters is that to gain his desired end—somehow employing these letters with an ecumenical purpose—he needs to rob the rhetoric of its full force, as we have seen above. And, I don't believe we can do that.[135] What we have observed in reading the letters is that for each man the stakes were as high as they could possibly have been—the eternal salvation of men and women in their charge. This would tend towards number 7 of Mannion's list of themes ('an understanding of salvation'), but his list is too objective or passive for what the two correspondents are driving at. We have seen that what is important is not only 'an understanding of salvation' but salvation *itself*, not so much the theology of salvation (though that is clearly important to both) but the eternal wellbeing of the Genevan populace. What is threatened is the endless destruction of those who disagree. What is promised is eternal life and confidence before God, himself. The stakes could not have been higher!

There are several important things that need briefly underlining before we close this chapter: Calvin's sense of call, the believer's first consideration, the nature and purpose of the Church, the centrality of Jesus Christ, the significance of justification by faith, the final tribunal and a matter of truth.

Calvin's sense of call.

Alexandre Ganoczy rightly states that the reformer's reply to Cardinal Sadoleto 'testifies to Calvin's self-understanding as a pastor directly chosen by God and commissioned to the task of reform'.[136] It is interesting to consider that Calvin takes the task of responding to Sadoleto, offered to him, not because there was no one else who could write the rejoinder, but because he felt divinely called to the church in Geneva and to its people's wellbeing. It is clear that writing the letter is for Calvin a pastoral undertaking, first and foremost. It is secondarily a masterful piece of polemic in the cause of the Reformation. And, of course, some have discerned an attempt to reconcile with the Genevan authorities, too, and this should not be dismissed. However, all this rests on the strong and gripping sense of vocation that Calvin evidenced in high measure.[137]

The believer's first consideration.

We have observed that Sadoleto's stated objective in writing is to safeguard the recipients' eternal life and wellbeing. That certainly appears to be the underlying and genuine concern of the Cardinal. Time and time again he stresses that their spiritual safety is at stake. If they return to the Catholic Church, he says, their security is assured because salvation is found in that Church alone. And,

---

[134] Mannion, 'Calvin and the Church,' 10.
[135] See pages 80-81, above.
[136] Ganoczy, 'Calvin's Life,' 14. See, also, Mullett, *John Calvin*, 72.
[137] See chapter 1 of the present volume.

so, he urges them to consider the worth of their own soul before God and in the light of eternity. However, Calvin counters this with the claim that the believer is to be primarily concerned with the glory of God—that is their first consideration, not that of their own salvation.[138] This is entirely in line with the reformer's Trinitarian theology, generally, of course, that God is central, that we are made for him and in Christ we return to him in gratitude and worship by the Holy Spirit. Though he is concerned for the wellbeing of the letter's recipients, of course, his first consideration and his responsibility is to point to their obligation to venerate the Lord. In true worship and piety is their salvation.

The nature and purpose of the Church.

In this salvific context the Church is described by Calvin as being ruled by the Word of God and the Holy Spirit in tandem, as it were. He is not afraid to say that we are saved in the Church, we are nurtured by her and formed in her. But the reformer is speaking of the living Church where the gospel is preached, Jesus Christ is declared and God is worshipped, in which people are being transformed by divine grace and in which Jesus Christ is central.

The centrality of Jesus Christ.

The reformer states that Jesus Christ is absolutely central to our salvation. The truth is that in him we have *everything* necessary. He speaks, typically, of 'Christ in whom every part of our salvation is complete'.[139] He is totally sufficient and as such there is no place for our works—good or otherwise! Indeed, against Sadoleto's argument for the importance of 'good works', in an Augustinian manner, Calvin appears to deny all human capability before God. In ourselves, we bring nothing to it. We simply receive Christ by faith. Salvation is exclusively of divine grace.

In this context Michael Mullett suggests that Calvin's theology 'cancelled out the notion of a benign God open to our petitions for pardon'.[140] This seems very strange in the face of what we find in his letter to Sadoleto, for there the reformer is at pains to state that our salvation is all of God and that, therefore, he is entirely 'open to our petitions for pardon'. This is part of the significance of the important doctrine of justification by faith—without this gift there is no salvation at all. Brian Gerrish asks the following important rhetorical questions in relation to this:

> The crucial question is this: Who *are* the ones who are touched by grace? Is it those who, because their resources are limited, can climb no higher but may count on the assistance of grace because they have done all they can? Or is it those who can slip no lower because they have hit the bottom of frustration and despair and

---

[138] 'We are created to no other end, and live for no other cause than that God may be glorified in us'—Calvin, quoted by Timothy H. Wadkins, 'A Recipe for Intolerance: A Study of the Reasons behind John Calvin's Approval of Punishment for Heresy,' *Journal of the Evangelical Theological Society* 26.4 (1983), 433.

[139] Calvin, 'Reply,' 61.

[140] Mullett, *John Calvin*, 94.

expect only condemnation? Is grace aid for the weak, or is it the promise of new life for the dead?[141]

The final tribunal.

The climax of Sadoleto's argument is the suggestion of the tribunal scene, the final judgement of God in which two men are scrutinised by the all-seeing Judge. He postulates the dread that awaits those who have left the Catholic Church as they realise, perhaps, just what they have done. As we have observed, Calvin counters this by describing the judgement scene of two such Reformed men in which there is no fear at all for they are both confident, not in themselves—and this is exactly the point—but confident in Jesus Christ and the righteousness that comes through him. This, he asserts, is 'a day to be desired by the faithful'.[142]

A matter of truth.

For John Calvin truth is essential. It is discovered in the scriptures and as far as he was concerned, although remaining imperfect, of course, the Reformed Church taught the truth of the Gospels and sought to live it. That truth centred on Jesus Christ. As he states in his Reply, his confidence and that of his fellow believers stems from being conscious of that truth.[143]

As we will see in chapters 6 and 7 of the present volume, it is that truth which gives fortitude in the midst of persecution, martyrdom, grief and loss—or, rather, it is knowing the God of that truth through the work of the Spirit that allows that. It is also that truth which forms the foundation of Calvin's argument against Servetus, as we will see now in the following chapter.

---

[141] Brian A. Gerrish, 'Sovereign Grace. Is Reformed Theology Obsolete?' *Interpretation* 57 (2003), 45-57. I used this perceptive quotation before in a similar argument, in Parsons, 'Everything is forgiven by grace,' 14, which see.
[142] Calvin, 'Reply,' 75.
[143] See Calvin, 'Reply,' 75.

CHAPTER 5

'Even in your criticisms, judge me with equity.' Calvin's letters on Servetus[1]

Whilst I understand and, to an extent, concur with the cautionary remark by John Hasley Wood Jr., that 'interpretation of Michael Servetus's execution [says] as much about the interpreter as it [does] about Servetus and Calvin,'[2] I am willing to take that chance, believing it to be worthwhile reflecting further on this dramatic and tragic episode in the reformer's career, if for no other purpose than that it allows us to consider again the possible reasons that lay behind the reformer's choices and the subsequent outcome—an outcome that has, arguably and understandably, accrued over time generally greater significance than it had in its occurrence.[3]

Few would dispute the fact that John Calvin seems best known to many for two matters: his doctrine of predestination and his contribution to the execution in Geneva of the heretic, Servetus. Indeed, his reputation for some critics and historians appears to stand or fall on these two somewhat unrelated, seemingly unpalatable aspects of the reformer's work.[4] However, the situation still dis-

---

[1] Letter to Bullinger, February 27, 1554, quoted by Cottret, *Calvin*, 227. For the most part, throughout this present volume I am employing John Calvin, *Letters*, 4 volumes (edited by Jules Bonnet; translated by Marcus R. Gilchrist; Philadelphia: Presbyterian Board, 1858). See, also, John Calvin, *Lettres françaises*, 2 volumes (edited by Jules Bonnet; Paris: Meyrueis, 1854) and *Ioannis Calvini Opera quae supersunt omnia* [CO] (Corpus Reformatorum: Brunswick: Schwetschke et Filium, 1863–1900).

[2] John Hasley Wood, Jr., 'Making Calvin Modern: Form and Freedom in Abraham Kuyper's Free Church Ecclesiology' in Gerard Mannion and Eduardus Van der Borght (eds), *John Calvin's Ecclesiology. Ecumenical Perspectives* (London: T&T Clark, 2011), 169-84 (178).

[3] William G. Naphy, *Calvin and the Consolidation of the Genevan Reformation* (Louisville: John Knox, 2004), 231, points out that in the nineteenth century, for instance, 'Too often spectacular cases were treated outside their historical context and allowed to gain an importance and weight far beyond what they actually deserved.' He concludes that the Servetus case is perhaps the best example of this.

[4] See, for example, comments by the following who all stress the incongruence of this in the reformer's life: Timothy George, *Theology of the Reformers* (Nashville: Broadman, 1988), 167; T.J. Davis, 'Images of Intolerance: John Calvin in 19th Century History Textbooks,' *Church History* 65 (1996), 248; Marilynne Robinson, 'The Polemic Against Calvin: The Origins and Consequences of Historical Reputation' in David Foxgrover (ed.), *Calvin and the Church. Calvin Studies Society Papers 2001*

turbs us all enough to question the reasons why Calvin could approve of capital punishment for the crime of heresy. And his correspondence from 1546 to 1555 around the subject becomes significant to our reflection on the matter, as we will see.[5]

There is little need and no space in the present chapter to retell the story in great detail; that has been done admirably by many Reformation historians in the past.[6] In the previous retelling, itself, we discover a whole spectrum of opinions, as we would expect. Some, including T.H.L. Parker and, apparently, following him, Richard Gamble, claim Servetus to have been mentally unstable,[7] whilst others see what would appear to be almost a Shakespearian fatal flaw in his tragic character. Michael Mullett, for example, speaks of him as brilliant, deeply learned, endlessly versatile as well as combative, maddening and 'fatally impudent'.[8] Hans Hillerbrand, on the other hand, speaks of Servetus as 'the outstanding representative of antitrinitarian tendencies during the early years' of the Reformation, underlining a positive estimation; as does Michael Mullett, who speaks of him as 'the boldest literary challenger of his age to the Trinitarian doctrine'.[9]

This present chapter, then, simply gives the briefest outline of both the narrative and the heretical views that condemned Servetus in order to put the later

---

(Grand Rapids: Calvin Studies Society, 2002), 97; Herman J. Selderhuis, *John Calvin. A Pilgrim's Life* (Downers Grove: IVP Academic, 2009), 203; Michael A. Mullett, *John Calvin* (Abingdon: Routledge, 2011), 243-57.

[5] Timothy H. Wadkins, 'A Recipe for Intolerance. A Study of the Reasons behind John Calvin's Approval of Punishment for Heresy,' *Journal of the Evangelical Theology Society* 26.4 (1983), 431-41 (432).

[6] See footnotes for details. Also, for short, helpful summaries, see Alister McGrath, *A Life of John Calvin. A Study in the Shaping of Western Culture* (Oxford: Blackwell, 1990), 114-20; Carter Lindberg, *The European Reformations* (Oxford: Blackwell, 1996), 267-70; Robert L. Reymond, *John Calvin. His Life and Influence* (Geanies House, Fearn: Christian Focus, 2000), 111-25; Bernard Cottret, *Calvin. A Biography* (Grand Rapids: Eerdmans / Edinburgh: T&T Clark, 2000), 213-17; Naphy, *Calvin and the Consolidation*, 182-84; Rudolph W. Heinze, *Reform and Conflict. From the Medieval World to the Wars of Religion, AD 1350-1648* (Grand Rapids: Baker, 2005), 188-90; Selderhuis, *John Calvin*, 203-206; Mullett, *John Calvin*, 151-55. For extensive critical accounts of the history, see the following early full-length works: Roland Bainton, *Hunted Heretic. The Life and Death of Michael Servetus, 1511-1553* (Boston: Beacon, 1953); Jerome Friedman, *Michael Servetus: A Case Study in Total Heresy* (Geneva: Librairie Droz, 1978).

[7] T.H.L. Parker, *John Calvin. A Biography* (Philadelphia: Westminster, 1975), 118; Richard C. Gamble, 'Calvin's Controversies' in Donald K. McKim (ed.), *The Cambridge Companion to John Calvin* (Cambridge: Cambridge University Press, 2004), 197.

[8] Mullett, *John Calvin*, 153.

[9] Hans J. Hillerbrand, *The Reformation. A Narrative History Related by Contemporary Observers and Participants* (Grand Rapids: Baker, 1979), 273, see 273-75; Mullett, *John Calvin*, 152.

considerations into a concrete context, before deliberating upon Calvin's response to the situation as he is drawn crucially into it by the protagonist, himself. This is followed by an examination of relevant correspondence and a critical consideration of the possible reasons for Calvin's reaction, before concluding with brief reflections.

Michael Servetus (1511-1553)

Michael Servetus (Miguel Serveto), 'a Spanish Radical,' 'an evangelical rationalist,'[10] went to reside in Basel as early as 1530 but soon fell out with Johannes Oecolampadius (1482-1531), the city's very influential and greatly respected reformer, over the nature of the sonship of Jesus Christ. Leaving Basel, Servetus journeyed to Strasbourg hoping to find more liberty in a city that already tolerated Anabaptists in its midst—Casper von Schweckfeld and Melchoir Hofmann lived there at that time. However, Servetus soon fell out with the city's reformer, Martin Bucer, over his work against the Trinity (*De trinitatis erroribus*, 1531). His dogmatic assertions against received creedal doctrine were not going to be ignored by the reforming churches, nor, for that matter, by the Catholic Church. In his work, Servetus states, for example, that 'Jesus, surnamed Christ, was not a hypostasis but a human being is taught both by the early Fathers and in the Scriptures.'[11] He is no less assertive regarding the concept of the Holy Spirit, writing that the creedal statements 'land us in practical tritheism no better than atheism'.[12] He claims that 'The Holy Spirit as a third person of the Godhead is unknown in Scripture,' concluding that 'It is not a separate being, but an activity of God himself.' Servetus blames what he terms 'scholastic philosophy' or 'Greek philosophy' for introducing what he considers to be the irrelevant and mistaken terms into Christian dogma.[13] Of course, Bucer rejected the work outright and refuted it forcefully.

Seemingly backed into a corner, Servetus promised a recantation of his views but his next publication, a short pamphlet, *Dialogorum de trinitate libri duo*, published just a year later (1532), though more moderate, was anything but a retraction. In it he attacks those who oppose his views because, according to him, they ignore Scripture and 'by shouting, and by appeals to the great councils' simply state their doctrine, rather than arguing in a reasonable and logical manner.[14] Again, Protestant and Roman Catholic theologians vigorously rejected the work, forcing Servetus, under his pseudonym Michael de Villeneuve, to travel to Paris and from there to Lyon, Montpellier, and again to Lyon, where he went into publishing. Whilst in Paris (1534) he arranged to

---

[10] N.R. Needham, *2000 Years of Christ's Power. 3. Renaissance and Reformation* (London: Grace Publications Trust, 2004), 225; George, *Theology*, 20, respectively.
[11] Hillerbrand, *The Reformation*, 275.
[12] Hillerbrand, *The Reformation*, 275.
[13] Hillerbrand, *The Reformation*, 276.
[14] Hillerbrand, *The Reformation*, 277.

meet with John Calvin in the Rue Saint-Antoine. The reformer travelled to the city, despite the journey being extremely dangerous for him—having been condemned to death in France—but Servetus was nowhere to be seen.[15]

In 1540 Servetus settled in Vienne, in Dauphiné, and stayed there for twelve years. In 1546, in the words of Daniel Cottret, 'with an assurance close to impudence, Servetus, immediately began giving Calvin lessons in Christology and the baptism of the new born,'[16] criticising the reformer's magnum opus, *The Institutes of the Christian Religion*, which Calvin had asked him to read, presumably with the purpose of correcting his faulty views. In 1553 Servetus' *Christianismi restitutio*, written in Vienne, became the material cause of his trial and subsequent death. Arguing that the Church should return to the purity of the age before Constantine, he criticised pivotal doctrines, those of the Trinity, original sin, infant baptism and justification by faith. The Inquisition of Vienne cited 'Monsieur Villeneuve' on the April 5, 1553. Initially, he responded by denying that he was Servetus and saying, 'I never wished to dogmatise or assert anything contrary to the Church and the Christian religion.'[17] He was subsequently arrested, but managed somehow to escape. On leaving Vienne, Servetus passed through Geneva[18] where he was discovered on Sunday, August 13, 1553, at the church of St Pierre (Calvin's church) and was arrested. It was Calvin and others who had him arrested by the town council. The reformer later prepared the charges against the heretic and defended them in the civil court.

Having had Servetus condemned to death, Calvin attempted to have the mode of execution altered to a more humane form of execution. He also visited the heretic in prison, begging him to return to the mercy and grace of God, even at this hour. Calvin's account is as follows:

> I simply protested . . . that I had never pursued any personal grudge against him. . . . I reminded him gently how I spared no effort more than sixteen years ago to win him to Our Lord, even to the point of hazarding my own life. . . . Then afterwards, saying that I put aside everything that concerned me personally, I prayed him rather to think of begging mercy of God, whom he had so villainously blasphemed, wanting to efface the three persons who are in his essence and saying that those who recognize in one God the Father, the Son, and the Holy Spirit with a real distinction invent a three-headed hound of hell. I prayed him to devote his efforts to asking pardon of the Son of God, whom he had disfigured with his fantasies, denying that he had worn our flesh and that he was like us in his human nature, and whom by this means he had renounced as his Savior. Seeing that I gained nothing by exhortations, I did not want to be wiser than my master permit-

---

[15] According to Cottret, *Calvin*, 217, there *was* contact between the two men in the form of correspondence; Servetus sending Calvin as many as thirty letters, but the reformer preferred not to 'respond to this amateur theologian'.
[16] Cottret, *Calvin*, 216-17.
[17] Hillerbrand, *The Reformation*, 283.
[18] Wadkins, 'A Recipe for Intolerance,' 432, speaks of Servetus' fatal fascination in this context.

ted me to be. Therefore, following the rule of Saint Paul, I withdrew from a self-condemned heretic who carried his mark and brand on his heart.[19]

The reformer is clearly disappointed in Servetus' adamant refusal to recant. There really seems little necessity or reason for Cottret's sarcasm at this point: 'His duty done, Calvin could return with his vast serenity of conscience that the spectacle of the vicissitudes of fortune has always provided to men of faith.'[20] Michael Servetus was burned at the stake on October 27, 1553. In the years following this, Calvin spent a good deal of energy refuting Servetus' errors and counselling others to do the same.[21]

So, Servetus' radical, uncompromising, though amateur, theology was adoptionist in relation to Jesus Christ, denying his pre-existence. Stephen Edmondson rightly claims that 'The central question of Calvin's debate with Servetus appears to be whether there was a second person of the Trinity, the Eternal Word and Son of God, before the incarnation.'[22] Claiming the doctrine of the Trinity to be a sophistry invented by the Council of Nicaea, Servetus taught that the names 'Jesus' and 'the Holy Spirit' were merely terms designed to express divine activity or manifestations.[23] The terms 'Father,' 'Son' and 'Holy Spirit,' for Servetus, suggest three modes of activity, or three forms of the divine manifestation.[24] He asserted that all creatures are of the same substance as God and Servetus was, therefore, accused of pantheism, and, of course, therefore, of heresy. It might be noticed, too, that Servetus became more and more radically apocalyptic later in his theology.[25]

---

[19] Quoted by Cottret, *Calvin*, 224. The final comment probably refers to the mark of reprobation. Calvin generally discerned three signs of this: rejection of God's Word, deliberate rebellion against God and the denial of the conscience. See Randall C. Zachman, *Image and Word in the Theology of John Calvin* (Notre Dame: University of Notre Dame, 2007), 413-15. See, also, 415-19.

[20] Cottret, *Calvin*, 224.

[21] See, for example, his letter to the pastors of the church in Frankfurt, August 27, 1553; Calvin, *Letters*, 2.422-23. See, also, his letters to Bullinger, Geneva, December 30, 1553; Calvin, *Letters*, 2.447; to Bullinger, Geneva, February 23, 1554; Calvin, *Letters*, 3.19-21; and, to Ambrose Blaurer, Geneva, February 6, 1554; Calvin, *Letters*, 3.16-18, in which he promises the recipients his short refutation of Servetus' heresies.

[22] Stephen Edmondson, *Calvin's Christology* (Cambridge: Cambridge University Press, 2004), 211. 'Again, the heart of Calvin's battle with Servetus lies in Calvin's insistence on the eternal and divine existence of Christ as the second person of the Trinity before Christ's incarnation' (217).

[23] See Calvin's Sermon on Micah 5.3-6 (1550), where he appears to develop his doctrine of the Trinity in opposition to Servetus—*Sermons on the Book of Micah* (translated and edited by Benjamin W. Farley; Phillipsburg: P&R, 2003), 275-77.

[24] The inconsistent writings of Servetus appear to speak of both subordinationism and modalism.

[25] For a helpful brief introduction to Servetus and his theology, see Martin I. Klauber, 'Servetus, Michael (1511-53)' in Trevor A. Hart (ed.), *The Dictionary of Historical Theology* (Grand Rapids: Eerdmans / Carlisle: Paternoster, 2000), 520-522. He sug-

Servetus was linked disparagingly by Calvin with other sixteenth century humanists—'Epicureans,' he calls them—including Agricola of Nettesheim, Doletus, Rabelais, Deperius and Goveanus.[26] He considers them to be 'atheists'.[27] He also links Servetus with the Anabaptists ('those reprobate spirits')[28] several times, concluding at one point, for example, 'I trust I have made it plain how weakly Servetus has supported his little Anabaptist brothers.'[29] However, from a reading of his *Institutes* it seems that the reformer certainly understood the theology of his opponent. And, as a pastor, he shows as much concern with the consequences of Servetus' theology as with the statements, themselves, believing that his teaching has the effect of alarming and confusing the uninstructed,[30] of extinguishing the hope of salvation,[31] of diminishing somewhat the glory of the divine goodness[32] and of encouraging impious ingratitude towards God and 'a certain negligence about instructing our children in piety'.[33] Calvin reads Servetus' theology as a callous resurrection of old heresies and of new deceptions: 'What is this,' he once asks of Servetus' doctrine, 'but to raise Marcion from hell?'[34]

The reformer castigates the heresy in no uncertain terms calling it 'this monstrous fabrication,'[35] an 'impious notion,'[36] 'delusion,'[37] 'devilish imagina-

---

gests that the doctrine of the Trinity served as a stumbling block in evangelising Jews and Muslims; and that Servetus rejected infant baptism because of his experience in Spain with forced baptisms of Jews and Muslims (521^b-22^a). On Servetus' theology of Christ see the useful brief summary by Byung-Ho Moon, *Christ the Mediator of the Law. Calvin's Christological Understanding of the Law as Rule of Living and Life-Giving* (Milton Keynes: Paternoster, 2006), 130-39, 144-147.Cottrett, *Calvin*, 218, reminds us that Servetus wrote to Abel Poupin, Calvin's colleague in Geneva, predicting his own death:

Woe, woe, woe! This is the third letter I have written to warn you that you may know better. I will not do it again. It may shock you that I meddle in this battle of [the Archangel] Michael's and that I want to involve you in it. Study this passage carefully, and you will see that they are men who will fight there, offering their souls to death in blood and for a testimony to Jesus Christ. Before the battle the world will be seduced. Then the battle will come, and the time will be near. . . . I know that I shall certainly find death on this account, but I do not lose the hope of being a disciple like the Master.'

[26] See Thomas F. Torrance, *The Hermeneutics of John Calvin* (Edinburgh: Scottish Academic Press, 1988), 153.
[27] Ironically, Servetus thought of Calvin as an 'atheist'.
[28] *Inst.* 4.16.31 (OS 5.340). Cottrett, *Calvin*, 208, says that Calvin sees the Anabaptists as 'the internal enemy'.
[29] *Inst.* 4.16.31 (OS 5.340). See, also, *Inst.* 2.10.1 (OS 3.403).
[30] *Inst.* 1.13.22 (OS 3.137).
[31] *Inst.* 2.14.8 (OS 3.471). See, also, *Inst.* 4.16.32 (OS 5.340).
[32] *Inst.* 4.16.32 (OS 5.340).
[33] *Inst.* 4.16.32 (OS 5.341).
[34] *Inst.* 4.17.17 (OS 5.363). See, also, *Inst.* 1.13.22 (OS 3.137); 1.15.5 (OS 3.181-82).
[35] *Inst.* 1.13.22 (OS 3.138).

tion,'[38] 'slander,'[39] 'deception'[40]—in short, 'the crafty evasions of this foul dog'.[41] And, according to the reformer, behind the malice is the cunning of Satan and of hell, itself.[42] These repeated rhetorical devices in Calvin's works and letters clearly demonstrate the reformer's strong antagonism towards Servetus' heretical theology[43] and, it must be admitted, towards Servetus, the man, himself. What they don't do is to give us the specific reasons for the reformer's support of the death penalty for this condemned man's heresy. Before we consider these, however, it will be instructive to consider how the reformer frames the subject of heresy in his work on scandals.

Heresy and *Concerning Scandals*

Calvin wrote his short treatise, *Concerning Scandals* (*De Scandalis*) and had it printed in Geneva by Jean Crespin (Crispinus) in 1550—just three years before the trial and execution of Michael Servetus. According to Bonnie Pattison, it provides one of the most focused and extensive treatments of his perspective on the persecuted Church[44] and, as we will notice below, this is a significant perspective for a backdrop to his comments on heresy. And, though in this treatise, Calvin covers a whole range of scandalous issues—the many things in the gospel of Christ from which human reason shrinks back (*a quibus humanum ingenium penitus abhorreat*)—this short segment will concentrate only on his comments regarding heresy, found in a short section on 'sects and heresies,' towards the end of the work. We do so because it will give us further evidence of Calvin's thought on the matter, particularly when the section is framed by its literary and theological context within the treatise.

---

[36] *Inst.* 1.13.22 (OS 3.138).
[37] *Inst.* 1.15.5 (OS 3.181).
[38] *Inst.* 2.9.3 (OS 3.400). See, also, *Inst.* 1.15.5 (OS 3.181).
[39] *Inst.* 2.14.7 (OS 3.469).
[40] *Inst.* 2.14.8 (OS 3.470).
[41] *Inst.* 2.14.8 (OS 3.471). See, also, *Inst* .1.13.10 (OS 3.122), where Calvin says that 'Servetus *yelps* that God took on the person of an angel' (emphasis added). Elsewhere, *Inst.* 2.14.5 (OS 3.464), the reformer speaks of Servetus as 'a deadly monster'.
[42] *Inst.* 4.16.32 (OS 5.340-41). In his sermons on Isaiah (1558) Calvin speaks of 'that devil Servetus'—see *Serm. Isa.* 53.9-10 in *Sermons on Isaiah's Prophecy of the Death and Passion of Christ* (translated and edited by T.H.L. Parker; London: James Clarke, 1956), 111 and 112.
[43] See Randall C. Zachman, 'What Kind of a Book is Calvin's *Institutes*?' in *John Calvin as Teacher, Pastor, and Theologian. The Shape of his Writings and Thought* (Grand Rapids: Baker, 2006), 92.
[44] For an excellent relevant examination of this work, see Bonnie Pattison, 'The suffering church in Calvin's *De Scandalis*: an exercise in Luther's *Theologia Crucis*? in Michael Parsons (ed.), *Since we are Justified by Faith. Justification in the Theologies of the Protestant Reformation* (Milton Keynes: Paternoster, 2012), 117-37.

Scandals

Calvin defines scandals as 'obstacles of all kinds, whether they divert us from the right direction, or keep us back by being in the way, or provide the means for making us fall'.[45] Christians must not be tempted by scandals to forsake Christ, he says. His pastoral sensitivity recognises the urgency, and recognises, too, that there are differences in people's responses to scandals. Accordingly, he delineates four 'classes' of people who might turn from Christ or who might make scandals an excuse for their own antagonism towards the gospel:

> those who dread scandals,
> those who are simply lazy;
> those who are arrogant; and,
> those who are malicious, hating the gospel.[46]

The first two classes ('the weak and ignorant') should be dealt with leniently, he advises; he insists that the second two ('the ungodly,' those 'beyond hope') 'must be repulsed more sharply'.[47]

The pattern of history and Satan's activity

On a close reading of the text we can see that the pastoral urgency derives from at least two broader considerations: the reformer's consciousness of what he sees as past patterns repeating themselves throughout history and his mindfulness of the reality of Satan's attacks on the Church. At one point in the writing Calvin makes an important digression from his argument[48] in which he presents the idea that history repeats itself and that, importantly, the Reformation Church is actually somehow caught up in that recurrence. He points out that 'Men's constant revolts from God are what have interrupted the otherwise constant and unimpeded course of his grace.'[49] He then selectively lists times of such impediment. For example, the post-flood inhabitants of the earth begin to worship the Lord in truth, but then many rebel and sin, for which God punishes them. The Church, purified by the flood is reduced to unrighteousness. Again, he discerns the same pattern when the people flee from Egypt: 'Who would not predict from such auspices a perpetual state of blessedness?' he asks.[50] Each time the Lord restores his people to what the reformer calls 'a tolerable form of life'[51] they heap disasters upon themselves. Again, he recalls, the people's return from exile must have been 'like a second birth to them',[52] but again,

---

[45] John Calvin, *Concerning Scandals* (translated by John W. Fraser; Edinburgh: Saint Andrew Press, 1978), 8 (OS 2.166). See, also, his letter to Farel, Geneva, August 19 1550; Calvin, *Letters*, 2.279-82, particularly, 280.
[46] Calvin, *Concerning Scandals*, 11 (OS 2.167).
[47] Calvin, *Concerning Scandals*, 11 (OS 2.168).
[48] The digression covers pages 31-36 of *Concerning Scandals* (OS 2.181-84).
[49] Calvin, *Concerning Scandals*, 32 (OS 2.181).
[50] Calvin, *Concerning Scandals*, 32 (OS 2.182).
[51] Calvin, *Concerning Scandals*, 32 (OS 2.182).
[52] Calvin, *Concerning Scandals*, 33 (OS 2.182).

through their own fault, they fall from grace through sin. It is clear that the pattern appears relentless to Calvin. He sees it again at the time of Jesus Christ ('the source of peace and blessing'[53]):

> When God brought forward the gospel, the ultimate cure for so many deadly diseases, they rejected it in their pride, and like men devoted to destruction they continued to rush from bad to worse.

It is this incongruous combination of the gracious introduction of the gospel and its arrogant rejection that drives home the contemporary conclusion:

> The same thing can also be observed *in our own time*. A few years after the remarkable beginnings of the reborn Church had appeared, we then saw them collapse back into ruins.[54]

History is unmistakeably a mirror for Calvin's own time and vice versa.[55] The reformer comes with such self-consciousness about the Reformed Church—'the true Church,' as he refers to it in this treatise[56]—in which 'the gospel has begun to be revived'[57] that he sees as urgent the call to persevere in the faith and in truth at this crucial time of gracious gospel blessing.

The fact that makes this the more urgent is that behind human rebellion and sin is the malicious activity of Satan, himself. At the moment of most promise—post-flood, the exodus, the return from exile, the coming of Jesus Christ, the reintroduction of the true gospel in the sixteenth century—Satan throws up different and many obstacles in order to rid humanity of its joy and to tempt people from the straight path of righteousness.

This idea repeats throughout the work from the very beginning. In his dedicatory letter to Laurent de Normandy the reformer speaks of Satan preparing 'a confusing labyrinth for [him] out of the endless stock of scandal'.[58] In the introduction of the work Calvin mentions the devil's cunning 'in raising obstacles of every kind'.[59] He speaks of Satan as 'the worst tyrant of them all'.[60] The rhetorical weight of this repetition makes what Calvin believes and what lies at

---

[53] Calvin, *Concerning Scandals*, 34 (OS 2.183).
[54] Calvin, *Concerning Scandals*, 35 (OS 2.184), emphasis added.
[55] Calvin, *Concerning Scandals*, 33 (OS 2.182); 44 (2.190).
[56] Calvin, *Concerning Scandals*, 47 (OS 2.192). See, also, Calvin, *Concerning Scandals*, 46-50 (OS 2.181-94).
[57] Calvin, *Concerning Scandals*, 57 (OS 2.198). For the reformer's consciousness of the revival of the gospel in his own day see the following: Calvin, *Concerning Scandals*, 7 (OS 2.165); 10 (OS 2.166-67); 60-61 (OS 2.200); 64 (OS 2.203); 65 (OS 2.204); 83 (OS 2.216); 88 (OS 2.220).
[58] Calvin, *Concerning Scandals*, 3 (OS 2.163).
[59] Calvin, *Concerning Scandals*, 7 (OS 2.165).
[60] Calvin, *Concerning Scandals*, 56 (OS 2.197). For the repeated idea, see the following: Calvin, *Concerning Scandals*, 13 (OS 2.169); 16 (OS 2.171); 20 (OS 2.173); 21 (OS 2.174); 53 (OS 2.196); 56 (OS 2.198); 57 (OS 2.198); 58 (OS 2.199); 74 (OS 2.210); 78 (OS 2.212); 81 (OS 2.214); 81 (OS 2.215); 90 (OS 2.221); 91 (OS 2.221); 104 (OS 2231); 115 (OS 2.237); 116 (OS 2.238); 118 (OS 2.240).

the back of his thinking on heresy very clear. Heresy is one way—a significant way—in which Satan attacks the Church in times of blessing.[61] He has done it before, many times throughout history, when men and women have experienced the grace of God. And, in a mirror-image of previous occasions, the devil is attacking the Reformed Church in the reformer's day and in his own city of Geneva. This, for the reformer, is not merely theoretical, not simply speculative, but it is the ground for many of the Church's difficulties as he writes his treatise.

Sects and heresies

Calvin asserts that the gospel is the pure and clear truth of God and that it forms the bond of unity between churches and believers. In opposition to this is Satan seeking to 'obscure the light' and to 'tear to pieces the unity into which the sons of God are growing'.[62] All that the Church needs at this crucial time has been divinely given: access to truth (see Matt. 7.7), the Holy Spirit, the Lord has promised to teach his people, and the way of life (application) is apparent, as well. But there are those, he notes, who are gripped by error, who have 'perverted ambition' and arrogance, who are 'dragged this way and that by their own inconclusive speculations'—creating 'intellectual tortures for themselves and others'.[63] Out of many he could choose, he notes Michael Servetus as exemplary.[64]

> Out of many let the one example of Servetus suffice. For this man, who was already puffed up with Portuguese pride, and is now even more swollen with his own arrogance, made up his mind that the best way to make a name for himself was to overthrow all the principles of religion. Accordingly, not only does he repudiate as absurd all that was taught by the Fathers ever since the Apostolic Age itself, and accepted by all believers all down the course of the ages, but he also criticizes it and tears it to pieces with the cruellest of insults. Now, that furious dog-like biting and barking which fills all the pages of his writings is evidence enough of the kind of spirit that drives the man. Indeed, if one looks into the matter he will clearly see that, burning with a desperate thirst for vainglory, he has eagerly swallowed all the craziest and absurd things and made himself drunk with them. . . . At the same time Servetus collects many wagon-loads of speculations which are so meaningless that it is easy for any sensible man to see that only someone bewitched by a blind love of himself can be so foolish. But as soon as the truth of God has come onto the scene, if both their ambition rouses and Satan

---

[61] Heresy is one way in which Satan attacks the Church; persecution is another. See Calvin's letter to the brethren of Chambery, October 8, 1555; Calvin, *Letters*, 3.233. He says, 'It is thus that Satan, when he sees the reign of the Son of God advancing and the number of the faithful increasing, makes still greater efforts to overturn every thing.'

[62] Calvin, *Concerning Scandals*, 65 (OS 2.204). Note the significant present continuous tense, 'are growing,' indicating some hope. The reformer sees this as a developing situation.

[63] Calvin, *Concerning Scandals*, 66 (OS 2.205).

[64] Note that this is three years before Servetus is brought to trial in the Genevan court.

stimulates arrogant inclinations so that they either conceal or overthrow it with perverse fictions and fanatical opinions, that is no reason why we need to be upset as if it were something unusual.[65]

Several things may be pointed out briefly in relation to this paragraph. First, following Augustine's dictum that pride is the mother of all heresies, Calvin is convinced that pride and arrogance lie at the back of Servetus' speculative heresies. The reformer considers him, in fact, 'bewitched by a blind love of himself'. This emphasis on the heretic's ambitious pride underlines the reformer's insistence that only those who submit themselves to God in humility, modesty, sobriety and reverence will sustain their faith in the gospel.[66] It becomes, by implication, a call to Christian piety.[67] Second, the images of Servetus tearing to pieces accepted and received doctrine, coupled with the phrase, 'furious dog-like biting and barking' to describe his writing style and written tone adds to the bestial impression that Calvin wishes to give of the man. Third, the reformer's mention of Satan in the context of what is usual reminds the reader of the two considerations that frame his thinking throughout the treatise: the reformer's consciousness of what he sees as past patterns repeating themselves throughout history and his mindfulness of the reality of Satan's attacks on the Church. Servetus (and others like him, of course) is seen as central to both these matters.

Later, Calvin asks the following rhetorical and pastorally-charged questions.

> Why then does it please wretched men to grasp at the chance of staggering and tottering in the changeable breezes of the world when God makes us firm on the eternal foundation of the Word? Why do they prefer to be tossed about in the midst of the storms of opinions rather than lie quietly in the safe harbour of certain truth, where God invites us?[68]

The contrast between the uncertainty and changeableness of worldly thinking (heresy) and the certainty of divine truth (the Reformation gospel) is significant. The fact that the reformer sets this idea in two rhetorical questions demonstrates its essential pastoral intention.

---

[65] Calvin, *Concerning Scandals*, 66-67 (OS 2.205).
[66] See Calvin, *Concerning Scandals*, 6 (OS 2.204), where the reformer lists these qualities.
[67] For a very helpful essay on Calvin's important concept of piety see S.-Y. Lee, 'Calvin's understanding of Pietas' in W.H. Neuser and B.G. Armstrong (eds), *Calvinus Sincerioris Vindex* (Kirksville: Sixteenth Century Journal Publishers, 1997), 225-40. See, also, F.L. Battles, 'True Piety According to Calvin' in R. Benedetto (ed.), *Interpreting John Calvin* (Grand Rapids: Baker, 1996), 289-306; J.R. Beeke, 'Calvin on Piety' in D.K. McKim (ed.), *The Cambridge Companion to John Calvin* (Cambridge: Cambridge University Press, 2004), 125-52; Matthew M. Boulton, *Life in God. John Calvin, Practical Formation, and the Future of Protestant Theology* (Grand Rapids: Eerdmans, 2011), 45-58.
[68] Calvin, *Concerning Scandals*, 110 (OS 2.234).

Calvin's letters and Servetus

What, then, of Calvin's letters about Servetus? What do they indicate of his opinion on this issue? He wrote several letters on the subject—some to Servetus, himself, and others to his reforming colleagues and to the pastors of other Reformed churches.

To John Frellon, February 13, 1546

In a letter to Servetus, written in 1546,[69] the reformer speaks to him in the third person throughout. In his short work on the reformer's letters, Henry Henderson implies that this shows Calvin's disdain for the man,[70] but the third person may well have been a rhetorical device employed to keep consistency with the pseudonyms both Calvin and Servetus utilise in their correspondence at this early period—Charles D'Espeville and John Frellon, respectively.

Having informed Servetus that he has written as soon as he could he outlines his (albeit, weakening) hope that he may profitably use a last opportunity to help him, 'in order to try once more if there shall be any means of bringing him back, which will be, when God shall have wrought in him so effectually, that he has become entirely another man'.[71] His diagnosis is stark: God needs to work in the heretic in recreating grace (that is, miraculously). The problem, as Calvin sees it, is the man's pride: 'For I do assure you that there is no lesson which is more necessary for him than to learn humility,' he says, 'which must come to him from the Spirit of God, not otherwise.' The reformer assures Servetus that he will sincerely rejoice if he changes his thinking, but, if not, then Calvin flatly refuses to waste more time on him.[72] He has, he insists, more pressing affairs to deal with, more useful reading to do. And, significantly, he refers to Satan who, no doubt, he says, seeks to tempt the reformer from his work by the distraction of Servetus' theology. He beseeches the Lord to have Frellon (Servetus) in his keeping and closes with the phrase, 'Your servant and hearty friend, Charles D'Espeville'.

However, on the same day as this letter Calvin wrote to his colleague, William Farel with less than warm and conciliatory language towards Servetus.[73] Towards the end of the letter he remarks: 'Servetus lately wrote to me, and coupled with his letter a long volume of his delirious fancies.' He continues, 'He takes it upon him to come hither, if it be agreeable to me. But I am unwilling to pledge my word for his safety, for if he shall come, I shall never permit

---

[69] Letter to John Frellon, February 13, 1546; Calvin, *Letters*, 2.30-31.
[70] Henry F. Henderson, *Calvin in his Letters* (Eugene: Wipf and Stock, 1996), 99-108.
[71] Calvin, *Letters*, 2.30.
[72] He mentions this in a letter to Viret, September 1, 1548; Calvin, *Letters*, 4.409-410, where he says, 'I think you must have read by this time the answers I made to Servetus. At length I have resolved not to contend any longer with the incorrigible obstinacy of a heretical man' (4.409).
[73] Letter to William Farel, February 13, 1546; Calvin, *Letters*, 2.31-34.

him to depart alive, provided my authority be of any avail.'[74] Before we judge this comment too soon and too harshly, it may be that Calvin's austere language underlines his intolerance of heresy, perhaps, in contrast with the warmth of his comments to Servetus, himself, which indicate a pastoral concern for the man as he is before God. We need to return to this idea below.

To Farel, August 20, 1553

When Servetus was discovered in Geneva listening to Calvin's preaching he was subsequently arrested. The reformer wrote to Farel the following detailed account.[75]

> We have now new business in hand with Servetus. He intended perhaps passing through this city; for it is not yet known with what design he came. But after he had been recognized, I thought that he should be detained. My friend Nicolas [de la Fontaine – Calvin's servant] summoned him on a capital charge, offering himself as security according to the *lex talionis*. On the following day he adduced against him forty written charges. He at first sought to evade them. Accordingly we were summoned. He impudently reviled me, just as if he regarded me as obnoxious to him. I answered him as he deserved. At length the Senate pronounced all the charges proven. Nicolas was released from prison on the third day, having given up my brother as his surety; on the fourth day he was set free. Of the man's effrontery I will say nothing; but such was his madness that he did not hesitate to say that devils possessed divinity; yea, that many gods were in individual devils, inasmuch as deity had been substantially communicated to those, equally with wood and stone. I hope that sentence of death will at least be passed upon him; but I desire that the severity of the punishment may be mitigated.[76]

Several matters are made clear through this brief report. First, the responsibility of capture was Calvin's, he thought that '[Servetus] should be detained'. Second, the trial was secular; Calvin and other pastors were summoned later and only as experts on theological issues. Third, there was clearly antagonism on both sides: Servetus reviles the reformer, the reformer 'answered him as he deserved'. Fourth, it seems that the overall impression that Calvin wishes to give of Servetus' heresy ('his madness') is that he was a pantheist—that everything, according to him, was divine in some sense. Fifth, though Calvin deems the death sentence as appropriate, he wishes to mitigate the severity of its accomplishment.

It is not without considerable significance that the editor notes Farel's reply, around two weeks later (September 8, 1553): 'In desiring to mitigate the severity of his punishment, you act the part of a friend to a man who is most hostile to you. But I beseech you so to manage the matter that no one whatever may rashly dare to publish new dogmas, and throw all things into confusion with impunity for such a length of time as he has done.' Then, he adds, dramatically, but

---

[74] Calvin, *Letters*, 2.33. See, also, Calvin's letter to Madame de Cany, Geneva, January, 1552; Calvin, *Letters*, 2.338-41.
[75] Letter to William Farel, Geneva, August 20, 1553; Calvin, *Letters*, 2.416-17.
[76] Calvin, *Letters*, 2.417.

to the point, 'I must be prepared to suffer death if I should teach anything contrary to the doctrine of piety. . . . I should be most worthy of any punishment whatever, if I should seduce any one from the faith and doctrine of Christ.'[77] Again, as we noted above concerning Calvin, Farel's concern is not with heresy per se, but with the fact that heresy can seduce believers from the faith. That is, his concern, as Calvin's, is pastoral.

To Bullinger, September 7, 1553

On 5th September, 1553, the Genevan Council decided to consult other cities—Bern, Basel, Schaffhausen and Zurich—respecting Servetus' guilt. They did this against Calvin's wishes; and, as a matter of fact, the reformer appears wearied by the tensions over the case when he writes to Bullinger on the problem.[78] He presents the members of the Council as in his mind cantankerous. He complains, for example, that the Council had 'reached such a pitch of folly and madness, that they regard with suspicion whatever we say to them. So much so,' he says, 'that were I to allege that it is clear at mid-day, they would forthwith begin to doubt it.' This impatient letter concludes with the words, 'My colleagues—all very dejected—salute you earnestly, etc.'[79]

The pastors of Zurich wrote the following after unanimously agreeing that the condemned heretic should die.

> We think that you ought in this case to manifest much faith and zeal, inasmuch as our churches have abroad the bad reputation of being heretical, and of being particularly favourable to heresy. Holy providence at this time affords you an opportunity of freeing yourselves and us from that injurious suspicion, if you know how to be vigilant and active in preventing the further spreading of that poison.[80]

Consequently, Calvin wrote to Farel of this decision a day before the execution: '[The Swiss Churches] are unanimous in pronouncing that Servetus has now renewed these impious errors with which Satan formerly disturbed the Church, and that he is a monster not to be borne.' Again, he mentions his failed attempt to 'alter the mode of his death'.[81] Subsequent to the execution, Calvin wrote again to Bullinger to thank the church in Zurich, through him, for their 'faithful and pious response' given in the case of Servetus.[82]

---

[77] Calvin, *Letters*, 2.417n.2.
[78] To Bullinger, Geneva, September 7, 1553; Calvin, *Letters*, 2.425-27.
[79] Calvin, *Letters*, 2.427.
[80] Calvin, *Letters*, 2.435n.2.
[81] To Farel, Geneva, October 26, 1553; Calvin, *Letters*, 2.426. Cottret, *Calvin*, 224, reminds us that though the majority of ministers of the churches in Zurich, Bern, Basel and Schaffhausen, were in agreement on the verdict, it was not actually unanimous. Amongst the exceptions were the pastor Vergerio and the former Anabaptist, David Joris.
[82] To Bullinger, Geneva, November 26, 1553; Calvin, *Letters*, 2.440-42 (2.441).

To Melanchthon, March 5, 1555

Almost eighteen months after the event, the reformer wrote to thank his Lutheran colleague, Philip Melanchthon, for his endorsement of Calvin's 'zeal in crushing the impiety of Servetus' (Calvin's words).[83] For his part, Melanchthon had commended Calvin's handling of the situation and the involvement of the city's magistrates: 'I maintain that your magistrates have acted with justice, in having put to death a blasphemer, after having regularly judged the affair.'[84] Of particular interest is the fact that Calvin's response is set in the context of his rebuke of Melanchthon's slowness to refute error in his own setting—a rebuke he continues later, in August of the same year.[85]

Calvin's reasons for having Servetus put to death

Our modern and postmodern tolerance of religious pluralism is anachronistic for the sixteenth century, confessional churches of the Reformation and we must be careful not to judge them for not being like us. However, neither should we defend them as if everything is acceptable in the way they dealt with issues such as the punishment for heresy. We recognise that they too had the gospel of Jesus Christ to guide their ecclesial decisions and actions, though their comprehension of that gospel (like ours, it must be said) was steeped in hundreds of years of traditional reading and response, and cultural and intellectual framing.

The present section is not meant to condone or to exonerate Calvin and his peers; nor is its purpose to judge them too harshly. Though I would wholeheartedly agree with Gerard Mannion, where he says, in the context of the Servetus affair, 'What is contrary to the Word of God can never be an appropriate or true means of defending the Word of God, itself',[86] Henry Henderson's conclusion, that 'Nothing is more certain than that Calvin did wrong'[87] smacks to me of what Alister McGrath calls 'a selectivity approaching victimization'— singling Calvin out for criticism as if his involvement in the affair was single-handed and more than 'oblique'.[88] What follows is a critical list of reasons gen-

---

[83] To Melanchthon, Geneva, March 5, 1555; Calvin, *Letters*, 3.157-58.

[84] Calvin, *Letters*, 3.157n.1. See William Monter, 'Heresy Executions in Reformation Europe, 1520-1565' in Ole Peter Grell and Robert W. Scribner (eds), *Tolerance and Intolerance in the European Reformation* (Cambridge: Cambridge University Press, 1996), 48-64.

[85] To Melanchthon, Geneva, August 23, 1555; Calvin, *Letters*, 3.219-20. In this letter Calvin calls Melanchthon 'sluggish'.

[86] Gerard Mannion, 'Calvin and the Church: Trajectories for Ecumenical Engagement Today – Volume Introduction' in Gerard Mannion and Eduardus Van der Borght (eds), *John Calvin's Ecclesiology. Ecumenical Perspectives* (London: T&T Clark, 2011), 1-30 (17).

[87] Henderson, *Calvin in his Letters*, 107.

[88] Alister E. McGrath, *A Life of John Calvin: A Study in the Shaping of Western Culture* (Oxford: Blackwell, 1990), 116.

erally given for Calvin's participation in the execution of Michael Servetus, recognising the sixteenth century nature of the situation, but recognising, too, the fallibility of all the men caught up in the tragic circumstances of his death.

Calvin was a man of his time

An overarching reason sometimes given to understand Calvin's involvement in Michael Servetus' death is that the reformer was a man of his time, a child of his age. Richard Gamble suggests this and concludes, 'Thus, when contemporary readers understand the sixteenth century cultural context in which Calvin lived, this act of execution, though not to be regarded with approval, is much more understandable.'[89] There are a number of factors that go some way to making the situation more understandable; though, as Gamble says, not endorsed, nor excused.

First, it is widely pointed out that execution for heresy was in fact a legal requirement in central Europe in the sixteenth century. Michael Mullett, for example, states that '[Servetus'] offence, seen in neutral and jurisprudential terms, was not that of being wicked or deranged but consisted of the objective, almost impersonal, crime of being wrong.'[90] Indeed, that heresy was a capital crime had been a commonplace medieval concept for some time. More recently, the Emperor Charles V had established a law against anyone found within his empire who contradicted the received doctrine of the Trinity—they were to be punished by death. Even Henry Henderson, negative and critical though he is at this point, states that heresy was regarded as the most dangerous and worst of all forms of treason against the state.[91] John Calvin, trained in law, would undoubtedly have known the requirement of the death penalty for heresy. Certainly, the affair seems to have been conducted with legality and legitimacy in view. Philip Melanchthon's letter to Calvin, quoted above, seems to have that in mind: 'I maintain that your magistrates have acted with *justice*, in having put to death a blasphemer, after *having regularly judged* the affair.'[92] So as a backdrop to Calvin's reaction to Servetus, the fact that heresy was punishable by death amounts to something, but it doesn't account for Calvin's rather personal attack on Servetus. His tone, both in his letters and his other works, is anything but judicial or objective, and suggests other, more pressing reasons.

Second, it is significant that there was broad contemporary consensus about what should be done with Michael Servetus, a consensus that covered Lutherans, Roman Catholics and the Reformed churches, all of whom wanted him

---

[89] Richard C. Gamble, 'Calvin's Controversies' in Donald K. McKim (ed.), *The Cambridge Companion to John Calvin* (Cambridge: Cambridge University Press, 2004), 188-203 (198).See, also, McGrath, *A Life of John Calvin*, 114.
[90] Mullett, *John Calvin*, 154.
[91] Henderson, *Calvin in his Letters*, 106. See, also, Derek Thomas, 'Who was John Calvin? in Burk Parsons (ed.), *John Calvin. A Heart for Devotion, Doctrine and Doxology* (Orlando: Reformation Trust, 2008), 24.
[92] Calvin, *Letters*, 3.157n.1, emphasis added.

done away with. The fact that the milder mannered and peaceful Melanchthon was in full agreement with the sentence is evidence of the spectrum. As we noted, the churches of Bern, Basel, Schaffhausen and Zurich all concurred in the matter—though, not entirely unanimously. Peter Martyr's response testifies to the same: 'Regarding Servetus, I have nothing to say but that he was the devil's own son, whose evil and detestable doctrine must everywhere be banished . . . his blasphemies simply could not be tolerated.'[93] In the sense that almost everyone who was asked to make a judgement on the situation agreed with the verdict, Calvin was clearly a child of his age.

Third, we should also take into account the fact that as nearly every confessional church held it to be right to execute heretics, so too there were others in Calvin's day who passed the death sentence for 'lesser' theological reasons than for anti-trinitarian propaganda. In her intriguing and nuanced essay on the polemic against Calvin, Marilynne Robinson is adamant that this, at least, be recognised.[94] It is worth quoting her at length.

> Calvin is routinely blamed for torture and executions carried out in Geneva, without reference to the fact that both were utterly commonplace in Europe—judicial torture was established in Roman law—or that Geneva had a civil government which Calvin did not control.

She then compares John Calvin and Thomas More to good effect.

> Calvin called for the death of Michael Servetus, a Basque physician who wrote an attack on the doctrine of the Trinity. More called for the death of William Tyndale, the priest who made the translation of the New Testament and early books of the Old Testament into English which became the basis for the so-called King James Bible. Both men were burned, as were their books.[95]

Indeed, to change the comparison, at the same time as Calvin was arguing for Servetus' death for heresy, the Catholic Church in Lyon, for example, held five young students prisoner until their trial and death—punished for being Calvinists, for holding Reformed doctrines. During this period, from June 10, 1552 to May 15, 1553, the reformer wrote to them encouraging them to stand firm in the faith despite their fate.[96] Many similar examples could be adduced from every side to show that Calvin was a man of his own age.

In passing, two other matters might come into consideration under this subheading. Some argue that Calvin demonstrates intolerance against heretics; that he is a religious fanatic who cannot allow differences. Bernard Cottret says as much: '[B]y definition the Calvinist enterprise could not envisage the least compromise.' And, again, 'Calvin's *logic* could no more accommodate a con-

---

[93] Quoted by Needham, *2000 Years*, 227.
[94] See Robinson, 'The Polemic Against Calvin,' 96-122.
[95] Robinson, 'The Polemic Against Calvin,' 98.
[96] See chapter 7 of the present volume. He speaks of these students as 'martyrs'.

tradition than his conscience could a business arrangement.'[97] In sharp contrast to this, it is not insignificant that William Naphy points out that immediately before the Servetus affair two other cases of heresy were tried in Geneva, with very different results. In July, Robert le Moine from Normandy claimed and taught that prostitution and fornication were not contrary to the Word of God. Later in the year, and more theologically serious and closer to Servetus' arguments, perhaps, Jean Baudin of Lorraine maintained that Jesus was not a real human being, but a mere phantom and that the Bible was just another book. Neither man was sentenced to death, but both were banished from the city. Naphy, understandably, suggests that these two cases might well have made the reformer more sensitive to heresy.[98] That is true. And, it adds weight to the argument that Calvin's treatment of Servetus was at least a judicial response against a heretic teaching that the doctrine of the Trinity, specifically, was untrue, unbiblical and against the Church Fathers' opinions.

It should also be noted, briefly, that Calvin did not have the final word, nor, indeed, a great deal of weight in the final decision. We have already seen that Calvin and other pastors were brought in by the civil government as specialists because of the theological nature of the crime.[99] Naphy is resolute. The Servetus situation, he says, was 'a wholly secular affair'.[100] Similarly, in his largely positive account, McGrath underlines the authority of the Messieurs de Genèva, not that of Calvin, who was, after all, a foreigner in the city.[101] Alongside this, we note that the reformer says to Sulzer that he instigated the arrest and imprisonment of Servetus,[102] though he is somewhat less adamant in his account of the episode to his friend, Farel.[103]

---

[97] Cottret, *Calvin*, 207, italics added. The italicised word surely betrays an opinion of Calvin which cannot really be substantiated.

[98] See Naphy, *Calvin and the Consolidation*, 183-84. See, also, Oliver Millet, 'le thème de la conscience libre chez Calvin' in *La liberté de conscience (xvie-xviie siècles)* (Geneva: Droz, 1991), 21-37, cited by Cottret, *Calvin*, 207n.7.

[99] See his letter to William Farel, Geneva, August 20, 1553; Calvin, *Letters*, 2.417. Calvin, himself comments elsewhere that 'there is no doubt that [Christ] wished to bar the ministers of his Word from civil rule and earthly authority,' *Inst.* 4.11.8 (OS 5.203).

[100] Naphy, *Calvin and the Consolidation*, 183.

[101] McGrath, *A Life of John Calvin*, 114.

[102] 'At my instigation, one of the Syndics ordered [Servetus] to be conducted to prison'—letter to Sulzer (1553), quoted by Henderson, *Calvin in his Letters*, 104. In reference to the church and state working together see the following: Timothy E. Fulop, 'The Third Mark of the Church? – Church Discipline in the Reformed and Anabaptist Reformations,' *Journal of Religious History* 19.1 (1995), 37-38; Stephen M. Johnson, '"The Sinews of the Body of Christ." Calvin's Concept of Church Discipline,' *Westminster Journal of Theology* 59 (1997), 92-94; William G. Naphy, 'Calvin's Geneva' in Donald K. McKim (ed.), *The Cambridge Companion to John Calvin* (Cambridge: Cambridge University Press, 2004), 32-33.

[103] Calvin, *Letters*, 2.417.

The reformer, then, is clearly a man of his time. We would expect this to be the case, of course, though this broad reflection only adds to our wider understanding, but cannot exonerate, excuse or blame the reformer. We need to try to get closer to the question: what makes his response so personal against Servetus? The next three short sections attempt this.

The historical situation

Some commentators give weight to the suggestion that the trial and execution of Servetus served Calvin's interests well, and that this may help to explain his reasoning in the case. William Bouwsma, for instance, says that 'The confrontation between Calvin and his adversaries may help to explain the trial and execution of Servetus, which occurred when tensions in Geneva were at their height.' He adds that 'each side needed to demonstrate its zeal for orthodoxy'.[104] Others, understandably, agree.[105] On this matter, Cottret, for instance, says, 'To become fully acceptable among Christians, it was desirable for him in his turn to identify a heretic, a heresy, a blasphemer, an apostate.'[106] However, the explicit evidence appears to demonstrate that the plea to demonstrate orthodoxy came from outside, and not entirely from the reformer himself, if at all. Bullinger and the pastors of the church in Zurich, for example, speak of this to Calvin in very adamant terms: 'We think that you ought in this case to manifest much faith and zeal, inasmuch as our churches have abroad the bad reputation of being heretical, and of being particularly favourable to heresy.'[107] We might say that defending orthodox trinitarian faith against Servetus certainly did no harm to Calvin's position in Geneva. Indeed, it may have been a turning point in his situation. His trinitarian orthodoxy had been questioned, by Caroli, in particular, for over fifteen years.[108] Nevertheless, surely, Cottret argues too strongly that 'Caroli and Servetus forced [Calvin] to specify his support of the trinitarian dogma' and that Servetus' execution 'was almost without a doubt a demonstration of *the uncertainty of the exegete* overcome by the vertigo induced by the text.'[109]

There is ample confirmation that the reformer held firmly to traditional, orthodox belief in the Trinity before the situation under review, but that he sought

---

[104] William J. Bouwsma, *John Calvin. A Sixteenth Century Portrait* (New York: Oxford University Press, 1988), 27.

[105] See, for example, J.T. McNeill, *The History and Character of Calvinism* (London: Oxford University Press, 1954), 175; Mullett, *Calvin*, 42-43; Needham, *2000 Years of Christ's Power*, 225; Wadkins, "A Recipe for Intolerance,' 441. Bernard Cottret, *Calvin*, 221, suggests that there was a fear of a popish plot to destabilise Calvin's position in Geneva; and there is evidence that Wolfgang Musculus, the reformer's colleague, assumed that Servetus had come to the city to take advantage of the Council's dissatisfaction with Calvin—see Selderhuis, *John Calvin*, 205-206.

[106] Cottret, *Calvin*, 220.

[107] Calvin, *Letters*, 2.435n.2.

[108] See Cottret, *Calvin*, 221.

[109] Cottret, *Calvin*, 322, 308, respectively, emphasis added.

to expound that belief in more soteriological terms and for soteriological reasons. Timothy George, for example, says that the purpose of Calvin's Trinitarianism is soteriological, because it is a witness to the deity of Jesus Christ and thus points to the certainty of our salvation through him. And, in her extremely important work, *Calvin's Ladder*, Julie Canlis sums this up:

> Calvin always points us to the Trinitarian economy: how the Trinity works to bring us to itself. . . . Nor is it a simplistic dichotomy between the immanent and the economic Trinity. Rather, it is a robust theology of the communion, cooperation, and interrelationship between Father, Son, and Holy Spirit for the salvation and sanctification of humanity.[110]

Indeed, in his influential work on the subject, Philip Butin concludes that 'Calvin reveals his own sense that the battle he is fighting' is to 'safeguard believers' redemption via the orthodox doctrines of the Trinity and the person of Christ'.[111] Therefore, it will not do to say that Calvin was able to sharpen his doctrine of the Trinity and thereby to strengthen his position, as if this were reason enough to have the heretic, Michael Servetus, executed.

Calvin's theology

In an interesting article on the subject, Timothy Wadkins suggests that there are several underlying theological reasons behind Calvin's approval of the death penalty for heresy.[112] He argues for the following three areas: the reformer's doctrine of God, his understanding of ecclesiology and his hermeneutics. From the evidence, it is clear that these do have weight in the reformer's thinking, though a brief summary will have to suffice at this point.

First, Calvin's doctrine of the nature of God is significant. Wadkins says that 'a false belief [on the Trinity], especially if made public, was considered an affront to the divine majesty, thus promoting the idea that God must be vindi-

---

[110] George, *Theology of the Reformers*, 200-201. Julie Canlis, *Calvin's Ladder. A Spiritual Theology of Ascent and Ascension* (Grand Rapids: Eerdmans, 2010), 94; see 92-98. On this important subject see, also, Allan M. Harman, 'Speech about the Trinity: with Special reference to Novatian, Hilary and Calvin,' *Scottish Journal of Theology* 26.4 (1973), 385-400; T.F. Torrance, *Trinitarian Perspectives* (Edinburgh: T&T Clark, 1994), 41-76, particularly, 44-48; John McIntyre, *The Shape of Pneumatology. Studies in the Doctrine of the Holy Spirit* (Edinburgh: T&T Clark, 1997), 109-33; Philip W. Butin, *Revelation, Redemption and Response. Calvin's Trinitarian Understanding of the Divine-Human Relationship* (Oxford: Oxford University Press, 1995), particularly, 39-53, 55-94; T.H.L. Parker, *Calvin. An Introduction to his Thought* (London: Geoffrey Chapman, 1995), 31-34; Kurt A. Richardson, 'Calvin on the Trinity' in Sung W. Chung (ed.), *John Calvin and Evangelical Theology. Legacy and Prospect* (Milton Keynes: Paternoster, 2009), 32-42.

[111] Butin, *Revelation, Redemption and Response*, 34.

[112] Wadkins, 'A Recipe for Intolerance,' 431-41.

cated'.[113] 'Without blinking an eye,' the reformer says, 'we should be willing to take up the sword.'[114] Wadkins quotes Calvin's rather stark comments on Deuteronomy, chapter 13:

> Hence, too, we are admonished, that zeal for God's glory is but cold among us, unless true religion is held to be of more value than the preservation of a single city or people.... And since we are created to no other end, and live for no other cause than that God may be glorified in us, it is better that the whole earth should perish, than that men should enjoy the fruits of the earth in order that they may contaminate it with their blasphemies.[115]

Second, Calvin's ecclesiology is important to the situation. It is the saints' task to build up and to defend the Church against heresy and the inroads of Satan. He is adamant where responsibility lies. Third, the reformer's hermeneutics are not irrelevant to his response to Servetus' heresy. Reading and commenting on Deuteronomy 13, Calvin likens heresy to a disease or a deadly pestilence that should be met 'with extraordinary means'. And, this image brings us closer to answering the question why Calvin was so personal in his attack on Servetus. It was his pastoral understanding of the situation that gave rise to the reformer's annoyance and determination.

Calvin's pastoral urgency

The fuller quotation from his commentary on Deuteronomy 13 is instructive:

> Because more severe remedies are applied to *perilous diseases*, so it is right that so *noxious*, and altogether *deadly pestilence* as this should be met with extraordinary means.... For although it might seem cruel to betray such as have not publicly transgressed, yet inasmuch as sectaries fly from the light, and creep in by clandestine and deceitful acts, it is necessary to prevent them from fraudulently *infecting* individual houses with their *poison*, as always is the case with them.[116]

Though not unusual rhetoric, of course, the prolonged medical image is very significant in this context. I noted above that the reformer, in the *Institutes*, appears as anxious about the repercussions of Servetus' doctrine as about the doctrine itself.[117] Calvin, the pastor, discerns the true destructive nature of heresy and fears for his congregation; fears that the sacrilege will spread like a dreadful disease (significantly, like the plague—'deadly pestilence') and snatch people from life and from God.[118] Truth is absolutely necessary to salvation.[119] If

---

[113] Wadkins, 'A Recipe for Intolerance,' 432. 'The motif of rendering glory to God is absolutely dominant in Calvin's theology and in his personal writings as well,' Susanne Selinger, *Calvin Against Himself* (Hamden: Archon, 1984), 57; see 57-58.
[114] Quoted by Wadkins, 'A Recipe for Intolerance,' 433.
[115] Quoted by Wadkins, 'A Recipe for Intolerance,' 433.
[116] Quoted by Wadkins, 'A Recipe for Intolerance,' 438, italics added.
[117] See footnotes 30-33.
[118] We noted above that William Farel speaks of heresy as seducing people from faith and from Christ, Calvin, *Letters*, 2.417n.2.

untruth was allowed to prevail the salvation of those in the pastors' charge would be at risk. This accounts for Calvin's urgency when writing to the pastors of the church in Frankfurt in the year of Servetus' death: '[I]t is your duty to see to it that this pestiferous poison does not spread farther . . . purge the world of such noxious corruptions.' The strength of Calvin's understanding comes across in the following emphatic words: '[T]he magnitude of the affair demands that I beseech you, by Christ, faithfully to strive to discharge your duty, lest the opportunity should slip from you.'[120]

Elsewhere, in his sermon on Deuteronomy 5.13-15, Calvin is clear that the Christian has 'two principal articles in the law of God: the one concerns what we owe him; the other what we owe our neighbours with whom we live [*conversans-vivants avec*]'. Later, he seems to apply this duality of the law's concern to pastors who must not tolerate heresy. He gives two reasons, which correlate with the two principal articles: first, they must not tolerate heresy because unbridled heresy creates a corruption which is difficult to cure (note, again, the medical image); second, he insists that if the ground on which God wants people to live is polluted, '*nothing will make him*,' that is, God, '*come to us*'.[121] Salvation, then, is at stake, but not simply because untruth or heresy somehow disqualifies *us* as its recipients, or because it drives us away from God, but because the holy God himself will not 'come to us' in that condition. For Calvin, the pastor, this situation is a question of whether the church may engage in worship, in true Christian piety and in the daily experience of the living God.

This brings us closer to Calvin's angry and passionate response to Servetus, I think. It is the angry response of a pastor charged with looking after the wellbeing of his congregation; the angry response of someone who realises that sin and heresy are not, as it were, static, but that they spread their contagion from person to person and from church to church. It seems to me, therefore, illegitimate to conclude, with Alexandre Ganoczy, that the *confession's* value 'stood higher than a person's life' in this situation.[122] This misses the crucial point that troubled Calvin. The confession was not the pivotal determinant of the situation and of his response; the salvation and eternal wellbeing of many in Geneva (and central Europe) was the point. The continued, present, lived experience of God was the objective. Calvin and his colleagues saw heresy as a deadly threat

---

[119] 'A correct belief in God was deemed to be absolutely essential to salvation,' Wadkins, 'A Recipe for Intolerance,' 432. See, also, George, *Theology of the Reformers*, 200-201.

[120] Letter to the pastors of the Church of Frankfurt, Geneva, August 27, 1553; Calvin, *Letters*, 2.423. See, also, his letter to Bullinger, Geneva, March 28, 1554; Calvin, *Letters*, 3.32-35 (35).

[121] Calvin, *Serm. Deut.* 5.13-15; *Sermons on the Ten Commandments* (edited and translated by Benjamin W. Farley; Grand Rapids: Baker, 1980), 122, 130, respectively, emphasis added.

[122] Alexandre Ganoczy, 'Calvin's Life' in Donald K. McKim (ed.), *The Cambridge Companion to John Calvin* (Cambridge: Cambridge University Press, 2004), 18.

to living faith itself. It is significant that the charge of the Genevan Council included the following words about Servetus' heresy, 'This,' they say, 'entails the murders and ruin of many souls.'[123] What made matters worse for them was the belief that behind all of this lay the malicious activity of Satan, himself.[124] As we observed above, in his work *Concerning Scandals* Calvin is adamant that past patterns of grace followed by sinfulness and rebellion repeat themselves throughout history and he is mindful of the reality of Satan's attacks on the Church in all of this, together with the sense that the Reformation Church (the Genevan Church, in particular) might fall foul of the same destructive tendency.[125]

Reflections

In examining John Calvin's letters and other works in which he mentions Michael Servetus we have discovered that the reformer is perhaps driven in his response by urgent pastoral concern for his own congregation and for the wider Reformed Church as well. We have come to the obvious conclusion that he is a man of his time, but that this does not excuse or blame him—it is simply the backdrop to his decision-making in the specific situation. We noted, too, that the complexities of the historical situation, in which Calvin was opposed by those who might have supported him, may have underlined the importance of a decision against Servetus, the heretic. Calvin's theology also leant its weight towards such a verdict. But, in answer to the question of why Calvin supported the death penalty against Servetus, these reasons are simply not enough to explain his exasperation with the man.

We have concluded that the crucial reason for Calvin's attitude and decision against Servetus is to be found in his very real pastoral concern for the Church of his day. As strange as it may seem, this pastoral concern extends at crucial times to the victim as well. During the early years of their correspondence, as we have seen above, the reformer attempts to dissuade Servetus from his path and to convince him of his errors. He rather despairingly hopes for change, but fears that it will take divine re-creation of the man to make what would amount to a radical difference.[126] He refuses to give Servetus permission to enter Geneva, or to encourage him, before he has had a chance to read the reformer's *Institutes* and to change his thinking.[127] He seeks to change the mode of execution

---

[123] Quoted by Heinze, *Reform and Conflict*, 189. See, also, Calvin's letter to Sulzer (1553), quoted by Henderson, *Calvin in his Letters*, 105.

[124] See Calvin's letter to Farel, Geneva, October 26, 1553; Calvin, *Letters*, 2.426. Also, Calvin, *Inst.* 1.15.5 (OS 3.181); 2.9.3 (OS 3.400); 4.16.32 (OS 5.340, 341); Calvin, *A clear explanation of sound doctrine concerning the true partaking of the flesh and blood of Christ in the Holy Supper* (1561) in J.K.S. Reid (ed.), *Calvin: Theological Treatises* (Philadelphia: Westminster, 1954), 261.

[125] See the section, *The pattern of history and Satan's activity*, above.

[126] Letter to John Frellon, February 13, 1546; Calvin, *Letters*, 2.30-31.

[127] Letter to Guiluame Farel, February 13, 1546; Calvin, *Letters*, 2.33.

to a more humane form; and visits the prisoner on the penultimate day of his life, the day before his execution. This focused pastoral concern does not excuse Calvin, of course, but it should be taken into account in our consideration. Indeed, it must be. But, of necessity, the reformer's primary concern lies with the people under his charge as a pastor in the Reformed Church, and as a reformer in the European Reformed movement.

In conclusion we may ask where this leads our thinking? This brief chapter has demonstrated that it is simply not possible to come to any easy answers on the question of the reformer's involvement in Servetus' death. But we can make a plea for a just reading of the situation. In February 1554 Calvin wrote to Bullinger

> You at least, even in your criticisms, judge me with equity. Others attack me savagely, reproaching me with professing cruelty, with pursuing with my pen a man who died by my hand.[128]

From our twenty-first century, ecumenical and relatively 'liberal' viewpoint Calvin is not above criticism in the situation.[129] However, perhaps we should be willing to criticise 'with equity' the man who sought to put the lives and salvation of his congregants and the glory of God as his priority in a complex and tragic situation.

---

[128] Letter to Bullinger, February 27, 1554, quoted by Cottret, *Calvin*, 227.

[129] It is worth recalling that during his final illness, on his death-bed, the reformer said, 'I have meant well, *my faults have always displeased me*, and the root of the fear of God has been in my heart'—cited by Gwyn Walters, *The Sovereign Spirit. The Doctrine of the Holy Spirit in the Writings of John Calvin* (Edinburgh: Rutherford House, 2009), 228, italics added.

CHAPTER 6

'To find consolation in our Lord.' Calvin's letters on grief[1]

In his intriguing book, *Lament, Death and Destiny* (2004),[2] R.A. Hughes suggests, rightly I think, that there has been a marked decline in the practice of lament in the church and blames the growing significance of the doctrine of providence since the time of Augustine, who, it is argued, 'bequeathed to the ages a general theodicy of justifying suffering, evil, and death by the providential will of God'.[3] In this broader context, Hughes' examination of John Calvin begins by asserting that 'the two guiding concepts at the heart of Calvin's theology [are] those of providence and the abyss'. In a rather stereotypical manner, he claims that Calvin's doctrine of providence is the reformer's method of overcoming the anxiety and powerlessness that he felt. Illustrating his thesis on a reading of the reformer's exposition of Psalms 13.1 and 22.1, Hughes suggests that 'Calvin does not read lament in its own terms but subordinates it to providence.' He continues, 'If lament was accepted *in itself*, this would mean a spiritual blindness and failure to discern God's hidden order in history. It would also imply an inability to realize that God determines both natural and human events.'[4] It is not clear what the italicized words imply. They seem to indicate the experience of lament within its own context, essentially, as it were, divorced from providence; and, if that is the case, Hughes is perhaps asking the wrong question of Calvin, because, for the reformer, every experience necessarily happens within the broader context of God's relationship with humanity—that is, in the very context of divine providence. In that sense, lament *has* to be subordinated to divine providence. There is *no* context, unless it is the context of God's providential care of creation and of his people. This, in a

---

[1] This chapter is a much revised version of Michael Parsons, *Luther and Calvin on Grief. Life Experience and Biblical Text* (Lewiston: Edwin Mellen, 2013), 42-62, used with permission.
[2] R.A. Hughes, *Lament, Death and Destiny* (New York: Peter Lang, 2004). See, also, two other excellent and thought-provoking works: Nicholas Wolterstorff, 'The Wounds of God. Calvin's Theology and Social Injustice,' *Reformed Journal* 37 (1987), 14-22, and K.D. Billman and D.L. Migliore, *Rachel's Cry: Prayer of Lament and Rebirth of Hope* (Cleveland: United Church Press, 1999).
[3] Hughes, *Lament, Death and Destiny*, 151.
[4] Hughes, *Lament, Death and Destiny*, 109, emphasis added.

sense, is the balance that Calvin seeks—the balance between experience and faith, between grief and trust—and so lament is important to him within that broader perspective.

Hughes examines Calvin's sermons on Job in much the same way. He states that providence is the central aspect of the sermons and that lament is delimited and subordinated beneath that central doctrine. Hughes quotes Calvin, 'Now he who murmurs against God *as if He were cruel and inhuman* thereby curses God,'[5] but makes no comment upon these important words. However, the italicized words are vitally important to our understanding of Calvin, as he believes that lament is actually *good* as long as it does not throw us into sin. Hughes does, however, use as synonymous the phrases 'laments' and 'extravagant statements'—as if by them Calvin meant exactly the same thing. He does not. It seems to me that they are *not* synonymous in the reformer's reading of Job, nor are they in his exposition of lament found elsewhere. Lament is not 'extravagant' according to the reformer unless the person lamenting goes beyond the limits of piety and loses control in self-pity or fear.[6]

Hughes' conclusion is unsurprisingly dogmatic. He says that within a long line of theological tradition from the Church Fathers (particularly, Augustine) through Thomas Aquinas to Martin Luther that claimed lament as a form of sin, 'Calvin's rigorous and comprehensive arguments for providence essentially prevented any further consideration of lament in theology.'[7] According to Hughes, Calvin identified lament with the sin of blasphemy. His theology 'culminated the critique of lament in classical theology'.[8]

Can Hughes' conclusions be sustained? Elsewhere, in the monograph *Luther and Calvin on Grief. Life Experience and Biblical Text* (2013), I have written a full-length rebuttal of them.[9] This chapter asks the question in a rather more limited context. What of the reformer's letters of condolence to those who are grieving the loss of loved ones? What do these show us of Calvin's understanding of grief and lament in the very concrete situation of loss? This chapter examines several letters and seeks, then, to reflect on Calvin's pastoral approach and understanding in the light of Hughes' conclusions.

Calvin's pastoral letters to those who grieve

To Monsieur de Richebourg, 1541

Calvin writes a relatively long letter to his friend de Richebourg after the death of his son, Louis.[10] Apparently, Louis was pious, gentle, lively, patient and

---

[5] Hughes, *Lament, Death and Destiny*, 110, emphasis added.
[6] See Parsons, *Luther and Calvin on Grief*, for a full exploration of this view.
[7] Hughes, *Lament, Death and Destiny*, 113.
[8] Hughes, *Lament, Death and Destiny*, 114. More generally, Hughes argues that reformers rejected lament as a sin of blasphemy or a kind of venial sin (161).
[9] See footnote 1.
[10] Letter to Monsieur de Richebourg, Ratisbon, April, 1541; *Letters*, 1.246-53.

modest and Calvin knew him well. He had a quick intellectual apprehension and the ability to apply what he had learned. Sadly, he had succumbed to and died of the plague whilst studying in Strasbourg. The aspect of the letter that most strikes us is the way the reformer expresses his own grief over this death even as he seeks to console the father in his sorrow. The first paragraph that he writes contains the following words.

> When I first received the intelligence of the death of Claude[11] and of your son Louis, I was so utterly overpowered that for many days I was unfit for nothing but to grieve; and albeit I was somehow upheld before the Lord by those aids wherewith he sustains our souls in affliction, among men, however, I was almost a nonentity; so far as regards my discharge of duty, I appeared to myself quite as unfit for it as if I had been half dead.[12]

This is clearly not simply hollow rhetoric; there is that discernible ring of authenticity about Calvin's words. In prayer, in reading scripture, in meditation,[13] the reformer was barely able to sustain himself, but in the company of other people he was 'almost a nonentity', 'half dead'—unable to concentrate, disinterested, preoccupied, perhaps.[14] Later, he speaks of Louis' brother, Charles, in much the same realistic manner, suspecting that he also must be 'steeped in sorrow and soaked in tears'.[15] So Calvin is certainly not afraid of his emotions when confronted with grief and sorrow; neither is he afraid of exposing them to others.[16] In a letter to William Farel concerning the same tragic death Calvin indicates that his 'house was in a state of sad desolation';[17] he speaks of 'the bitterness of [his] grief' and of being 'grievously distressed' by the situation.[18] He speaks, too, of his melancholy: he states that there is 'so much sadness, that it seems as if they [ie. his sad thoughts] could utterly upset the mind and depress the spirit'. He adds, '[Y]ou cannot believe the grief which consumes me'.[19]

However, he is explicit about his reason for sharing them with his friend de Richebourg. This expression of grief is foundational to the exhortations and encouragement which follow. Calvin wants de Richebourg to value his consolation because it comes from a genuine friend, one who loved his son 'as

---

[11] Claude Féray was a distinguished professor in Strasbourg, a friend of Calvin and the son's tutor there.
[12] Calvin, *Letters*, 1.246.
[13] Later, Calvin mentions prayer and 'private meditations, which are suggested by His word'. Without them, he says, he would have been 'utterly cast down'—Calvin, *Letters*, 1.247.
[14] Subsequently, Calvin speaks again of the situation as 'this crushing blow'—Calvin, *Letters*, 1.250.
[15] Calvin, *Letters*, 1.247. He returns to the subject of grief at the end of the letter.
[16] Letter to Farel, Ratisbon, March 28, 1541; Calvin, *Letters*, 1.237-46.
[17] Calvin, *Letters*, 1.237.
[18] Calvin, *Letters*, 1.238.
[19] Calvin, *Letters*, 1.238.

a father'. The reformer then offers some reminders that might help de Richebourg to obtain some comfort in the terrible circumstances into which he is forced.

First, Calvin reminds the father that it is the Lord who has taken his son: 'The son whom the Lord had lent you for a season he has taken away.'[20] He therefore cautions that the situation should not be read in the light of impersonal factors as some would do: 'There is no ground, therefore, for those silly and wicked complaints of foolish men; O blind death! O horrid fate! O implacable daughters of destiny! O cruel fortune!' There is no ground for this, says Calvin, because 'The Lord who had lodged him here for a season, at this stage of his career has called him away.'[21] The situation, for Calvin, reflects something of the nature and, importantly, the mystery of God—it has to: if he works according to 'special providence'[22] then the circumstance, however difficult to bear, needs to be seen in that light.

> What the Lord has done, we must, at the same time, consider has not been done rashly, nor by chance, neither from having been impelled from without; but by that determinate counsel, whereby he not only foresees, decrees, and executes nothing but what is just and upright in itself, but also nothing but what is good and wholesome for us. Where justice and good judgement reign paramount, there it is impious to remonstrate. . . . [H]ow great would be the degree of ingratitude not to acquiesce,[23] with a calm and well-ordered temper of mind, in whatever is the wish of our Father![24]

This is an interesting and significant passage. It reads similarly to a theological argument from the *Institutes*. It reminds us that, for Calvin, beneath every circumstance through which we journey is the providence of God who remains a loving Father toward us. And, so, every circumstance must reflect something of the nature of God—every circumstance, good *and* ill, positive *and* negative, is both just and upright and good and wholesome because it is a circumstance actively given by God the Father for our good. There is certainly a sense here that this is not obvious to us when we are immersed *in* the situation—there is mystery too, but we accept it by faith. Calvin puts this instruction in the realm of our piety before God (*coram Deo*). Pastorally, Calvin realises, as well, that questioning within the situation is dispiriting for those who suffer, and he suggests to de Richebourg that he asks God to bring good from evil, to humble him and to make him patient[25]—though he admits that God doesn't always answer: 'Should it be his will to exercise you even farther, by concealing it

---

[20] Calvin, *Letters*, 1.248.
[21] Calvin, *Letters*, 1.248.
[22] Calvin, *Letters*, 1.249.
[23] Later, Calvin counsels de Richebourg on this subject: '[Y]ou must not be ungrateful to God'—Calvin, *Letters*, 1.253.
[24] Calvin, *Letters*, 1.248-49.
[25] Calvin, *Letters*, 1.249.

from you, submit to that will, that you may become wiser than the weakness of your own understanding can ever attain to.'[26]

Second, the reformer reminds de Richebourg that, though we are prone to consider it such, 'long life [is not] to be reckoned so great a benefit of God'. It is not the length of life that is significant, he says, but its quality before the Christian community and before God. The frustration we feel about lives seemingly ending prematurely should be countered by the sense of those lives coming to completion in the plans and purposes of God the Father: 'However brief, therefore, either in your opinion or in mine, the life of your son may have been, it ought to satisfy us that he finished the course which the Lord had marked out for him.' He continues, 'Moreover, we may not reckon him to have perished in the flower of his age, who had grown ripe in the sight of the Lord.'[27] That which should soothe 'the bitterness of death' is the marked devotion of the young man: that he was pious, that he had an understanding of the faith, that he had 'been faithfully imbued with the unfeigned fear and reverence of God'.[28]

Third, Calvin reminds de Richebourg that his son has not been lost, though it seems like it, but has gone on before. In a powerfully charged phrase Calvin claims that 'he has regained the real immortality of being'. Eventually, in time, the father will recover the son 'in the blessed resurrection in the kingdom of God'.[29] Calvin then encourages de Richebourg to press forward toward the goal already reached by the son. But he cautions him to 'Beware . . . that you do not lament your son as lost, whom you acknowledge to be preserved by the Lord.'[30]

Having been open about his own grief at the start of the epistle, Calvin now concludes it by returning to the subject and advising de Richebourg against excessive grief—a significant issue to which we return below.

> It is difficult . . . you will say, so to shake off or supress the love of a father, as not to experience grief on occasion of the loss of a son. Neither do I insist upon your laying aside all grief. Nor, in the school of Christ, do we learn any such philosophy as requires us to put off that common humanity with which God has endowed us, that, being men, we should be turned into stones. These considerations [the reminders, above] reach only as far as this, that you do set bounds, and, as it were, temper even your most reasonable sadness; that, having shed those tears which were due to nature and to fatherly affection, you by no means give way to senseless wailing.[31]

In this instructive passage Calvin says some significant things. We notice, for example, how the reformer insists that he does not ask de Richebourg to abandon the grieving process. And, more significantly, he underlines the fact

---

[26] Calvin, *Letters*, 1.249.
[27] Calvin, *Letters*, 1.251.
[28] Calvin, *Letters*, 1.250.
[29] Calvin, *Letters*, 1.251.
[30] Calvin, *Letters*, 1.251.
[31] Calvin, *Letters*, 1.253.

that true piety or discipleship ('the school of Christ') does not have such a philosophy—which implies that others as the Stoics, for example, do. Again, we have the image that Luther before him is fond of employing; that we are not stones, but flesh and blood—with 'nature', feelings, affection and familial love. Calvin desires that de Richebourg, in this instance, gives expression to his grief but limits or moderates his sorrow so that it does not become excessive ('senseless wailing'). Calvin, focusing on the future perspective, then closes with words that remind de Richebourg and his remaining family that it is Christ the Lord who keeps them, directing them by his Spirit, 'until [they] may arrive where Louis and Charles have gone before'.[32]

To the Budé family, 1547

Jeannine Olsen reminds us that 'The Budé family had a long acquaintanceship with Calvin, which dated from Calvin's student days in Paris, when he was welcomed in their home and when their father, the renowned Hellenist, Guillaume Budé (1468-1540), was still alive.'[33] This short letter was written to the Budé family on the occasion of the death of one of its members.[34] We are uncertain who this might have been, though Jules Bonnet, the letter's editor, suggests the possibility that it was Mathieu de Budé. Calvin offers the remaining relatives consolation on at least two fronts. First, he speaks of the man's death as 'happy and blessed' in the sense that he was evidently and explicitly a Christian, someone who knew God to be his Father, and in the sense, also, that his passing occurred 'in the face of him [that is, God] and of all his angels'.[35] Second, the reformer alludes to what he considers to be a divine secondary purpose in the death.[36] He comments that Mathieu de Budé (if, indeed, it was him) had shown his brother how to live a disciplined and faithful Christian life, and suggests as a corollary to that that God has something to say in the circumstance, as awful as it currently is: 'Know, then,' he says, 'that the death of your brother is as God's trumpet, whereby he will call upon you to serve him alone, and this more loudly than if your brother had lived ten years longer to exhort you.'[37]

This, then, naturally comes with an implied caution through the instruction he offers, and here Calvin appears to have in mind the problem of excessive grief distorting vision and crippling the Christian's walk with and witness of God. 'If you have begun well, which, indeed, ought to prove a help to you in

---

[32] Calvin, *Letters*, 1.253.
[33] See Jeannine E. Olsen, 'The Friends of John Calvin: The Budé Family' in David Foxgrover (ed.), *Calvin Studies Society Papers 1995, 1997* (Grand Rapids: Calvin Studies Society, 1998), 161.
[34] Letter to the Budé family, 1547; Calvin, *Letters*, 2.154-57.
[35] Calvin, *Letters*, 2.154-55.
[36] I am not suggesting here that Calvin sees this as the primary purpose of the man's death, of course—that remains a mystery to those left behind. However, this, for Calvin, becomes a purpose consequent to that death.
[37] Calvin, *Letters*, 2.155.

going forward, do not slacken,' he says, 'but rather redouble your ardour, so as to run with greater diligence.' The reformer empathises with them, 'I am not ignorant of the dangers which environ you, and am not so devoid of fellow feeling as not to have that sympathy which I ought.'

To Peter Viret and to William Farel, 1549

In an excellent essay on the subject of Calvin's friendship with Peter Viret Robert Linder says of the relationship between the three reformers (including William Farel), 'The closeness of the triangular friendship between Calvin, Farel and Viret became legendary. Contemporaries and modern scholars have noted the intensity of their relationship.'[38] For us, coming later, this is to be observed in particular in their correspondence. In these short and rather intense letters to his close friends, Peter Viret and William Farel, Calvin speaks of the recent tragic death, after a lengthy illness, of his own wife, Idelette de Bure.[39] It will, in fact, be more helpful to take the letters together at this juncture. In each letter the reformer speaks of both grief and his moderation and control of that grief. Given his earlier advice to de Richebourg, for example, it is worth our while considering this dove-tailing of ideas and experience in Calvin's own private life.

In the context of an exchange of letters to Viret in 1549, Calvin's letter to Viret begins with the words, 'Although the death of my wife has been exceedingly painful to me, yet I subdue my grief as well as I can.' Later, in the same correspondence, he speaks of 'a powerful self-control' that had been given to him in relation to his grief.[40] On a cursory glance it might be felt that here we have a stereo-typical portrait of a self-disciplined, controlled and unemotional John Calvin—generally the sort of picture given by those who

---

[38] Robert Linder, 'Brothers in Christ: Pierre Viret and John Calvin as Soul-Mates and Co-Laborers in the Work of the Reformation' in David Foxgrover (ed.), *Calvin Studies Society Papers 1995, 1997* (Grand Rapids: Calvin Studies Society, 1998), 137. On Calvin's friendships, see, also, two older works, D. Hourticq, *Calvin, mon ami* (Geneva: Labor et Fides, 1963); A. Perrto, *Le visage humain de Calvin* (Geneva: Labor et Fides, 1986).

[39] Letter to Viret, April 7, 1549; Calvin, *Letters*, 2.216-17; letter to Farel, Geneva, April 11, 1549; Calvin, *Letters*, 2.217-19. Viret and Farel were reformers in their own right, of course, and Calvin's predecessors in Geneva—see M.A. Van den Berg, *Friends of Calvin* (Grand Rapids: Eerdmans, 2006), 78-89.

[40] Calvin, *Letters*, 2.216. In his reply, Viret recalls the death of his first wife, Elizabeth Turtaz Viret, in 1546. 'As friends they commiserated with each other in their mutual grief over the loss of spouses whom they described as beloved partners and companions,' Linder, 'Brothers in Christ,' 150. Significantly, Linder quotes Viret's letter to Nicholas de Wattville, 'The Lord has taken the half of myself from me; he has deprived me of a faithful companion, an excellent homemaker, and a wife admirably gifted to share my life, my studies, and my ministry. I am so affected by this blow that I feel like a stranger in my own home' (150; citing Viret to Nicholas Wattville, 6th March, 1546, CO 12.306).

have not read much of him!⁴¹ R.A. Hughes, for example, states that this shows Calvin's 'need to control grief and to understand his wife's death as providentially determined'. However, the reality is very different to this. To Viret he says that had he not been self-controlled, 'I could not have borne up so long.' To Farel he says, 'I do what I can to keep myself being overwhelmed with grief.' He speaks of his own 'mental suffering'.⁴² It is very significant too that Calvin himself accredits the strength to continue in this way to the grace of God in Christ and not to his own ability or nature. In concluding his letter to Farel he speaks of 'this heavy affliction, which would certainly have overcome me, had not he, who raises up the prostrate, strengthens the weak, and refreshes the weary, stretched forth his hand from heaven to me'.⁴³ There is a real sense here of knowing and of experiencing the grace of God in this terrible circumstance.

The loss of his wife and companion was extremely felt by the reformer, who was evidently left in excruciating pain and the sense of being abandoned. He underlines the reason for his uncommon grief:

> I have been bereaved of the best companion of my life, of one who, had it been so ordered, would not only have been the willing sharer of my indigence, but even of my death. During her life she was the faithful helper of my ministry. From her I never experienced the slightest hindrance. She was never troublesome to me through the entire course of her illness; she was more anxious about her children than about herself.⁴⁴

Again, much might be read into this brief vignette of Calvin's wife and their relationship. However, it must be stressed that the reformer sees her as 'the best companion of my life'—someone who shared, someone who helped, someone whom he evidently loved.⁴⁵ Indeed, Calvin gains his consolation from his wife's evident piety toward the end. He tells Farel that some of her last words were, 'O glorious resurrection! O God of Abraham, and of all our fathers, in thee have the faithful trusted during so many past ages, and none of them trusted in vain. I also will hope.' Interestingly, Calvin insists that these were her

---

⁴¹ Hughes, *Lament, Death, and Destiny*, 108. In contrast, and more realistically, speaking of this tragic episode, Michael Mullett understandably says, 'Nothing so much explodes the myth of the laconic, self-concealing and even unemotional Calvin as his outpouring of grief to his friends'—M.A. Mullett, *John Calvin* (Abingdon: Routledge, 2011), 78.

⁴² Calvin, *Letters*, 2.216, 217. The editor of his letters, Jules Bonnet, quotes a letter from Viret to Calvin in which he speaks of the reformer's 'heart so broken and lacerated' by grief and the sense of loss— Calvin, *Letters*, 2.216n.1.

⁴³ Calvin, *Letters*, 2.219.

⁴⁴ Calvin, *Letters*, 2.216.

⁴⁵ See Michael Parsons, *Reformation Marriage. The Husband and Wife Relationship in the Theology of Luther and Calvin* (Eugene: Wipf and Stock, 2011), 280-88. See, also, chapter 2 of the present work.

own words, they had not come from the suggestion of others.[46] Later, just before the end, he movingly recounts how she asks those surrounding her to pray for her.

So here, in these two short letters, we have a glimpse of the reformer who suffers acute grief through the untimely loss of his wife. It shows us that he takes his own advice, as it were; he lives consistently with his own pastoral theology and practice. He clearly and evidently grieves, but he tries not to allow that grief to control him, nor to drive him into despair—though he recognises that it could easily do so. He desires to moderate his sorrow, naturally finding it difficult, but trusting in God's grace and apparently experiencing it even at the worst moments.

To Madame de Cany, 1549

Calvin writes this rather unusual but instructive letter to Madame de Cany giving her an account of the death of Madame Laurent of Normandy, so that she might pass the news on to Madame Laurent's father whom she had introduced to the Reformed faith and doctrine.[47] Significantly, the reformer wants the recipient to comfort the father 'that he may not be beyond measure disconsolate'.[48] What follows is a rather full description of the woman's last days and of her death with which narrative de Cany might be able to comfort the woman's father. Calvin recognises, less than four weeks after his own bereavement and ensuing grief, that the father will 'be wrung with grief',[49] but encourages de Cany to speak to him of his daughter, reminding her that the apostle Paul tells us to 'weep with those who weep;' that is to say, 'to have compassion and sorrow for our neighbours, that we should willingly take part in their tears, and thus comfort them'.[50]

What is the comfort or consolation that Calvin suggests is offered in this particular circumstance? He underlines throughout the letter that the primary consolation is in knowing that the daughter belongs to God, through her faith in Christ. He begins the letter, 'Our consolation is, that he has gathered her unto himself; for he has guided her even to the last sigh, as if visibly he held out the hand to her.'[51] It is worth pointing out the personal, tender nature of this comment: the hand of God himself is held out to his own at their death; he gathers and guides them into his eternal presence. Calvin appears to have the Fatherhood of God in mind here; even in the moment that seems most dreadful,

---

[46] Letter to Farel, Geneva, April 11, 1549; Calvin, *Letters*, 2.218.
[47] Letter to Madame de Cany, April 29, 1549; Calvin, *Letters*, 2.219-23. The letter is written in French.
[48] Calvin, *Letters*, 2.220.
[49] Calvin, *Letters*, 2.223.
[50] Calvin, *Letters*, 2.222-23. Previously, he had spoken of the husband who had been 'possessed with such grief . . . and weighed down by extremity of sorrow'—Calvin, *Letters*, 2.222.
[51] Calvin, *Letters*, 2.219.

he is there in grace. In a change of biblical image Calvin points out that even during her sickness, which apparently was extremely painful, 'she proved herself to be a true sheep of our Lord Jesus, letting herself be quietly led by the Great Shepherd'. However, through it she relied and had confidence not in herself but in God as Father: 'I know what a poor sinful woman I am, but my confidence,' she asserts near the end, 'is in his goodness, and in the death and passion of his Son. . . . I go to him as to a Father.' A little later Calvin speaks of her faith as 'the certainty which she entertained of her salvation, putting her sole confidence in Jesus, and having her whole trust in him'.[52] As far as Calvin's pastoral engagement is concerned he sees consolation as leading to submission and self-denial, that is, to 'bowing to the will of God' in this situation.[53] Those left behind, he advises, ought to seek to follow her example, 'willingly complying with the disposal of God'.[54]

Calvin's approach to those who grieve

At this point, having examined four or five of Calvin's consolatory letters to those who grieve, we may discover something of the reformer's general approach to the question of grief in the experience of Reformed believers. This will also give us a chance to widen the scope of letters examined. We pause to consider what Calvin has to say about grief expressed, comfort given and pastoral exhortations offered.

Grief is to be expressed, in moderation

The first thing we learn from an examination of the letters gathered in Bonnet's edited collection is that Calvin says that grief is to be expressed, not stoically ignored or subdued. In this he appears to be not as self-conscious as Martin Luther. Rather than the explicit assertion of the earlier reformer, Calvin demonstrates this more by an authentic openness and an appropriate vulnerability in the situation (not entirely lacking in Luther, of course[55]). Indeed, there is plenty of evidence in the letters we have already explored and a whole host of others that Calvin expresses his own grief time and time again in this open and vulnerable manner. Herman Selderhuis, in his exceptional biography of the reformer, states that 'Calvin of all people cannot be behind the image of Calvinists as people who show no emotion at death. . . . Calvin's

---

[52] Calvin, *Letters*, 2.221.
[53] 'Self-denial is the sacrificial dimension of *pietas*. . . . [U]nconditional obedience to God's will is the essence of piety'—J.R. Beeke, 'Calvin on Piety' in D.K. McKim (ed.), *The Cambridge Companion to John Calvin* (Cambridge: CUP, 2004), 141, 143, respectively.
[54] Calvin, *Letters*, 2.223.
[55] See Michael Parsons, 'Luther's pastoral letters: his insights into grief,' in Michael Parsons (ed.), *Aspects of Reforming. Theology and Practice in Sixteenth Century Europe* (Milton Keynes: Paternoster, 2013), 68-82, particularly, 75-76.

letters are . . . full of tears over loved ones who had died.'[56] An early letter written to his colleague William Farel, for example, demonstrates this well. Calvin relates how he feels since the recent death of Augustin Courault, a zealous preacher, a pastor in the city of Orbe and a colleague in the Reformed ministry.[57] He writes that 'The death of Courault has so overwhelmed me, that I can set no bounds to my grief.' He finds that he cannot concentrate on the daily tasks in which he is supposed to be engaged during the day. Night time is no better; indeed, it is worse: 'Distress and wretchedness during the day seems only to prepare a lodging for the more painful and excruciating thoughts of the night.' He writes that he is 'utterly exhausted' by melancholic thoughts.

> It is not merely the want of sleep, to which custom has so inured me, by which I am harassed, but I am utterly exhausted by these melancholy thoughts all night long, than which I find there is nothing more destructive of my health. . . . What else, therefore, dear brother, can we do than lament our calamity?[58]

Another letter written to Farel less than three months later finds Calvin lamenting the loss of his friend, Peter Robert Olivétan[59]—a loss that appears to leave him not only sorrowful but confused and preoccupied in the daily tasks he faces.[60]

For a man who is sometimes judged to say very little about himself Calvin's vulnerability in grief is somewhat astonishing, even though voiced in personal correspondence.[61] To his friend Peter Viret on the very significant deaths of Martin Bucer and Joachim Vadian Calvin speaks openly.

> The grief which I have suffered at the death of Bucer increases my anxiety and fear. I have now again experienced a fresh wound from the death of Vadian. . . . I feel my heart almost like to break when I think of the great loss the church of God has sustained in the death of Bucer.

The grief-stricken reformer concludes rather pathetically (but, given the occurrence, quite understandably) with the wish that 'The Lord grant that I may leave in life all those whose death I should mourn, that I may the more joyfully

---

[56] Herman J. Selderhuis, *John Calvin. A Pilgrim's Life* (Downers Grove: IVP Academic, 2009), 251.
[57] Letter to Farel, Strasbourg, October 24, 1538; Calvin, *Letters*, 1.99-104.
[58] Calvin, *Letters*, 1.99-100: See, also, his letter to Farel, Geneva, June 16, 1542; Calvin, *Letters*, 1.331.
[59] Having translated the Bible into French (1534) Peter Robert Olivétan was both a friend and a significant evangelical.
[60] Letter to Farel, January 1539, Calvin, *Letters*, 1.104-106. The reformer realises toward the end of the letter that grief and its preoccupation has caused him to forget to write about some important matters.
[61] S.B. Ferguson, 'Calvin the Man: A Heart Aflame' in J.R. Beeke and G.J. Williams (eds), *Calvin. Theologian and Reformer* (Grand Rapids: Reformation Heritage, 2010), 8, says, understandably, that 'it is noteworthy how reticent Calvin was throughout his life to entrust his inner emotional life to writing, and then only within the context of his deepest and most secure friendships'.

leave the world.'⁶² A month later we find the reformer apologising to Farel for not mentioning in a letter the death of Bucer—he fears that had he done so he may have opened his own wounds afresh.⁶³

The reformer's anxiety—alluded to above—comes to the fore in an almost inexplicable way later in his ministry. On at least two occasions Calvin's fear appears to get the better of him, for apparently he begins to grieve and lament even before those who are ill pass away, and, in fact, before they eventually recover! The first occasion, in 1551, relates to an illness that Theodore Beza was suffering, but from which he eventually improved.⁶⁴ Calvin speaks of his alarm at his friend's ill health and concerning the way he (Calvin) 'felt almost overpowered, as if I was already lamenting his death'. And though he denies that this was personal, relating the loss such a death would be for the church and for reform at large, it is undeniable that Calvin's anguish largely sprang from his genuine love of Beza: 'Indeed, I were destitute of human feeling, did I not return the affection of one who loves me with more love than a brother's love, and reveres me like a very father.'⁶⁵ The next occasion, two years later, is very similar, but this time in connection with Farel,⁶⁶ in which, after Farel's recovery, he speaks of 'the grief which was incidental to your premature death' and 'the pain of lamenting your death' even before it had happened.⁶⁷

In his correspondence Calvin speaks explicitly of moderating grief much more rarely, on the face of things, than does Luther, for example.⁶⁸ However, two occasions will suffice to indicate that, as we have noted above, he has the same pastoral belief—that grief must be moderate, and not allowed to become dangerously excessive. We notice, though, that Calvin stresses duty, rather than comfort at this point—and, given the subject of the correspondence, that may

---

[62] Letter to Viret, Geneva, May 10, 1551; Calvin, *Letters*, 2.310-11. See, also, similar expressions of grief in a letter to Bullinger, Geneva, September 6, 1560; Calvin, *Letters*, 4.125–26. Selderhuis, *John Calvin*, 253, says of a similar situation, 'There is no hardened Calvin here, who, rooted in God's almighty power, undauntedly and emotionlessly lets things pass over him. Rather we see Calvin at his wit's end, overwhelmed by grief.'

[63] Letter to Farel, Geneva, June 15, 1551; Calvin, *Letters*, 2.312. See Van den Berg, *Friends of Calvin*, 99-109. For further expressions of grief see his letter to Viret, Geneva, August 19, 1542; Calvin, *Letters*, 1.344, where the reformer speaks of being inflicted by 'a severe and bitter wound'; his letter to Bullinger, Geneva, November 8, 1542; Calvin, *Letters*, 1.363. See, also, Calvin's letter to Viret, Geneva, March 8, 1546; Calvin, *Letters*, 2.37-38, in which he encourages his friend to bear with sorrow in moderation, revealing his own empathy: 'Would I also could fly thither, that I might alleviate your sorrow, or at least bear a part of it!'

[64] See his letter to an undisclosed French gentleman, June 30, 1551; Calvin, *Letters*, 2.314-15.

[65] Calvin, *Letters*, 2.314.

[66] Letter to Farel, Geneva, March 27, 1553; Calvin, *Letters*, 2.395-96.

[67] Calvin, *Letters*, 2.395.

[68] See Parsons, "Luther's pastoral letters,' 78-80.

be more understandable. To Christopher Goodman Calvin writes, 'Though I am a little grieved to hear that our brother Knox has been bereaved of his affectionate wife, I rejoice nevertheless that he has so far mastered his affliction as not to suffer it to prevent him from strenuously discharging his duty to Christ and the church.'[69] Again, regarding control, he advises Peter Viret, whose wife is seriously ill, to hold himself 'ready to bear with moderation the issue, whatever that may be'.[70]

Calvin, in his commentary on Isaiah 6, is adamant that grief should not prevent us from our calling:

> Natural affections (στοργαι φυσικαι), therefore, ought not to prevent us from performing what is our duty. . . . [I]t ought to be checked and restrained, so that we may chiefly consider what is suitable to our calling, and what the Lord commands. . . . [W]hen we wish to give loose reins to ourselves, we commonly plead this excuse, that we are willing and ready to do what God requires, but are overpowered by natural affection. But those feelings ought to be restrained in such a manner as not to obstruct our calling.[71]

Nevertheless, on at least one occasion we catch a fascinating and frank glimpse of Calvin's own weakness in regard to the grieving process. Writing on the occurrence of the deaths of his friends Claude Féray and Louis de Richebourg (1541) he says,

> Although I am recovering my composure by degrees, I still feel nothing more than a slight abatement of the pressure. Nay, even, what one ought to feel shame in confessing, *there is some such sort of consolation in grief*, as that it may be somewhat pleasing in itself not to be entirely delivered from sorrow.[72]

This is both extraordinarily perceptive and honest. This is very vulnerable, too, isn't it?[73] Calvin knows that those bereaved are tempted to cling hold of grief and sorrow because it seems the only way of not letting go, of not moving on, and there is some sort of consolation in that stagnation, that inactivity, as it were. He knows it through experience, but he knows too that it is not good in the long run, though it seems 'pleasing' at the time.

Comfort in the face of death

We have noticed that Calvin takes the opportunity to speak into the lives of the grief-stricken families and friends something of the consolation that comes from his understanding of the gospel of God in Christ. Briefly, there appear to be three ways in which he does this.

---

[69] Letter to Christopher Goodman, Geneva, April 23, 1561; Calvin, *Letters*, 4.186.
[70] Letter to Viret, Geneva, February 22, 1546, Calvin, *Letters*, 2.37.
[71] *Comm. Isa.* 6.11.
[72] Letter to Farel, Ratisbon, April 24, 1541; Calvin, *Letters*, 1.254, emphasis added.
[73] This is a good example of what Wolterstorff, 'The Wounds of God,' 21, finds in Calvin's reflections—that he believes 'we must preserve our vulnerability to suffering'.

God is fully involved. First, the reformer points out that however dreadful the experience that they are going through, God the Father is fully involved in it. This is certainly a difficult balance to keep in such extreme moments, but even concerning the death of his own child, for example, he says, 'The Lord has certainly inflicted a severe and bitter wound in the death of our infant son. But he is himself a Father, and knows best what is good for his children.'[74] It is noticeable, of course, that though somehow the death of the child has been caused ('inflicted') by God[75] Calvin clings to the fact, by faith, that the same God is Father to him and does everything for the good of his children.[76] To John Cavent, having lost his wife and mother, Calvin writes,

> If it is hard to bear their loss, you have good cause to find consolation in our Lord, who enabled them to glorify his name in their death, and who gave them strength in the hour of need, and, who, I do not doubt, will give you grace to view all these things aright.[77]

We might note, briefly, that this certainly seems at odds with Karant-Nunn's assertion that 'Calvin's doctrine of unyielding double-predestination moved him to focus his main attention on edifying the living . . . [because] the most that could be done was to encourage the dying to feel confident that they were among those elected to salvation—*even though neither subject nor observer could be certain.*'[78] As we have observed, the reformer's understanding of the fatherhood of God gives him confidence because salvation rests entirely on fatherly grace and love.

God measures our days. Second, Calvin assures some that however short the deceased person's life has been it has run its God-given course. This is particularly the case as he addresses John Clauburger and his family mourning the death of Adolph Clauburger in 1556.[79] He admits to them that the life appears to have been 'snatched from us . . . not very seasonably', but concedes that it appears thus only when we are allowed 'to frame judgments according to our desires'. Because they long to have the deceased with them again, because they painfully miss him, he knows that it is natural to feel the abruptness and the unfairness of his end. If, on the other hand, they allowed themselves to abide by divine judgement, rather than by their own poor reasoning, they would understand that the deceased had, in fact, 'finished the allotted course of his life'.[80] Calvin also reminds the family that in taking their son God had delivered

---

[74] Letter to Viret, Geneva, August 19, 1542; Calvin, *Letters*, 1.344.
[75] Significantly, elsewhere, he speaks of the Lord 'in whose hand are life and death'—letter to Peter Martyr, Geneva March 2, 1559; Calvin, *Letters*, 4.32.
[76] Wolterstorff, 'The Wounds of God,' 21, points out that Calvin teaches that we must seek to discern God's goodness in our suffering and respond accordingly.
[77] Letter to John Cavent, June, 1545; Calvin, *Letters*, 1.464.
[78] Karant-Nunn, *The Reformation of Feeling*, 202, emphasis added.
[79] Letter to John Clauburger, Geneva, February 28, 1556; Calvin, *Letters*, 3.252-54.
[80] Calvin, *Letters*, 3.252-53.

him from 'the numerous and terrible corruptions that, in our days, prevail everywhere over the world'. He assures them that he awaits them in heaven now, in peace. The implication is that God knows best and that it is the quality of Adolph's life that counts, not the measurement of his days on earth.

God gives us hope. Third, Calvin gives the hope that comes from God to those who have lost their loved ones to death, and who grieve that terrible loss. Indeed, he asks profoundly, 'unless this sure hope held us firm and steadfast, what ground of despair encompasses us round about?'[81] He sets before those dying the cross and the grace of Jesus Christ and the hope, through them, of eternal life and to those who are left the fact that it is enough for believers to know that 'I live and die for Christ, who is to all his followers a gain both in life and death.'[82]

Exhortations to those who grieve

There are three particular exhortations that stand out in the correspondence under examination.

Consider the nature of reality. The first is that the reformer calls upon those who have been left to consider the nature of reality and to realise that, because 'in the midst of life we are in death' it is necessary to apprehend what is real, not by or through the natural senses, but by spiritual reality as it is in Jesus Christ.[83] The specific recipients of this advice were Denis Peloquin and Louis de Marsac who were, at the time, prisoners heading for Protestant martyrdom, and so perhaps the instruction takes on far more poignancy than it might have. Joel Beeke reminds us that such an exhortation may only be valid because of the eschatological presence of the Holy Spirit in the lives of those who believe.[84] He quotes Calvin's *Institutes*, 3.2.24, to good effect:

> Nothing prevents believers from being afraid and at the same time possessing the surest consolation. . . . Fear and faith [can] dwell in the same mind. . . . Surely this is so. We ought not to separate Christ from ourselves or ourselves from him. Rather we ought to hold fast bravely with both hands to that fellowship by which he has bound himself to us.[85]

---

[81] Letter to Farel, Strasbourg, October 24, 1538; Calvin, *Letters*, 1.100.

[82] Letter to Farel, Geneva, June 16, 1542; Calvin, *Letters*, 1.332; letter to Farel, Geneva, May 2, 1546; Calvin, *Letters*, 4.364. See Cornelius Van der Kooi, 'Life as Pilgrimage. The Eschatology of John Calvin' in Henk van den Belt (ed.), *Restoration through Redemption: John Calvin Revisited* (Leiden: Brill, 2013), 185-98.

[83] See his letter to Denis Peloquin and Louis de Marsac, August 22, 1553; Calvin, *Letters*, 2.421.

[84] J.R. Beeke, 'Making Sense of Calvin's Paradoxes on Assurance of Faith' in D. Foxgrover (ed.), *Calvin Studies Society Papers, 1995, 1997* (Grand Rapids: Calvin Study Society, 1998), 13-30.

[85] *Inst.* 3.2.24 (OS 4.35), quoted by Beeke, 'Making Sense of Calvin's Paradoxes,' 20.

That is, the true, spiritual apprehension of our situation even in grief and the pain of loss must be in the context of our union (or 'fellowship') with Jesus Christ. One cannot apprehend that by natural sight or by the senses, but only through accepting faith.

Be prepared for death. In terms of the logic, at least, the other two exhortations are a corollary of that one. For instance, Calvin teaches that because we are always in the face of death and grief we must be prepared for it whilst we still live: 'But let us now live so for Christ,' he says, 'that we may be daily prepared to die for him.'[86] Again, to Monsieur de Falais on the death of his sister he writes, '[M]eanwhile, let us think of preparing ourselves to follow her, for the time will soon come.'[87] In a lengthier passage, this time from a letter to Madame de Coligny (1563), we see the vital connection between preparation and an apprehension of our context with God.

> It is certain that all diseases ought not only to humble us in setting before our eyes our frailty, but also cause us to look into our selves, that having recognised our own poverty we may place all our trust in his mercy. They should, moreover, serve us for medicines to purge us from worldly affections, and retrench what is superfluous in us, and since they are messengers of death, we ought to learn to have one foot raised to take our departure when it shall please God.[88]

The occurrence of illness itself should, according to the reformer, forcefully remind us that we are frail (and, therefore, finite), that we have nothing ('our own poverty') and, consequently, it should turn us to rely on the riches found in Christ ('his mercy'). The image of walking ('one foot raised to take our departure') is apposite in a world in which death can come unannounced at any moment in the good pleasure of God.

Be submissive to the divine will. This brings us to the third exhortation: that is to be submissive to the will of him who has life and death in his hands—to be submissive, that is, to the providence of God.[89] This, as Wolterstorff points out, is the discipline of becoming patient in our suffering.[90]

Reflections

The first matter that might usefully be addressed and briefly reflected upon is the involvement that Calvin allows God in the situation of grief. He insists that

---

[86] Letter to Farel, March 27, 1553; Calvin, *Letters*, 2.396. See, also, his letter to Bullinger, April, 1553; Calvin, *Letters*, 2.414-15.
[87] Letter to Monsieur de Falais, Geneva, November 20, 1546; Calvin, *Letters*, 2.85.
[88] Letter to Madame de Coligny, Geneva, August 5, 1563; Calvin, *Letters*, 4.331.
[89] See Calvin's letter to Farel, Basel, August 20, 1538; Calvin, *Letters*, 1.78, where he speaks of Farel after the death of his friend's nephew through the plague, that he is 'both learning and teaching others willingly to submit to his [God's] providence'.
[90] Wolterstorff, 'The Wounds of God,' 17.

God is central to the circumstance of grief: he is actively involved because he takes the deceased; he is a father to the one who has passed away and the one who is left; he is the one who ultimately shows mercy and grace, and so forth. Calvin indicates that comfort will come from God (and through Christ). Pastorally, this affirmation of the centrality of God in the circumstance is a difficult road to take. What I mean by this is that the juxtaposition of pain and trust is a difficult balance in the traumatic event of bereavement. Interestingly, the reformer appears to realise this problem. So why does he insist on this recurrent theme? Theologically, he is convinced that everything that happens is in the control of God. Oliver Crisp says of Calvin that he thinks God ordains all that comes to pass. He quotes *Institutes* 1.16.3, 'For he is omnipotent . . . because, governing heaven and earth by his providence, he so regulates all things that nothing takes place without his deliberation.'[91] Later, he explains this.

> He is set against what he calls 'bare permission', that is, the idea that God merely allows certain things to occur. Calvin wants a full-bloodied determinism: God ordains all that comes to pass. . . . So, in essence, Calvin's response is the response of Job: trust in God, sometimes despite circumstances, in the knowledge that he works all things to the good, even though we cannot comprehend that from our limited epitemic vantage.[92]

This poses obvious problems for theodicy, but Calvin speaks and writes *from* theological understanding *towards* a situation, *from* doctrine *to* practice, not the other way around. The divine centrality in times of crisis and hurt is important

---

[91] *Inst.* 1.16.3 (OS 3.191-92). O.D. Crisp, *Retrieving Doctrine. Explorations in Reformed Theology* (Milton Keynes: Paternoster, 2010), 13. Similarly, Paul Helm, *John Calvin's Ideas* (Oxford: Oxford University Press, 2004), 96, 'There [in the *Institutes*] Calvin claims that all events are governed by God's secret plan and that nothing takes place without his deliberation. God so attends the regulation of individual events, and they all so proceed from his set plan, that nothing takes place by chance.' Earlier he insists that this includes 'evil events and actions' (93). See, also, William J. Bouwsma, *John Calvin. A Sixteenth Century Portrait* (New York: Oxford University Press, 1988), 172-73; Susan Schreiner, *Where Shall Wisdom be Found? Calvin's Exegesis of Job from Medieval and Modern Perspectives* (Chicago: University of Chicago Press, 1994), 151, Susan Schreiner, *The Theater of His Glory: Nature and the Natural Order in the Thought of John Calvin* (Durham: Labyrinth, 1991), 7–37; Derek Thomas, *Calvin's Teaching on Job. Proclaiming the Incomprehensible God* (Geanies House, Scotland: Mentor, 2004), 43–45. For two older, excellent studies, see Charles Partee, *Calvin and Classical Philosophy* (Leiden: Brill, 1977); Richard Stauffer, *Dieu, la creation et la providence dans le predication de Calvin* (Berne: Peter Lang, 1978), particularly, 261-302.

[92] Crisp, *Retrieving Doctrine*, 21. See, also, Selderhuis, *John Calvin*, 251, who says that Calvin 'thought that grief did not conflict with his belief that God was in control over all things'. D. Keck, 'Sorrow and Worship in Calvin's Geneva: their place in Family History' in M.R. Forster and B.J. Kaplan (eds), *Piety and Family in Early Modern Europe* (Aldershot: Ashgate, 2005), 207, agrees: 'The depth of anguish is too great for [Calvin] to ascribe its causes to chance or necessity.'

pastorally. He never refuses to separate sorrow from providence[93] for he knows that if someone suffering makes that severance they face the danger of unbelief, of ingratitude, of angering the Lord and of falling away. The emphasis on God-in-the-situation also allows the reformer a more concretely realistic view of grief.

The second matter that we might comment on, then, is the matter of grief, itself. Importantly, the reformer does not shy away from expressing his own grief, as we have seen. Calvin speaks with some tenderness of the death of his wife, Idelette, and at other times his friends. In this way, we might say that he encourages the expression of grief from others—certainly, that is the implication of his letters; he leads by example. The reformer sees grief as natural, but more than that he sees it as a consequence of the divinely-given familial situation in which the grieving lived with the deceased. Fellowship, closeness, the *alter Christus* situation in which families live by faith, are the background to the agony of grief being felt and expressed.

However, and this is important, Calvin insists that grief be expressed carefully, or moderately.[94] A secondary matter may be that of the importance of being dignified, perhaps;[95] but, this, fundamentally, has a theological basis for it clearly derives from his understanding of providence and God's intimate control of everything. But, importantly, it also derives from a pastoral appreciation of the psychology of those grieving. We saw that Calvin speaks of moderate grief as part of true piety, but of excessive grief as somehow blameworthy because it dangerously distorts perspective. So he exhorts those hurting to subdue their grief—not in a Stoical fashion of denial, nor following Augustine in ignoring grief,[96] nor as Karant-Nunn suggests simply to control emotion,[97] but in order for those he exhorts to move falteringly beyond the

---

[93] Keck, 'Sorrow and Worship,' 207. Mark R. Talbot, 'Bad Actors on a Broken Stage: Sin and Suffering in Calvin's World and Ours,' in John Piper and David Mathis (eds), *With Calvin in the Theater of God. The Glory of Christ and Everyday Life* (Illinois: Crossway, 2010), 59-63, speaks, in the context of Calvin's theology, of the very real difficulty of *not* blaming God for adverse things that happen.

[94] Interestingly, Bouwsma, *John Calvin*, 51, speaks of zeal controlled by the Holy Spirit.

[95] See J.M. Vorster, 'Calvin and Human Dignity' in Henk van den Belt (ed.), *Restoration through Redemption: John Calvin Revisited* (Leiden: Brill, 2013), 215-29.

[96] See the wonderful study by Nicholas Wolterstorff, 'The Wounds of God. Calvin's Theology and Social Injustice,' *Reformed Journal* 37 (1987), 14–22. Amongst other things, Wolterstorff shows Augustine's change of attitude regarding grief, a change that appears to have come about because of his conversion to Christianity. 'The general rule [according to Augustine],' says Wolterstorff, 'is that we are to struggle to eliminate grief from our lives by struggling to concentrate our love on God alone.' To grieve over the deaths of people we love is simply a 'childish' temptation (20).

[97] Susan Karant-Nunn, '"Gedanken, Herz und Sinn": (Göttingen, Vandenhoeck & Ruprecht 1999), 87, 91—cited by Reinis, *Reforming the Art of Dying*, 255. Karant-Nunn argues that an explicit goal of the reform movement was the control of emo-

terrible circumstance of distress towards peace and joy that the Lord alone can bring.

The third and final matter that might be touched upon is that of faith. We have noted that Calvin underlines the significance of faith in situations of suffering. Genuine faith, for example, in the midst of the terrible situation, is able to discern reality from that which we think is reality; the spiritual from the merely physical; the eternal from the temporal. It certainly does not deny the situation; but it does see it through a different lens, from a different perspective. Faith focuses on God and takes hold of Christ through the Word. Believers are encouraged by Calvin to look to the event of resurrection at which time those who have been taken will be recovered because Jesus Christ has overcome death once and for all. We must 'learn to have one foot raised to take our departure when it shall please God,' as the reformer writes to Madame de Coligny.[98] In the meantime, faith trusts God the Father and is encouraged to look at what has been retained, not so much on what (or, rather, on who) has been lost. In the view of the reformer, faith enables the struggling Christian to be further transformed into the image of Christ.

---

tion, replacing the affective piety of the Middle Ages with 'calm gratitude and unmoved obedience.'

[98] Cited by Sam Storms, 'Living with One Foot Raised: Calvin on the Glory of the Final Resurrection and Heaven,' in John Piper and David Mathis (eds), *With Calvin in the Theater of God. The Glory of Christ and Everyday Life* (Illinois: Crossway, 2010), 111.

CHAPTER 7

'It is too late to think of shrinking back.' Calvin's letters to contemporary martyrs[1]

In a significant article, the Lutheran scholar, Robert Kolb, makes the rather bleak statement that with the Protestant reformations of the sixteenth century 'the phenomenon of dying for the faith returned'. Christian Europe executed heretics throughout the medieval period, of course, but, as Kolb reminds us, 'they died largely alone, at the edge of Christendom, mourned by relatively few and remembered by fewer'.[2] Recently, in a short introductory article, Haruko Nawata Ward speaks of a 'renaissance' of Christian martyrdom in the Reformation period. Ward suggests that there were two distinct spheres of martyrdom at that time. First, martyrdom occurred in Europe 'due to conflicts among Christian groups'. Second, numerous Catholic missionaries, sent to Africa, Asia, and the Americas, for instance, 'became martyrs at the hands of the so-called "pagans"'.[3] It is with the former sphere of martyrdom that this chapter has to do; that of conflict among Christian groups. More specifically, we are concerned with the context of the martyrdom of those from the Reformed Church and Calvin's epistolary response, especially in three specific instances.

Following a brief introduction to the general theme, highlighting Martin Luther's understanding of martyrdom—an understanding that had significant, perhaps seminal, influence in protesting theology—the chapter examines several of John Calvin's letters to those about to be executed for their faith: three letters to five students in Lyon (1553), a letter to a small group in Chambery

---

[1] This chapter is a considerably revised version of Michael Parsons (ed.), '"It is too late to think of shrinking back." Calvin's letters to contemporary martyrs,' *Reformation Faith. Exegesis and Theology in the Protestant Reformations* (Milton Keynes: Paternoster, 2014), 122-37.

[2] Robert Kolb, 'God's Gift of Martyrdom: The Early Reformation Understanding of Dying for the Faith,' *Church History* 64.3 (1995), 399.

[3] Haruko Nawata Ward, 'Martyrdom' in David M. Whitford (ed.), *T&T Clark Companion to Reformation Theology* (Edinburgh: T&T Clark, 2012), 332. See, also, Auke Jelsma, *Frontiers of the Reformation. Dissidence and Orthodoxy in Sixteenth Century Europe* (Aldershot: Ashgate, 1998), 75-90; D. Nicolls, 'The Theatre of Martyrdom in the French Reformation,' *Past and Present* 121 (1988), 49; Lee Palmer Wandel, *The Reformation. Towards a New History* (Cambridge: Cambridge University Press, 2011), 103, 184, 132-33, 154, 196.

(1555), and one to women imprisoned in Paris (1557). Brief reflections on Calvin's theology and pastoral approach follow.

Protestant martyrdom

According to Robert Kolb, during the sixteenth century, 'sufficient numbers of the persecuted existed to enable every Christian confession to celebrate martyred brothers and sisters'.[4] Persecution was one significant aspect of a generally violent age.[5] Men and women died for their faith, believing that their form of confession was the true faith, over against those that were not, that were in significant error. He states that 'Martyrdom was not a matter of dying for just any faith but for what they regarded as the true faith. The truth, not heroic zeal for any cause, mattered.'[6]

Ward, helpfully, lists three requirements necessary for a death to be classified as martyrdom. First, martyrs had to be executed by secular authorities. Second, the martyrs had to have a certain self-perception. Generally, they believed that they belonged to the true Church. Third, the martyr's death was visualised and interpreted within a particular community. They were not isolated individuals, but members of communities of faith and, therefore, their deaths were 'interpreted through the lens of the community's shared beliefs'.[7] We might add another, I think: that the death of a martyr had to be seen as witnessing to divine truth, as the community saw it; after all, the word 'martyr' (μαρτύριον) literally means 'witness,' of course. This is the curatorial nature of faith, to protect and to defend truth against its adversaries.[8]

According to Robert Kolb, Luther was the first sixteenth century reformer to develop a *theology* of martyrdom.[9] His understanding of martyrdom, Kolb in-

---

[4] Kolb, 'God's Gift,' 399. For a wider perspective of this subject, see the excellent study by Brad S. Gregory, *Salvation at Stake. Christian Martyrdom in Early Modern Europe* (Cambridge: Harvard University Press, 1999). Also, William Monter, 'Heresy Executions in Reformation Europe, 1520-1565' in Ole Peter Grell and Robert W. Scribner (eds), *Tolerance and Intolerance in the European Reformation* (Cambridge: Cambridge University Press, 1996), 48-64; Peter Matheson, *The Imaginative World of the Reformation* (Edinburgh: T&T Clark, 2000), 77-82; Bernard Cottret, *Calvin. A Biography* (Grand Rapids: Eerdmans / Edinburgh: T&T Clark, 2000), 244-47.

[5] See Thomas M. Safley (ed.), *A Companion to Multiconfessionalism in the Early Modern World* (Leiden: Brill, 2011), to nuance this remark in this context. Also, from a different perspective, see Benjamin J. Kaplan, *Divided by Faith. Religious Conflict in the Practice of Toleration in Early Modern Europe* (Cambridge: Harvard University Press, 2009).

[6] Kolb, 'God's Gift,' 400.

[7] Ward, 'Martyrdom,' 332-33.

[8] See, Delwin Brown, *Boundaries of Our Habitations: Tradition and Theological Construction* (New York: Sate University of New York, 1994), 78-79.

[9] It is worth remembering that Luther, himself, thought he might be martyred for his stand against the established Church. This is partly why he delayed his own marriage, for instance. See Luther's letter to Spalatin, Wittenberg, November 30, 1524; *LW*

sists, illustrates the reformer's theology of the cross because it reveals a paradox 'which equates God's wisdom with what seems foolishness to the sinner and God's power with what seems impotence to the sinner (1 Cor. 1.18-2.16)'.[10] Therefore, confession of, or witnessing to, the truth of God is, for Luther, a gracious gift of God.[11] Kolb says the following,

> Because [the theology of the cross] led him to see martyrdom in the context of God's working through his Word, which finds its power and wisdom in what the world considers to be impotence and foolishness, he could define martyrdom as a gift from God, to the martyr who proved the power and wisdom of God in this ultimate sacrifice, and to the surviving people of God, who beheld the paradox of God's revelation of his love in the martyr's confession of the faith unto death.[12]

This certainly makes a great deal of sense. Kolb's conclusions are confirmed by even a cursory glance at the reformer's letters to those who are about to die for their faith or to others involved in grieving for them in their situation. For example, in writing to the believers in the Netherlands after the imprisonment and execution in Brussels of Henry Vos and John van den Esschen (the first Protestant martyrs),[13] Luther encourages them to be full of joy. We notice that hearing the gospel (the Word) and knowing Jesus Christ are foundational to their experience of suffering.

> For it has been your privilege before all others in the world not only to hear the gospel and know Christ but also to be the first to suffer shame and injury, anxiety and distress, imprisonment and death, for Christ's sake.[14]

In this eschatologically-charged letter the reformer suggests that they look at the persecution and subsequent deaths as God giving to them 'a new and fresh illustration of his own life'—that is, the kingdom, 'not in word, but in power'. And, on this basis, 'Let us renew our hearts,' Luther exhorts, 'and [let us] be of good courage and joyfully *allow the Lord to slay us.*'[15]

49.93 (*WA Br* 3.393-94); letter to Amsdorf, Wittenberg, June 21, 1525; *LW* 49.117 (*WA Br* 3.541); *Comm. 1 Cor.* 7.25-26, *LW* 28.49 (*WA* 12.134-35); Michael Parsons, *Reformation Marriage. The Husband and Wife Relationship in the Theology of Luther and Calvin* (Eugene: Wipf and Stock, 2011), 173-77.

[10] Kolb, 'God's Gift,' 401.

[11] Kolb, 'God's Gift,' 402. Later, Kolb says that 'Martyrdom was, for [Luther], literally witness to the faith, the Word of God in action' (403).

[12] Kolb, 'God's Gift,' 411. For a brief, excellent introduction to this theme in Luther, see Gerhard O. Forde, *On Being a Theologian of the Cross. Reflections on Luther's Heidelberg Disputation, 1518* (Grand Rapids: Eerdmans, 1997).

[13] See letter to the Christians in the Netherlands, August, 1523: Theodore G. Tappert (ed.), *Luther: Letters of Spiritual Counsel* (Vancouver: Regent College, 2003), 192-94; *WA* 12.73-80—hereafter, Luther: *Letters*.

[14] Luther: *Letters*, 193.

[15] Luther: *Letters*, 193, italics added.

In his letter to the martyr, Lambert Thorn,[16] Luther assures him of Christ's identification with him in his suffering; but notice here the antitheses: 'He himself suffers in you and is *glorified* in you. He is taken captive in you and *reigns* in you. He is oppressed in you and *triumphs* in you.'[17] The rhetorical intensity of the sentence, with the important italicised words (*glorified-reigns-triumphs*) in verbal opposition to their seeming counterparts (suffers-captive-oppressed), indicates Kolb's thesis concerning Luther. While Christ has become 'a reproach of men and despised of the people,'[18] in and through the suffering and the oppression of believers, Christ is glorified, reigns and triumphs.[19] In a letter to Sibyl Baumgaertner (July 8, 1544) Luther speaks again of this identification of Christ with suffering believers, '[W]e visit the Lord Christ himself,' he says, 'imprisoned in the person of a true member.'[20] In a letter to believers in Leipzig[21] Luther speaks of Christ 'who suffers and is put to death among you, but who will certainly rise again and reign'. He concludes on the same note of triumph through suffering: 'One must smite the devil in his face with the cross and not whistle his tune or flatter him. He must be made to know with whom he has to do.'[22] In another letter Luther assures the recipient that Christ is in the cell with him and encourages him to call upon Christ and to 'defy and ridicule the raging and arrogance of Satan'.[23] Suffering and persecution are necessary for the gospel to exist and to spread, according to the reformer,[24] and oppression of true believers in their inherent weakness sees the wonderful power of God in Christ manifest and reign.

Calvin's letters to contemporary martyrs

Interestingly, Andrew Pettegree sees John Calvin as first and foremost an evangelist and a preacher: 'He aimed at the conversion of society, and inevitably pursued traditional conversion strategies: the call to repentance, the appeal to

---

[16] See letter to Lambert Thorn, January 19, 1524, Luther: *Letters*, 197-99; *WA Br* 3.237-39.
[17] Luther: *Letters*, 198, italics added.
[18] Luther: *Letters*, 199.
[19] Luther: *Letters*, 198. The reformer quotes Ps. 91.14-15; Jn. 16.33.
[20] Luther: *Letters*, 225-27; *WA Br* 10.604-607 (227).
[21] Letter to the Evangelicals in Leipzig, April 11, 1533; Luther: *Letters*, 223-24; *WA Br* 6.448-50.
[22] Luther: *Letters*, 224. See, also, letter to the Christians of Miltenberg, February 14, 1524; Luther: *Letters*, 203; letter to the Christians in Bremen, March, 1525; Luther: *Letters*, 209.
[23] Letter to Leonard Kaeser, May 20, 1527; Luther: *Letters*, 214; for the whole letter see 213-15; *WA Br* 4.204-206.
[24] See Luther's letter to Casper Loener and Nicholas Medler, June 7, 1531; Luther: *Letters*, 216.

political elites, the call to witness and, if necessary, exile or martyrdom.'[25] On the other hand, when those who were converted to the Reformed faith witnessed that faith and were arrested and tried, Calvin, the pastor, supported and encouraged them—even from a distance, as we shall see. In that brief context, we now turn to examine some letters that John Calvin wrote to three groups of prisoners about to be executed, the five prisoners at Lyon in 1553, those in Chambery two years' later, in 1555, and also to the women in prison in Paris in 1557.[26]

Letters to the five prisoners of Lyon

Jules Bonnet, editor of Calvin's letters, describes the situation briefly as follows.[27] In April, 1552, five young Frenchmen, students of theology in Lausanne were returning to their own country. They are named by Bonnet as Martial Alba from Montauban, Peter Escrivain from Gascony, Charles Favre from Blanzac in Angoumois, Peter Navihères from Limousin and Bernard Seguin La Reole. After having spent some days in Geneva they were tricked and betrayed by

---

[25] Andrew Pettegree, 'The spread of Calvin's thought' in Donald K. McKim (ed.), *The Cambridge Companion to John Calvin* (Cambridge: Cambridge University Press, 2004), 222.

[26] These are not the only letters written in such circumstances. See, for example, Calvin's short letter to the Ministers of the Church of Basel, November 13, 1537; Calvin, *Letters*, 1.58-60, in which he speaks of two men who, after torture, have been burned for their faith in France. He speaks of the persecutors as those 'already drunk with the blood of these two victims, . . . not otherwise at all likely to set any bounds to their persecuting spirit'. He adds, 'Besides, the utmost care must be taken that the blood of the godly, which is so precious in the sight of God, may not be lightly esteemed by us' (59). See, also, Calvin's letter to Bullinger, Whitsunday, 1552; Calvin, *Letters*, 2.349, in which he grieves for the mistreatment of French Protestants, speaking of the faithful in Bretagne and Anjou being 'badly treated', and of a student being burned to death in Bordeaux. See, also, a letter to Sulzer, September 8, 1553; Calvin, *Letters*, 2.427-30, in which he speaks of four more suffering for the gospel. Also, letter to Denis Peloquin and Louis de Marsac, August 22, 1553; Calvin, *Letters*, 2.418-21, in which he states:

> For the rest, as in the midst of this life we are in death, you have now need to be well persuaded that in the midst of death you are in life. And thus we see that we must not be governed by sense merely in following Jesus Christ, but there is nothing more alien to our nature than to plunge ourselves into disgrace, and abase ourselves unto death, in order to be elevated to the glory of heaven. But in the end we shall feel, experimentally, that the Son of God has not disappointed us in promising that whosoever shall lay down his life in this world shall recover it to enjoy it for ever (421).

See, also, his letter to the Count of Wurtemberg, July 12, 1558; Calvin, *Letters*, 3.435-37, in which he pleads the cause of ministers being persecuted as heretics.

[27] See Calvin, *Letters*, 2.350n.1; 2.391n.1. These prisoners became famous as martyrs, being cited, for example, in Sebastian Meyer, *In apocalypsim Johannis Apostoli* (Zürich: Froschouer, 1559), fol. 42r.

a stranger they met on the road who insisted they visited him in Ainay. There, to their shock, they were arrested and led away to prison. Eventually, all five students were declared guilty of heresy and, forthwith, delivered to the secular Judge Ordinary of Lyon. From their imprisonment they appealed to the Parliament of Paris for clemency and their hoped-for release. The Reformed Church supported them, with the authorities of Bern, in particular, striving to have them released. Their long drawn-out trial lasted more than a year, during which time they were transferred from dungeon to bleak dungeon. Eventually, they were brought back to Lyon to await their sentence. On March 1, 1553, they received the communication which gave them over to their execution at the stake. During this whole ordeal they were supported by the reformer, John Calvin, and by others. Several letters are of significance to our study.

1. to the five prisoners of Lyon, from Geneva, June 10, 1552[28]
The first letter that Calvin wrote to the prisoners was written in response to a letter from one of the imprisoned students.[29] Calvin says that he had wished to write as soon as he had heard of their awful predicament, but admits that he had delayed somewhat in case his letter fell into the wrong hands in transit, fearing that it may have caused them greater harm by their resulting association with his name, condemned as he himself was. The letter was written before sentence had been passed on them, and it appears from what he says that there was at this point still room for hope of their release—at least, he assumes so. Calvin writes, then, to assure them of his genuine concern, but, also, to answer two questions that Bernard Seguin La Reole had asked, one concerning vows and the other, perhaps more understandably, about the nature of the glorified body. We need not enter into detail here. Suffice it to say, concerning vows, Calvin says that it is not lawful to vow to God anything but that of which God approves. Concerning the glorified body, the reformer argues, quoting Philippians 3, that it is the 'corruptible and fading nature of the world' which will be changed in our bodies.[30]

The major import of this letter is to assure them that God is intimately involved with them in their terrible situation and predicament. Calvin repeats what he has evidently heard, perhaps from John Liner (see below). 'I had been informed,' he says, 'how that God wrought so powerfully in you by his grace that you stood in no great need of my letters.'[31] Their constancy in this affliction is enough to demonstrate the divine presence and help. Upon this foundation, the reformer reassures the prisoners that God will give them strength to

---

[28] Calvin, *Letters*, 2.350-53.
[29] This letter is also quoted in Hans J. Hillerbrand, *The Reformation. A Narrative History Related by Contemporary Observers and Participants* (Grand Rapids: Baker, 1979), 203-204.
[30] Calvin, *Letters*, 2.351-52 and 2.352-53, respectively.
[31] Calvin, *Letters*, 2.350.

fulfil what they have begun.[32] They can rest in the divine promises, 'we know from experience that he has never failed those who allow themselves to be governed by him'.[33] Calvin, later, makes the point that this comes to those who suffer through Jesus Christ and their establishment in him (implying personal relationship and subsequent security): '[B]ut the firmness which is in Jesus Christ is sufficient for this, and all else that might shake us were we not established in him.'[34]

A secondary, but important, theme of the letter is the identification of the Reformed community with the students in their distress. This assures them that they are not isolated, not alone in their trial.

> Meanwhile, all the children of God pray for you as they are bound to do, not only on account of the mutual compassion which ought to exist between members of the same body, but because they know well that you labour for them, in maintaining the cause of their salvation.[35]

Interestingly, the motivation apparently runs in two directions, according to this short paragraph. On the one hand, the Church has compassion on the prisoners in their misfortune and anguish, 'as they are bound to do'. On the other hand, the Church realises that the prisoners 'labour for them, in maintaining the cause of their salvation'. They are united, then, by both Christian love and the defence of what they consider to be biblical truth, their own confession.

Calvin appears to draw the themes of God's and the Church's involvement together in his closing prayer for them.

> In conclusion, I beseech our good Lord that he would be pleased to make you feel in every way the worth of his protection of his own, to fill you with his Holy Spirit who gives you prudence and virtue, and brings you peace, joy, and contentment; and may the name of our Lord Jesus be glorified by you to the edification of his Church![36]

It is, of course, characteristic of the reformer to allude to the triune God in his prayers. Calvin is clear that it is the Lord who protects, it is the Holy Spirit who is able to furnish them with the qualities of prudence and virtue, and to allow them, even in this awful circumstance, to experience peace, joy and contentment; and, it is the Lord Jesus Christ who will be glorified by their perseverance. But we note that in all of this, the consequence is that the wider Church will be edified and built up.

---

[32] See, for example, Philippians 1.6 and 2.13.
[33] Calvin, *Letters*, 2.351.
[34] Calvin, *Letters*, 2.351.
[35] Calvin, *Letters*, 2.350-51.
[36] Calvin, *Letters*, 2.353.

2. to the five prisoners of Lyon, March 7, 1553[37]

This letter, the second of the reformer to the student prisoners, was written just six days after the sentence against them was passed. Calvin begins by confessing his own state of mind: 'We have been for some days past in deeper anxiety and sadness than ever,' he says, 'having heard of the resolve taken by the enemies of the truth.'[38] But, again, understandably, the theme of this short letter revolves around the presence and help of God.

Though he anticipates the worst, Calvin remains open to the possibilities of God's gracious providence, indicating that the Lord may yet dispose of the situation in an unexpected manner.[39] However, with that, the reformer speaks of continually praying to God 'to uphold you, and not permit you to fall away; in short, to have you in his keeping. I feel well assured that nothing shakes the firmness which he has put within you.'[40] God has given them constancy up to this point; Calvin's prayer is that he continues to do this for them. He exhorts them through consideration of the divine promises.

> If he has promised to strengthen with patience those who suffer chastisement for their sins, how much less will he be found wanting to those who maintain his quarrel—those whom he employs on so worthy a mission as being witnesses for his truth! You must therefore keep this sentence in mind, that 'He who dwells in you is stronger than the world.' We who are here shall do our duty in praying that he would glorify himself more and more by your constancy, and that he may, by the consolation of his Spirit, sweeten and endear all that is bitter to the flesh, and so absorb your spirits in himself, that in contemplating that heavenly crown, you may be ready without regret to leave all that belongs to this world.[41]

There are several points worth underlining in this important quotation. First, in encouraging the students to set their minds on the divine promise, Calvin speaks of them, not merely as believers, but as 'those who maintain his [that is, God's] quarrel,' 'those whom he employs,' 'witnesses for his truth'. This clearly establishes their position as Christian or, more particularly, Reformed *martyrs*. The work is God's, as is the truth that they defend and, consequently, so is the quarrel with the enemies of that truth, and the students have been called into

---

[37] Calvin, *Letters*, 2.391-93.
[38] Calvin, *Letters*, 2.391.
[39] It is worth noting that, when he writes to others at this time, Calvin is not optimistic in the least. Between the reformer's letters, dated March 7 and May 15 (1553), Calvin wrote a letter to his friend Pierre Viret (April 22, 1553) in which he gives an account of the situation—see Calvin, *Letters*, 2.401-402. According to Calvin, the majority of judges 'were disinclined to agree to the condemnation of the brethren, inasmuch as the king had given no express orders respecting it' (2.401). The Constable, Anne de Montmorency, 'stood alone in opposing' the decision (2.401). The reformer, also, points out Cardinal de Touron as being particularly obstinate in the matter. Calvin expresses the feeling that, though some still attempt to gain the prisoners' freedom, there is now no real hope for them.
[40] Calvin, *Letters*, 2.391.
[41] Calvin, *Letters*, 2.392.

this mission by God and for God. Second, Calvin suggests the second theme that generally pervades these letters, that of the Reformed community: 'We who are here shall do our duty in praying.' The prisoners are not alone in this situation, but have the Church supporting them in the difficult days that lie ahead. Third, Jesus Christ himself will be glorified by their constancy. Fourth, the Holy Spirit, by absorbing their spirits in himself, will bring consolation to them in their anxiety. By this, Calvin appears to mean that the Holy Spirit will so encompass their troubled spirits that they will be comforted (see, perhaps, 2 Cor. 1.4; Rom. 8.26-27). Fifth, the reformer reminds the young men of that important eschatological dimension and focus, speaking of them 'contemplating that heavenly crown'. This brings into focus the spiritual, eschatological perspective, so vital in times of affliction and anxiety, in which believers may be ready to leave this transient world, in pain and trouble but without remorse.

Calvin knows that, given the situation, the prisoners will have considered their deaths: 'It cannot be but that you feel some twinges of frailty.'[42] Therefore, he exhorts them to put their confidence in God alone, trusting that he will fill them with his Holy Spirit to the point of overcoming. Then comes the inevitable final prayer, together with a request that they pray for him—indicating their mutual dependence, even at this hour.

> And now, my brethren, after having besought our good Lord to have charge over you, to assist you in everything and through everything, to make you taste by experience how kind a Father he is, and how careful of the salvation of his own, I pray to be remembered in your prayers.[43]

Again, the understandable emphasis on the Lord's assisting presence. But, here is an interesting stress on experience, too. Calvin prays that, even in their distressing situation, they may *experience* 'how kind a Father he is and how careful of the salvation of his own'. Within the awful experience of their imprisonment and waiting for execution, Calvin prays that they may experience something else, something greater and more comforting, even the fatherly love and grace of God.

3. to the five prisoners of Lyons, May 15, 1553

Calvin's third letter to the prisoners was written a day before their execution.[44] The reformer commends the five men for not having wavered in their faith and

---

[42] Calvin, *Letters*, 2.392,
[43] Calvin, *Letters*, 2.393. It might be noted, too, that Calvin suggests that the prisoners write, warning the church of the false and malicious conspirator of the church whom they have met. Knowing the current weight of their testimony, the reformer believes this will help others.
[44] Calvin, *Letters*, 2.404-408. Between this letter and the last, on March 28 (1553), Calvin wrote to Christopher and Thomas Sollicoffre, merchants of Gall, dwelling in Lyon. A messenger on behalf of the prisoners had been to the French court to solicit pardon from the king, Henry II. Calvin asks the merchants if they would give the expenses of the messenger's journey. Of course, as we now know, the journey, itself,

trust in God, even in such difficult and trying circumstances. He exhorts them at this last hour to look towards heaven, to subdue their passions and to be humbly ready. Calvin speaks of God using their deaths 'to sign his truth'.

> You know, however, in what strength you have to fight—a strength on which all those who trust, shall never be daunted, much less confounded. Even so, my brothers, be confident that you shall be strengthened, according to your need, by the Spirit of our Lord Jesus, so that you shall not faint under the load of temptations, however heavy it be, any more than he did who won so glorious a victory, that in the midst of our miseries it is an unfailing pledge of his triumph.[45]

Here are those same characteristic comments. In seeking to encourage the prisoners in their final hours, Calvin identifies their misery with Christ's, only then to call attention to Christ's subsequent victory and ultimately their own triumph, through him. They are, he assures them, 'maintaining his [God's] quarrel'; their blood will *not* be spilt in vain. Their deaths will result in the name of Jesus Christ being 'powerfully' glorified.[46]

Calvin is sure that God will give to them the experience of his comfort and reminds them of the inheritance to which they go. Significantly, in this appalling context, the reformer speaks of them again as martyrs: 'That God should have appointed you his Son's martyrs, is a token to you of superabounding grace.'[47] He continues the eschatological theme by asserting the truth of resurrection:

> And seeing that he employs your life in so worthy a cause as is the witness of the Gospel, doubt not that it must be precious to him. The time draws nigh when the earth shall disclose the blood which has been hid, and we, after having been disencumbered of these fading bodies, shall be completely restored.[48]

Further, reflecting something of Luther's approach, his theology of the cross, perhaps, he claims that the Son of God will be 'glorified by our shame'.[49]

---

was to no avail—Calvin, *Letters*, 2.396-97. Apparently, to the brethren in Bern they wrote that their blood would be soon 'shed for the confession of his [Christ's] holy name' and that they were ready to suffer and to be received into God's heavenly kingdom. See the short, moving account of their deaths, Calvin, *Letters*, 2.404-405n.2.

[45] Calvin, *Letters*, 2.405-406.
[46] Calvin, *Letters*, 2.406, emphasis added.
[47] Calvin, *Letters*, 2.406.
[48] Calvin, *Letters*, 2.407.
[49] Calvin, *Letters*, 2.407. See the argument of Bonnie Pattison in her excellent essay, 'The suffering church in Calvin's *De Scandalis*: an exercise in Luther's *Theologia Crucis*? in Michael Parsons (ed.), *Since we are Justified by Faith. Justification in the Theologies of the Protestant Reformation* (Milton Keynes: Paternoster, 2012), 117-37, in which she concludes that Calvin resembles Luther in his approach and understanding of the suffering Church and that 'for Calvin as for Luther, there is no other way except through weakness and suffering to make manifest a knowledge of God in the lives of God's people' (137).

Calvin's final word to the prisoners, as one would expect, is a prayer. In it he asks God to protect them, to strengthen them 'more and more by his power,' 'to make [them] feel what care he takes of [their] salvation,' to increase the Spirit's gifts in them, and to let them serve 'his glory to the end'.[50] From the account of their death we know that this prayer was answered in good measure.

During the trial of these unfortunate students, Calvin wrote to John Liner, a rich merchant, originally of St. Gall, who had settled in Lyon. Apparently, he often visited the men in their dungeon and, on occasion, undertook errands for them.[51] Some of the contents of this short letter are worth considering at this juncture, as they add to our understanding of Calvin's view of the prisoners, themselves, and of martyrdom.

Naturally, Calvin thanks Liner for the zeal he has displayed on the prisoners' behalf. He comments that the tireless work of Liner is, in fact, God's work 'by the power of his Spirit'. By this, he means that the Spirit has disposed and directed Liner in his sacrificial efforts. He has been honoured by God and has been given grace and courage to perform his duty.[52] It is interesting, though, that the reformer speaks in this way more because of the Lord's high regard for the prisoners, than anything to do intrinsically with Liner and his efforts. Notice how he puts this.

> For however despised and rejected of men, the poor believers persecuted for the sake of the Gospel may be, yet we know that God esteems them very pearls; that there is nothing more agreeable to him than our striving to comfort and help them as in us lies.[53]

The gospel reverses perspective. In the eyes of the world and of 'the enemies of the faith'[54] they are 'despised and rejected'; in God's sight (*coram Deo*) they are precious jewels. They are God's 'agents, whom he appoints for the defence of his Gospel'.[55] Further, speaking of Liner's actions as 'fatherly,' Calvin cites Jesus' words about giving a cup of water to the least of his people (see Matt. 25.34-46): 'a cup of water given to them shall not be lost'. Significantly, the parable to which Calvin alludes suggests that water given to the least is water given to Jesus Christ, himself—such is his identification with those who suffer.[56] Then, in speaking of the prisoners as 'martyrs' Calvin, also, identifies Liner's efforts with theirs: 'It is said that they who comfort the children of God in their persecutions which they endure for the Gospel, are fellow-labourers for the truth.' And, more remarkably, he states that God upholds and approves *us*

---

[50] Calvin, *Letters*, 2.407.
[51] Letter to John Liner, August 10, 1552; Calvin, *Letters*, 2.358-60.
[52] Calvin, *Letters*, 2.358.
[53] Calvin, *Letters*, 2.358-59.
[54] Calvin, *Letters*, 2.358.
[55] Calvin, *Letters*, 2.359.
[56] Calvin, *Letters*, 2.359.

(Calvin and Liner, in this instance) as his martyrs, 'even though we do not personally suffer, merely because his martyrs are helped and comforted by us'—martyrdom by association, as it were.[57]

The theme of the Christian community is never far from the reformer's mind, in this or any other context. Again, he raises it here, reminding Liner that many believers glorify God for what he (Liner) is doing. The prisoners, for instance, are said to be encouraged and made more resolute in their stand because they can see God working in Liner's gracious actions on their behalf. 'Be of good courage, therefore, in this holy work, in which you serve not only God and his martyrs, but also the whole Church.' Calvin encourages Liner to persevere in the potentially dangerous work, speaking of the temptations involved: '[T]he devil,' he says, 'will not fail to whisper in your ear on many sides to divert you from it.'[58]

Letters to prisoners in Chambery

1. to the prisoners in Chambery, September 5, 1555[59]

Again, the editor, Jules Bonnet gives us the names of four of the five individuals imprisoned for the sake of the gospel.[60] They are John Vernou, student, native of Poitiers; Anthony Laborie of Caiar (formerly the royal judge of that place); John Trigalet (licentiate of law) of Nismes, and Bertrand Bataille, student, of Gascony. These young men set out with the intention of preaching the Word of God but were arrested and imprisoned, later to face death for their (Reformed) faith.

Characteristically, the reformer expresses his sorrow for the situation which these prisoners face: '[W]ith what anguish our hearts are filled on account of your bonds,' he says.[61] Likewise, he assures them of the affection of 'the whole body of the church'—a poignant reminder that they are part of a wider community, the Reformed Church.[62] Indeed, he alludes again to this wider context in the following comment: 'Since then so many of the brethren pray fervently for you, I doubt not but our heavenly Father will listen to their desires and groanings, and I see by your letters how he has already begun to work in you.'[63] The use of the word 'groanings' is significant; perhaps, it indicates that Calvin and the others praying for these brethren did not know exactly what to pray for but trusted in the Holy Spirit to aid their agonised prayers (see, perhaps, Rom. 8.26).

There is in this letter a tacit understanding that the situation might end in execution for the prisoners. The reformer is quite open about this, saying, for in-

---

[57] Calvin, *Letters*, 2.359.
[58] Calvin, *Letters*, 2.359.
[59] Calvin, *Letters*, 3.220-23.
[60] See Calvin, *Letters*, 3.220n.1.
[61] Calvin, *Letters*, 3.221.
[62] Calvin, *Letters*, 3.223.
[63] Calvin, *Letters*, 3.221.

stance, that he wishes they had, what he calls, 'worldly means' of deliverance; but encourages them to 'look higher' as he believes God urges them to do. He acknowledges their understandable weakness and fear, but sees even in that the activity of divine grace: 'For if the weakness of the flesh will sometimes show itself in such a manner as that you shall have hard and difficult struggles to maintain, this is not to me a matter of astonishment, but rather of magnifying God, because he raised you above it.'[64] Earlier, in a letter to Farel, July 24, 1555, the reformer had mentioned the prisoners' extraordinary courage and determination, commenting on their eagerness to undergo death, if that finally proves to be the Lord's will. 'The issue is in the hands of God,' he writes, 'it is as yet hidden from our sight.'[65]

In his letter to the prisoners, Calvin then explicitly uses terms that situate the prisoners within the concept of contemporary martyrdom, reminding them that God has called them into his service. Speaking of the doctrines for which they make a stand, he tells them that divine providence will cause their present witness to be even more effective than their preaching or teaching: '[T]he testimony which you are about to bear will not fail to confirm them [the doctrines] from afar. For God will bestow on it a virtue to resound further than voice of man can reach.' This is God's work, not theirs; its efficacy derives from the divine purpose and activity. But Calvin encourages them to practise what they have learned, to continue to do what they have begun.[66] The reformer continues in a similar vein,

[R]epose in his paternal goodness, not doubting but he will take your bodies as well as your souls under his protection, and if the blood of his faithful followers is precious, will effectually show it in you, since he has chosen you to be his witnesses. And should it be his will to demand the sacrifice of your lives to approve his truth, besides that this is as you know an oblation well pleasing in his sight, let it console you that in surrendering the whole into his hands you will lose nothing; for if he kindly deigns to take us under his protection during this perishable life, much more, having called us away from it, will he show himself the faithful Guardian of our souls.[67]

Here we find the reformer's characteristic themes: the fatherhood of God, the divine choice of these particular men to witness to the gospel truth, the necessity of suffering,[68] the believer's eternal safety, and so on. Calvin seeks to con-

---

[64] Calvin, *Letters*, 3.221.
[65] Letter to Farel, July 24, 1555; Calvin, *Letters*, 3.206. The prisoners had sent one or two letters to Calvin, which he forwarded to Farel and, later, to Viret: see letters to Viret, August 4th, 1555; Calvin, *Letters*, 3.217; September 9, 1555; Calvin, *Letters*, 3.230-31.
[66] Calvin, *Letters*, 3.221.
[67] Calvin, *Letters*, 3.222.
[68] See Calvin, *Letters*, 3.23, where, in writing to a gentleman of Piedmont (Geneva, February 25, 1554) he states that under the tyranny of antichrist, 'if a man will live

firm the prisoners' divine calling and their sense of worth within God's purposes. Even their death, should that be God's demand, is 'an oblation well pleasing in his sight'. Though the unimaginable situation must have challenged the faith of these men to the extreme, they are to cling tenaciously to the grace of God, 'the faithful Guardian' of their souls. Calvin's final exhortation, then, is this: 'Since God has brought you so far, it is too late to think of shrinking back. Cast all your cares on the providence of God.'[69]

Calvin's last comment, as always, concerns his prayer for them. It is noticeable that though the reformer is open about the very real possibility of their deaths, he prays that they may experience satisfaction in God during this terrible ordeal.

> I will pray our heavenly Father to have you in his holy keeping, direct you by his Spirit, arm you with courage and constancy, so to do battle that he may triumph in you either by your life or death, and that he would make you feel what it is to have our whole satisfaction in him alone.[70]

Importantly, the reformer's last word is of experience of God, an experience directly opposite to that which they undergo in prison, but an experience that gives them 'courage and constancy' in dire circumstances, by the grace of the Holy Spirit.

2. to the prisoners in Chambery, October 5, 1555[71]

This letter begins, deliberately, with a Trinitarian salutation: 'The love of God the Father, and the grace of our Lord Jesus Christ, be always upon you, by the communication of the Holy Spirit.' The triune God is involved with them, even in their dreadful situation. The reformer speaks of his anguish for their situation, an anguish which has 'paralysed' him in respect of writing to them. He laments, specifically, about the length of time the whole process is taking, commenting on it as one of Satan's devices to wear them down and praying that God will enable them to persevere. The situation is clearly far from resolved:

> like a Christian, he must by continual training learn to die, so that no difficulty plead an excuse for him when the honour of his God is in question'.

[69] Calvin, *Letters*, 3.222. The prisoners had apparently written a petition against their imprisonment, which, except for a few minor things, had gained Calvin's approval. He graciously acknowledges that it had been God who had put this into their minds.

> If the world approve not so a just and holy protestation, at least it will be approved of by God and his angels, by his prophets, apostles, and the whole church. Nay, every true believer, on seeing it, will have cause to glorify him for having dictated it to you by his Holy Spirit.

Again, we see the reference to that broad community who support the prisoners in their time of difficulty; a community expanded to include the whole company of heaven, itself (see, perhaps, Heb. 12.22-24)—Calvin, *Letters*, 3.222.

[70] Calvin, *Letters*, 3.223.
[71] Calvin, *Letters*, 3.231-32.

But I hope, however things turn out, that God will at last fill our hearts with joy, after having left you as it were to pine away; for he sees so many of his children in continual *anxiety on your account*, that he will not fail to lend an ear to their desires.[72]

We notice, again, in the italicised words, the communal aspect to what the reformer says. The prisoners are not on their own. Rather, they are surrounded by those who are anxious about them and evidently praying earnestly for them. Calvin concludes his short letter by assuring the men that he will pray to God that they might be kept, filled with the Holy Spirit 'to pursue the combat to which he has ordained you,' and given hope.[73] As is the reformer's custom, he asks them to pray for him, too, and concludes with a greeting from the brethren in Geneva.[74]

A letter to women detained in Paris[75]

Two years after the previous letters, written to prisoners in Lyon and Chambery, the reformer wrote a letter to some women imprisoned in Paris for their Reformed beliefs. One of their number, Phillippe de Lunz, had already bravely gone to execution. The remainder, les dames de Rentigny, d'Ouartis, de Champagne, and de Longemeau, as well as some of lower social rank, were the recipients of this letter of encouragement. As we have previously noticed in letters to prisoners, Calvin empathises with these women, knowing that naturally they will be repulsed by the physical possibilities of their situation should the death penalty be carried out, but encouraging them to trust in the grace and power of God to see them through their ordeal. He also encourages them to pray for strength.

Central to this letter is the reformer's use of 1 Corinthians 1.27-28 concerning the divine choice of foolish things to confound the wise, of weak things to confound the strong and despised things and of those 'of no account' to confound the presumptuous and the proud.[76] He reinforces this later by citing Joel's prophecy of God empowering by the Spirit both 'sons and daughters'.[77] There is in this use an inferred assumption that women are the weaker sex, sometimes despised and of no account, and that God is using them (even *them*, we might say) to confound the machinations of men who oppose the truth.[78] If they persevere to the bitter end, says Calvin, their inherent weakness will speak

---

[72] Calvin, *Letters*, 3.232, italics added.
[73] Calvin, *Letters*, 3.232.
[74] Three days later, Calvin wrote to the brethren who apparently met in secret in the French dominated town of Chambery, encouraging them to stay firm in their faith, despite persecution in the town—letter to the brethren of Chambery, October 8, 1555; Calvin, *Letters*, 3.233-34.
[75] Letter to the women detained in prison in Paris, Geneva, September 1557; Calvin, *Letters* 3.363-66.
[76] Calvin, *Letters*, 3.364.
[77] Calvin, *Letters*, 3.365.
[78] It is the truth that is 'the object of their hatred,' Calvin, *Letters*, 3.364.

the more powerfully of the might and ability of their God[79]—a power which 'they [the enemies] cannot gainsay'.[80]

Noticeable and perhaps surprising, too, is the battle imagery that is distributed throughout the letter. When Calvin speaks of being called to maintain God's cause, he says to the women,

> When he calls us to do battle, and puts us to proof before the enemy, it serves us nothing to allege our weakness as an excuse for abandoning or denying him, except to expose ourselves to be condemned for disloyalty. For he who marshals us to battle, arms and shields us at the same time with the necessary weapons, and gives us dexterity in wielding them.[81]

Here, explicitly, is Calvin's belief in the divine calling to suffering and to martyrdom in his cause. God is acutely involved in the whole situation and in their response to it.

To encourage the women, Calvin assures them that they have been specifically called by God and that he will give them grace to fulfil that vocation. He then encourages them by putting them into a broad context of those who have gone before: Jesus Christ, himself; the women of the New Testament at the death of Jesus, noticeably, 'when the apostles had forsaken him'; and women in history who have similarly maintained the cause of Christ.[82] Speaking of these historic witnesses as 'martyrs', the reformer asks, 'Has their faith not obtained the glory of the world as well as that of martyrs? . . . They have not feared to quit this perishable life to obtain a better, full of glory and everlasting.'[83] His final prayer for them is that they might experience the grace of God, even and especially in this situation, and that they might be conformed 'wholly to his holy will'.[84]

Reflections

John Calvin often comments on the difficulties that pastors face as they adhere to what he would consider the truth of Reformed teaching. In his reply to Sadoleto, for instance, he speaks, not only of the work that pastors do inside the Church to edify congregants and believers, but, also, of their readiness to work *against* those who would destroy that Church: '[T]hey are also armed,' he says,

---

[79] Calvin trusts that the women will be strengthened and will rest in the fact that in the past God 'has performed such great things by weak vessels,' Calvin, *Letters*, 3.366.
[80] Calvin, *Letters*, 3.364.
[81] Calvin, *Letters*, 3.365. The reformer uses the same imagery in his letter to Godfrey Varaglia, December 17, 1557; Calvin, *Letters*, 4.427-28 (428), where he speaks of the prisoner being called to martyrdom and reassures him that many others will come to the truth through his present suffering.
[82] Calvin, *Letters*, 3.365.
[83] Calvin, *Letters*, 3.365, 366.
[84] Calvin, *Letters*, 3.366.

'to repel the machinations of those who strive to impede the work of God.'[85] But, one might argue that that is specifically an integral part of the pastor's calling, *as pastor*. But Calvin thinks otherwise. He claims in *Concerning Scandals*, for example, that it is part of *every* Christian's calling, as *believers* in Christ, to set themselves against the enemies of Christ.

> But the fact is that the heart of a Christian ought to be so fortified that no matter what scandals burst on the scene he never yields ground or turns aside a hair's breadth from Christ. The man who is not equipped for perseverance like this, so as to overcome all scandals victoriously, does not yet understand the power of Christianity.[86]

In this context, this appears a rather dogmatic stance, lacking both nuance and, perhaps, concrete reality and sensitivity. However, our brief examination of Calvin's letters to contemporary martyrs has demonstrated that in the acute pastoral context, involving those who presently face execution for their faith, the reformer is quite different.[87]

Calvin, the pastor, is extremely aware of the dreadful situation which these prisoners encounter. He is open about the difficulties they endure, about the anxiety that this must cause them, about their natural weakness and frailty in the face of a painful, horrifying death. He is also open about his own feelings of anxiety for them, and tells them so. He sometimes hints at his longing for a hopeful outcome, but more often admits realistically that this is unlikely. In this, he shows himself to be very human and sympathetic, a pastor who feels their anguish. He clearly rests on the providence of God, but, importantly, not as a doctrine to be intellectually comprehended, certainly not understood as a cold Stoical determinism, but as a truth to be experienced, to be taken in faith and prayerful trust.

We have seen that Calvin has several recurrent themes in his letters, themes by which he seeks to encourage the prisoners in these dreadful circumstances: the centrality of God in the situation, the importance of the wider community and the prisoners' role as present witnesses of God's truth.

---

[85] See Calvin's reply to Sadoleto—*A Reformation Debate. Sadoleto's Letter to the Genevans and Calvin's Reply* (edited by John C. Olin; New York: Fordham University Press, 2000), 47. See, also, 86, where he remarks that 'those who first engaged in this cause (that is, the Reformation) could expect nothing else than to be spurned by the world'. See chapter 4 of the present work on that letter.

[86] Calvin, *Concerning Scandals* (1550) (translated by John W. Fraser; Edinburgh: Saint Andrew Press, 1978), 10; OS 2.167.

[87] W. Robert Godfrey, 'The Counsellor to the Afflicted' in Burk Parsons (ed.), *John Calvin. A Heart for Devotion, Doctrine and Doxology* (Lake Mary: Reformation Trust, 2008), 83-93, says, '[Calvin's] counsel had both a tough realism and a sensitive compassion to it. He faced the miseries and struggles of life straightforwardly, and he pointed Christians to God's fatherly care both in this life and in the life to come' (92).

The centrality of God in the situation

First, Calvin stresses the part God plays—he is central to the situation, even to the point of calling the prisoners to suffer for his cause.[88] For Calvin, God is absolutely pivotal to the circumstance, however difficult that is to grasp.[89] He emphasises divine involvement,[90] stressing that God's engagement is seen both in the present and in the future. At this moment, they see his presence by the way the prisoners themselves remain constant in the faith, persevering in their trial—this is the current work of the Holy Spirit upon them and in them. They are held closely by the Spirit and established, held firm, in Christ. The Father has given them promises and protects and strengthens them, even now. We noted the Trinitarian nature of Calvin's words. And, though there is not so much comment on personal eschatology as in Luther's letters to prisoners in similar circumstances, Calvin, also, says that in the future God will call them away from this perishable life towards eternal life, to a heavenly crown and to complete and full victory in Christ.

A notable feature of this theme is the way in which Calvin stresses experience to those who are presently suffering a terrible experience in the gruelling ordeal they face. When speaking about the promises of God to those in Lyon, for instance, the reformer underlines that *from experience* they know that God never fails them.[91] Further, he prays that they may be made to *feel* the divine protection; and, again, he prays that 'in everything and through everything' that God would 'make [them] taste *by experience* how kind a Father he is'.[92] For the prisoners in Chambery he prays that they may experience full satisfaction in God alone. This stress is entirely understandable, of course. Given that in their situation the experience through which they go is likely to press in upon them and overshadow all else, Calvin tries to direct their attention to the reality of spiritual experience that might get crowded out. The reformer attempts to cause them to see by faith, not by sight; to realise the spiritual reality of a paternal God who cares for them, even though circumstances might seek to persuade otherwise.

---

[88] See, for example, Calvin, *Letters*, 3.365.

[89] However, see the critical comments on this subject by Matthew Myer Boulton, *Life in God. John Calvin, Practical Formation, and the Future of Protestant Theology* (Grand Rapids: Eerdmans, 2011), 193-99.

[90] See Nicolls, 'The Theatre of Martyrdom,' 49.

[91] See the important early article, Charles Partee, 'Calvin and Experience,' *Scottish Journal of Theology* 26.2 (1973), 169-81, in which he concludes that Calvin's theology in general is not speculative, but, rather, that he believed 'in everything we deal directly with God' (181).

[92] Calvin, *Letters*, 2.393, emphasis added.

The importance of Christian community

Second, Calvin stresses the importance of the wider Christian community.[93] Even when he omits this specifically, he suggests it through the act of writing, itself, of course. More generally, Lee Palmer Wandel suggests that for Calvin 'human communities helped individual human beings work against their nature, fight that inner propensity to sin, in order to be godly'.[94] Into a more specific context which evokes isolation and despair Calvin wishes to instil a sense of communal empathy, support and prayer. He does this in several ways. He assures the prisoners that the Church has compassion on them and that they show this concretely by praying for them and supporting them, for example, in the way that John Liner has been doing.[95] Calvin is careful to suggest, however, that the relationship is two-way. The prisoners, in their stand for the truth, bless the Church: they edify the community of faith. This emphasis on the community to which the prisoners belong identifies them with something outside of their narrow and frightening situation as well as encouraging them to see that they are actually standing for something much bigger than their own personal faith—that is, the faith of the Reformed community. This gives them a sense of purpose and of their own worth.

Witnesses of God's truth

Third, Calvin underlines the prisoners' role as witnesses of God's truth and stresses that they are to view themselves as martyrs and their situation as mar-

---

[93] Church community was vital to the reformer's understanding of spiritual life, itself. As Gwyn Walters, *The Sovereign Spirit. The Doctrine of the Holy Spirit in the Writings of John Calvin* (Edinburgh: Rutherford House, 2009), 146, states, 'Calvin is the avowed enemy of spiritual isolationism and a champion of the social aspect of Christian life.' 'The church, for Calvin,' he says, 'is not merely an external organisation but a society, an "organism" of living beings, of men made spiritually alive by the Holy Spirit. These, being in vital communion with their living head, will also be in living communion with one another' (148). He cites *Inst* 4.1.22, 4.1.20. See, also, Roger Haight, 'Calvin's Contribution to a Common Ecclesial Spirituality' in Henk van den Belt (ed.), *Restoration through Redemption: John Calvin Revisited* (Leiden: Brill, 2013), 159-70.

[94] Wandel, *The Reformation*, 121.

[95] This emphasis on the community is emphasized by Calvin in his interpretation of Hebrews 13.3, 'Remember them who are in bonds.' He states,

> There is nothing that can give us a deeper feeling of compassion than to put ourselves in the place of those who are afflicted. [At which point the reformer dismisses other interpretations of the phrase 'in the body' (e.g., 'in their shoes' and the like), and gives his opinion.] I take this as referring to the body of the Church, with this meaning, "Since you are members of the same body, you ought to have a common feeling for one another's troubles, so that you are not divided amongst yourselves (*Comm. Heb.* 13.3).

tyrdom.[96] By doing this Calvin establishes an even greater sense of value or worth to their present situation. They are martyrs, Calvin says, those who maintain God's quarrel, divinely chosen and called, employed by God, agents or witnesses 'whom he appoints for the defence of his Gospel'[97] and, further, those who are identified with Jesus Christ in his suffering and therefore in the victory of his resurrection. These powerful images connect the troubled prisoners with the Church's esteemed martyrs of the past but, more importantly, with Jesus, himself, in his sacrifice for others in the mission of God. Their humble status allows them to re-evaluate their situation against the backdrop of eternal truth and their relationship with God. The image of being God's martyrs, itself, 'pulls [them] into its field of reality, which is also a field of energy,'[98] of obedience, perseverance, prayerfulness and hope.[99]

In the *Institutes* (1559), Calvin speaks of martyrs in the context of our acceptance of the credibility of Scripture. It is worth quoting fully here:

> Now with what assurance ought we to enlist under that doctrine which we see confirmed and attested by the blood of so many holy men! They, having once received it, did not hesitate, courageously and intrepidly, and even with great eagerness, to suffer death for it. Should we not accept with sure and unshaken conviction what has been handed on to us with such a pledge? It is no moderate approbation of Scripture that it has been sealed by the blood of so many witnesses, especially when we reflect that they died to render testimony to the faith; not with fanatic excess (as erring spirits are sometimes accustomed to do), but with a firm and constant, yet sober, zeal toward God.[100]

---

[96] This is evident, as well, in a letter the reformer writes to an Italian prisoner, Godfrey Varaglia – Calvin, *Letters* 4.427-28 – in which Calvin speaks of Varaglia's 'confession of the faith before a crooked and perverse generation' and his 'testimony to the gospel'. 'Remember, then,' he continues, 'that you are produced as a witness by that same Master who thought you worthy of so high an honour, that what you formerly taught with your lips you may, if need be, seal with your blood' (428).

[97] Calvin, *Letters*, 2.359. Gregory, *Salvation at Stake*, 137, states that martyrs deaths testified to the restoration of the gospel. See, also, 315.

[98] Eugene H. Peterson, *Under the Unpredictable Plant. An Exploration in Vocational Holiness* (Grand Rapids: Eerdmans, 1992), 6, usefully employs this telling phrase: 'Willpower is a notoriously sputter engine on which to rely for internal energy, but a right image silently and inexorably pulls us into its field of reality, which is also a field of energy.'

[99] See, generally, Bonnie Pattison, *Poverty in the Theology of John Calvin* (Eugene: Wipf and Stock, 2006), 189-223; specifically, 194-203.

[100] *Inst.* 1.8.13; OS 3.81. This comes in a section in which Calvin lists reasons why 'the dignity and majesty of Scripture' are 'affirmed in godly hearts,' in which he seeks to establish the credibility of Scripture (see *Inst*. 1.8.1-13; OS 3.72-81). However, and importantly, Calvin concludes that 'Scripture will ultimately suffice for a saving knowledge of God only when its certainty is founded upon the inward persuasion of the Holy Spirit' (*Inst*. 1.8.13; OS 3.81).

Martyrs confirm and attest scriptural doctrine to be true, according to Calvin. They died, he says, 'with a firm and constant, yet sober, zeal toward God'. The reformer's reassurance to these contemporary martyrs, through letters, is to encourage them to live and to die 'with a firm and constant . . . zeal toward God'. We have seen that Calvin does not enlist them as martyrs to glorify them in any way; nor to make them fanatical for Reformed doctrine, but, rather, he enlists the prisoners as martyrs to suggest to *them* (not to others) that they stand for truth, divine truth, and for the good and edification of the Church. They endure suffering and hardship, not for their own sakes, but for the sake of the gospel and the Church. They confirm the certainty of what that Church believes, and they encourage believers to fight for the gospel of Christ and the cause of God. Notice how Calvin puts it in what follows,

> Was it unprofitable for them to glorify God through their death? to attest his truth by their blood? to bear witness by their contempt of the present life that they are seeking a better life? by their constancy, to strengthen the faith of the church but to break the stubbornness of its enemies? . . . But the church in general receives benefit great enough, when by their triumphs it is kindled with a zeal to fight.[101]

Again, in his work, *Concerning Scandals*, he writes similarly,

> This generation of ours has seen a goodly number of martyrs going to their deaths eagerly and fearlessly. And this glory was not restricted to men, but God has let us see women possess a strength that was more than manly. . . . Will that sacred blood, the separate drops of which are so many seals to believing hearts, vanish away as valueless and ineffective? Even if it is worthless to those people [who have followed evil ways], yet it will not be inglorious to God.[102]

Through their suffering, martyrs, showing patience, fortitude, dignity, and, above all, faith, manifest the victory that is in Jesus Christ. They suffer as Christ's witnesses on account of righteousness.[103] They demonstrate the eschatological nature of the kingdom—in weakness is strength, in apparent defeat is actual and unsurpassed triumph. Calvin, the pastor, assures them, ultimately, of the fatherly love and providence of God. This, he knew, was the paramount encouragement for those facing death for Christ's sake,[104] as it is today.

Earlier in *Concerning Scandals* the reformer centres Jesus Christ in the thinking of those who would rather flee persecution and present difficulties than to go through them to glory and triumph. His last remark here is a good one to close with for it speaks volumes in relation to those prisoners, those mar-

---

[101] *Inst.* 3.5.3; OS 4.135-36.
[102] *Concerning Scandals*, 78; OS 2.213.
[103] See Calvin, *Sermons on the Beatitudes* (translated by Robert White; Edinburgh: Banner of Truth, 2006), 61.
[104] Jennifer Campbell makes the important point that Calvinist martyrs were also killed in war – a topic we have not had space to consider—Jennifer Campbell, *The Way of Prophetic Leadership. Retrieving Word and Spirit in Vision Today* (Milton Keynes: Paternoster, 2015), 134.

tyrs, to whom Calvin has been writing. Calvin speaks critically to those who face persecution but would rather flee, saying, 'To you persecution is so grievous that you are retreating from Christ.' He asks them, 'Why?' Then he speaks with some rhetorical force: 'You have no idea how valuable Christ is.'[105]

---

[105] *Concerning Scandals*, 28 (OS 2.179).

CONCLUSION

'Let us then carefully consider to what end . . . the gospel is preached'[1]

In his remarkable book on Christian vocation, *Under the Unpredictable Plant*, Eugene Peterson makes this perceptive comment about those from Third World countries observing the North American Church—we might substitute 'the Western Church':

> They appreciate the size and prosperity of our churches, the energy and the technology, but they wonder at the conspicuous absence of the cross, the phobic avoidance of suffering, the puzzling indifference to community and relationships of intimacy.[2]

I question what believers in the sixteenth century would say, observing our churches today. I would imagine that their reflection would be much the same as that of the Third World, for during the Reformation, as we have seen through reading John Calvin's letters, there was manifestly a conspicuous presence of the cross, a spiritual acceptance of suffering, a recognition of the importance of community as well as relationships of genuine and lasting intimacy. Can we learn anything from Calvin's letters? And, if so, what can we learn?

To close, then, we turn to remind ourselves very briefly of some important themes in the reformer's correspondence.

Important themes

The significance of God

Central to Calvin's view of God is that we can know what he is like, but not what he is in himself. That is, we simply cannot discover what God is (*quid Deus sit*), only of what sort God is (*qualis Deus sit*) and how he relates to us and that only in so far as he has revealed himself in scripture and, of course, primarily in Jesus Christ. For Calvin, we are left doing business with this God (*negotium cum Deo*). Matthew Boulton speaks of this knowledge of God, in the important context of *pietas*, with the following words: 'knowledge . . . does not refer to a speculative, abstract, or merely mental affair, but rather to a concrete,

---

[1] John Calvin, *Sermons on the Beatitudes* (translated by Robert White; Edinburgh: Banner of Truth, 2006), 62: CO 46.809.
[2] Eugene H. Peterson, *Under the Unpredictable Plant. An Exploration in Vocational Holiness* (Grand Rapids: Eerdmans, 1992), 37.

relational, affective, and experiential one, what we might call a *knowledge of* as opposed to merely a *knowledge about*.[3]

We have seen time and again that Calvin prioritises God in his letters—as he does in the *Institutes*, his commentaries and elsewhere, of course. In response to Cardinal Sadoleto's letter to the Genevans, Calvin insists that the believer's first consideration is not their own salvation and eternal wellbeing. Their first consideration is always and only the glory of God. Even when believers are imprisoned and waiting for execution, their first consideration is to be the glory of God. In grief and loss, their first consideration is to be God. In marriage, too, and in their ministerial calling. This is an immensely important principle by which the reformer seeks to live and with which he encourages others in every circumstance. As we have observed above, this appears to be the backbone or foundation of what he writes to others. He has sympathy, even empathy, for those in trials and in loss, but what he desires for them is that they live—in grief, in persecution, in suffering, and in hope—to the glory of the God who has saved them.

Having said that, we noticed, too, that the God that Calvin presents is one with whom his recipients relate in a very particular way. He is, first and foremost, their Father—one who cares, loves, calls and sustains them through it all. He is one who, in Jesus Christ, has saved them, forgiving their sins and making them righteous. The reformer presents God to others as one who can be trusted even in the midst of tremendous difficulties, one who is faithful, patient, present and gracious. He is also the God who calls people to ministry and to marriage, drawing out from them their obedience and perseverance.

The significance of Jesus Christ

The significance of Jesus Christ for the reformer cannot be exaggerated. Calvin displays and encourages what Brian Gerrish calls an 'undivided attention to the Christ who is presented in the Word of the gospel' (*intuitus Christus*).[4] We noted that when Calvin considers his call to ministry in the church in Geneva, as difficult as it appeared, he considers Christ who has called him. It is his church. They are his people. Calvin is ultimately Christ's pastor. In his letter to Francis I, introducing the *Institutes*, the reformer is adamant that the persecuted church in France is Christ's and that he identifies with those being harassed and persecuted. He it is who will sustain the church against all the odds. In Calvin's response to Cardinal Sadoleto we found that, like the Cardinal, he centres Jesus Christ in the salvation of believers; but unlike the Cardinal, perhaps, he sees

---

[3] Matthew Myer Boulton, *Life in God. John Calvin, Practical Formation, and the Future of Protestant Theology* (Grand Rapids: Eerdmans, 2011), 47, emphasis original. In this context, Boulton uses words like trust, vigilance, learning, remembering, filial gratitude, love, reverence and willingness to serve – the 'restorative way of life' (65, 67, see 95).

[4] See Brian A. Gerrish, 'Sovereign Grace. Is Reformed Theology Obsolete?' *Interpretation* 57 (2003), 57.

Christ as absolutely sufficient for our salvation, in him we have *everything* we need.[5] In the situation of those grieving loved ones Jesus Christ comes alongside, identifying with those in mourning, sustaining them through their loss. To those imprisoned waiting execution Calvin presents Christ as the one who supports them in their misery and fear. Again, he identifies with them through their trial. Throughout his letters, then, we find that Calvin is truly Christ-centred—his understandings of different situations as well as his exhortations to his recipients originate in what he thinks of Jesus Christ.

It is fascinating that Calvin exhorts his recipients so often to *experience* the sustaining presence of God and of Jesus Christ through the Spirit—something we may not have expected. In the awful experiences of persecution, grief and imprisonment, in which those involved would feel particularly distraught, isolated and alone, Calvin prays for them the experience of the presence of God. He knows that nothing less than the Holy Spirit can sustain believers at such cruel times. We might add here the adamant conviction that Calvin had about his own call to ministry in Geneva, a conviction that arose from the impulse of the Holy Spirit as much as a dogged sense of duty, perhaps.

Faith amidst suffering

The sixteenth century was a period in which people knew only too well the fragility of life. Andrew Pettegree says that 'our sixteenth century forbears always had a greatly enhanced sense of the fragility of the human condition'.[6] The church during this time suffered from war, plague, imprisonment and persecution as well as the difficulties of accidents, domestic violence and the rest. It was an age in which people suffered. In this context, Bonnie Pattison states that for John Calvin 'Trials provide the necessary conditions under which God's grace marks the Church as true through its perpetuity'[7] A little later she says, 'Calling this a mark in his commentaries demonstrates the central role that faithfulness in suffering has in Calvin's ecclesiology.'[8]

We have already noted many times the importance of faith. This came to the fore in the reformer's response to Sadoleto. The latter assumed wrongly that the reformers meant by faith an intellectual assent to doctrine (*credulitas*), whereas they meant *fiducia* which emphasises 'a daring confidence in God, a trust in promises that could not be verified but that rested on the full faith and credit of a God who would not lie'.[9] Faith, then, is central to the believer's experience of

---

[5] Elsewhere, Calvin says the following: '[W]hatever we need and whatever we lack is in God, and in our Lord Jesus Christ'—*Inst* 3.20.1.

[6] Andrew Pettegree, *Reformation and the Culture of Persuasion* (Cambridge: Cambridge University Press, 2005), 212.

[7] Bonnie Pattison, *Poverty in the Theology of John Calvin* (Eugene: Wipf and Stock, 2006), 243.

[8] Pattison, *Poverty*, 244.

[9] James A. Nestingen, 'Challenges and Responses in the Reformation,' *Interpretation* 46.3 (1992), 267. Note, again, the centrality and significance of God in this definition.

God. According to Calvin, 'faith has to do with being deeply, existentially persuaded'.[10] As Lester de Koster states, 'Such faith is discovery, not construct, received, not made.'[11] It is faith that maintains a Christian vocation as much as it sustains believers in dire circumstances like persecution and grief. It is that belief that, despite appearances, we can take hold of the divine promises and believe them. So, in the face of death, for instance, Calvin exhorts the imprisoned students to faith greater than the circumstance they face. In bereavement, people are encouraged to lay hold of Christ in faith, knowing God's will is to sustain them in trials.

Persistent faith focuses on Jesus Christ without denial. That faith, says the reformer, engenders love for the brethren, hope in trials, perseverance through difficulties, and a strong assurance that all God does is for the good of those he loves. Faith enables us to continue, to see things as they are in Christ—not necessarily how they appear to our senses and in our lived-out experience—faith helps us to trust.

The community, the Church

We have often noticed through our reading of Calvin's letters the importance of community for Calvin, and by community he invariably means the true church of Jesus Christ, the Reformed Church, in Geneva, in France and throughout much of Europe.[12] It was the church in France to which he was particularly drawn, though. 'Calvin's ecclesiology was fashioned with primary reference to a church in exile—a church which sought to be an agent of cultural transformation even in the midst of great hostility and opposition.'[13]

The Christian faith is not, for Calvin, an individual faith but a communal one. Calvin had, what Philip Butin calls, 'a vital, organic concept of the church and its communal existence'.[14] In the church we are given birth, nurtured, fed and sustained. The reformer's letter to Francis I in support of the church in France is evidence of the significance of the church for Calvin. There he seeks to persuade the king to turn the tide against the believers in his country. Cal-

---

[10] Boulton, *Life in God*, 133. He cites *Inst* 3.2.8, 3.2.14, 3.2.15, 3.2.26.

[11] Lester de Koster, *Light for the City. Calvin's Preaching, Source of Life and Liberty* (Grand Rapids: Eerdmans, 2004), 108.

[12] Boulton, *Life in God*, 122: 'The true church, according to Calvin, is graciously granted not only faith *in* Christ, but also participation in the faith *of* Christ' (emphasis original).

[13] Philp W. Butin, 'Reformed Ecclesiology and Trinitarian Grace According to Calvin,' *Studies in Reformed Theology and History* 2.1 (1994), 3. He cites Robert M. Kingdon's two books, *Geneva and the Coming Wars of Religion in France (1553-1563)* (Geneva: Librarie Droz, 1956) and *Geneva and the Consolidation of the French Protestant Movement (1564-1572)* (Geneva: Librarie Droz, 1967).

[14] Butin, 'Reformed Ecclesiology, 16. Butin speaks of Calvin's distinctive emphasis on visibility. He says that 'God's people are called to embody visibly that grace in their corporate interrelationships and their common life' 13, 29, respectively. See, also, 18.

vin's strong sense of vocation, too, evidences his heightened appreciation of community—a community in which Christ dwells by his Spirit. The argument with Sadoleto circles around different thinking on the church, but Calvin defines it in terms of the Word and the Spirit in tandem, in which Christ and the gospel are preached in truth. To those suffering grief and those facing martyrdom he offers the support of their community, the church, as they face their torment. John Linder is seen as exemplary. Through his individual ministry to and support of those facing death the whole church identifies and supports their friends.

The importance of vocation

We have been reminded that vocation is important to John Calvin. We noted that by vocation (*vocatio*) the reformer means duty, being bound by the divine purpose, divine calling. To be called by God into salvation in Christ is then to be called into life's occupation—in marriage and / or in ministry. We noted Calvin's insistence, against the odds, that he retained his call to the ministry in the church of Geneva even when expelled from that place. His strong sense of call allowed him to hope for his return, albeit with some trepidation. His strong sense of call also enabled him to reply to Cardinal Sadoleto when he felt his church in Geneva was threatened by an aggressive Catholicism.

The importance of ministerial vocation is clear in Calvin's letter-writing.[15] We have noticed that it is related to the task in hand. The following important words of Calvin are symptomatic of this relationship.

> Every time a minister is inducted, we must remember to what end those called to the ministry labour among us, and how we may benefit from their labours. This is the sum and substance of it: while we were yet enemies of God he called to us and early found us, not waiting for us to seek him out; seeing us lost, in a state of perdition, he sought us out and called us to himself. This he did by forgiving all our sins, so that in turn we might learn to forgive our neighbours' sins. He desires to treat us with pity, so that we might treat others with pity.
>
> Let us then carefully consider to what end and for what purpose the gospel is preached, and the blessings God offers us in its teaching. The gospel is set before us in his name.[16]

---

[15] See Roger Haight, 'John Calvin and Ignatius Loyola on an Ecclesial Spirituality of Social Engagement' in Gerard Mannion and Eduardus Van der Borght (eds), *John Calvin's Ecclesiology. Ecumenical Perspectives* (London: T&T Clark, 2011), 31-49, 34-35.

[16] Calvin, *Sermons on the Beatitudes*, 62: CO 46.808-809. See, also, Calvin's letter to Wolfgang Musculus, Oct 22, 1549; CO 13.433; *Comm. Isa.* 53.6; CO 37.259. Also, Robert Kingdon, 'The Episcopal function in Protestant churches in the sixteenth and seventeenth centuries' in Bernard Vogler (ed.), *Miscellanea Historiae ecclesiasticae VIII.* (Brussels: Nauwelaerts, 1987), 207-20. See also, Julie Canlis, *Calvin's Ladder. A Spiritual Theology of Ascent and Ascension* (Grand Rapids: Eerdmans, 2010), 92;

His letters about his own calling to Geneva and his response to Sadoleto demonstrate this central idea in Calvin's ecclesiology. Ministers are called to preach the gospel precisely because through the gospel men and women are saved, their sins are forgiven. The minister as 'an ambassador bearing Light and Power not his own,'[17] brings salvation to a lost people. The rhetorical vigour and the robustness of Calvin's response to the Cardinal is evidence of what the reformer felt were the stakes involved. To allow the Genevans to leave the truth of the gospel, to return to a faithless church, would mean to endanger their eternal wellbeing and that Calvin was not going to do.

On another level entirely, we noted Calvin's insistence that he defines his marriage in terms of calling to ministry. He prioritises his ecclesial vocation above his familial one in order to fulfil his call to the Church. In this context, we noted his bifocal lens, as it were, through which he allowed for a public vocation to ministry and a private vocation to marriage. Idelette, then, becomes involved in his public vocation, ministering to the church of Christ, as well as being part of his private, domestic vocation, of course. As we observed, at the time of her death, his commendation of her to his friends is to be read in this way: she was never a hindrance to the public ministry. In a similar vein, those being persecuted as well as those awaiting trial and execution are called to be martyrs of Christ—a vocation they should not shrink away from, however difficult the road.

The significance of the cross

The cross and our personal crosses pervade and underlie the letters of Calvin. At times he speaks of Geneva, or at least his ministry there, as a cross to bear—sometimes as a cross too much. To Cardinal Sadoleto he stresses the essential importance of the cross of Jesus in our salvation; for example, in the following words:

> ... since, by His obedience, He has wiped off our transgressions; by His sacrifice, appeased the divine anger; by His blood, washed away our sins; by His cross, borne our curse; and by His death, made satisfaction for us. We maintain that in this way man is reconciled in Christ to God the Father, by no merit of his own, by no value of works, but by gratuitous mercy.[18]

Those preaching the gospel must uphold the centrality of Christ and of his cross. This, applied, leads to genuine piety.

We have also noted that Calvin echoes Martin Luther's theology of the cross (*theologia crucis*) in which he sees the weakness of the Church to be part and parcel of its calling because only in that state and its dependency on God can it

---

Rose M. Beal, 'Priest, Prophet and King: Jesus Christ, the Church and the Christian Person,' in Mannion and Van der Borght (eds), *John Calvin's Ecclesiology*, 95.

[17] de Koster, *Light for the City*, 38.

[18] Calvin's reply to Sadoleto from *A Reformation Debate. Sadoleto's Letter to the Genevans and Calvin's Reply* (edited by John C. Olin; New York: Fordham University Press, 2000), 60-61.

know the grace and power of God. The church is 'weak,' he says, 'to be sustained by him'.[19] To those suffering from grief, he sets before them the cross and grace of Christ which offer hope, comfort and eternal life. To those believers awaiting martyrdom, Calvin reflects that the Son of God will be glorified 'by our shame'.[20]

Intimate relationships

In his relationship with his colleagues, Peter Viret, Martin Bucer and William Farel, Calvin reflects an intimacy that somehow demonstrates the love of God in Christ and the fellowship of the gospel, to which they were called. The reformer's dependence on the two older men, Bucer and Farel, as mentors for him in his early ministry and beyond is exemplary. This relationship is again reflected in his letters, particularly to Peter Viret and William Farel, on the death of his wife, Idelette, in which he shows a vulnerability that demonstrates a closeness, together with a genuine love between the men. Calvin's ability openly to censure Farel about his proposed marriage to a much younger woman follows his earlier determined exhortations to have his friend at his own marriage ceremony. The length of friendships, the number of letters between these reformers and the obvious closeness signifies what for them was the nature of the true church.

We have discovered in John Calvin a correspondent who demonstrates his passion for the gospel, his love of God and of Jesus Christ, his desire for the church's wellbeing and a pastoral heart. He shows us his weakness and, at times, his failings, too, of course. He reveals vulnerability, faith, confidence and hope in equal measure. He shows his sympathy for those who suffer, his empathy, in fact. He shows determination and a persistent commitment to the church and to the gospel. He is God-centred, Christ-centred and pastoral in his correspondence. Perhaps we might delineate these aspects again in his more polemical writings and in the *Institutes* themselves and come to a trinitarian, pastoral image of the reformer.

---

[19] *Inst.*, prefatory letter, 13.
[20] Letter to the prisoners in Lyon, May 1553; Calvin, *Letters*, 2.407.

APPENDIX

'The gospel is set before us in his name.'[1]
A final comment

Since this is my final academic work on Reformation theology I thought it appropriate to offer readers a chance to resource their own research with the details of my previous monographs and edited volumes on aspects of theology and practice in the sixteenth century evangelical church of Martin Luther and John Calvin. My own doctoral research was on the marriage theology of Luther and Calvin against the backdrop of feminist readings of their theology. From that point onwards my interest and subsequent focus has been on their application of the biblical text to the life-experience of the believer, not so much on the polemical side of the Reformation, although that cannot be avoided or sidestepped so easily, of course.

I have discovered, as others more able than me, that the reformers were, in their own way, masters of exegesis, bound by the Word, lovers of Jesus Christ and of God through him, and earnest contenders for the truth as they saw it. Their search for a way to honour God in and through their lives is humbling to us today. They sought the God of the Scriptures both in those Scriptures and in their experience, too. Jesus Christ was all in all to them: in possessing him by faith we have everything. In a turbulent and violent period of history the reformers were certainly not beyond serious mistakes and weakness, but their resolute confidence in a sovereign and gracious God remains exemplary for the church today. A brief list of works follows.

My monographs include *Reformation Letters. A Fresh Reading of John Calvin's Correspondence* (2016), *Luther and Calvin on Grief and Lament. Life-experience and Biblical Text* (2013), *Martin Luther's Interpretation of the Royal Psalms. The Spiritual Kingdom in a Pastoral Context* (2009), *Calvin's Preaching on the Prophet Micah: The 1550-51 Sermons in Geneva* (2006), *Reformation Marriage. The husband and wife relationship in Luther and Calvin* (2005; republished in 2011) and *Luther and Calvin on Old Testament Narratives: Reformation Thought and Narrative Text* (2004).

---

[1] John Calvin, *Sermons on the Beatitudes* (translated by Robert White; Edinburgh: Banner of Truth, 2006), 62: CO 46.809.

Conclusion

Several edited works include *Reformation Faith. Exegesis and Theology in the Protestant Reformations* (2014), *Aspects of Reforming. Theology and Practice in Sixteenth Century Europe* (2013), *Since we are Justified by Faith. Justification in Protestant Reformation Theologies* (2012).

And, amongst my articles the following have not been reprinted in other works: 'Jude as Pastor: an aspect of Calvin's reading,' *South African Baptist Journal of Theology* 17 (2008), 111–116; '2 Samuel 11–12. Bathsheba: readings then and now,' *South African Baptist Journal of Theology* 15 (2006), 43–47; 'Difficult cases demand careful judgements.' A review article on J. Thompson's *Writing the Wrongs. Women of the Old Testament among Biblical Commentators from Philo through the Reformation* (Oxford: OUP, 2001), *Colloquium* 35:2 (2003), 149–160.

Finally, a more devotional work, for the 500th anniversary of the Reformation: *Praying the Bible with Luther* (2017)

BIBLIOGRAPHY

Primary works and translations

Calvin, John, *A clear explanation of sound doctrine concerning the true partaking of the flesh and blood of Christ in the Holy Supper* (1561) in J.K.S. Reid (ed.), *Calvin: Theological Treatises* (Philadelphia: Westminster, 1954), 257-324.

—. *A Reformation Debate. Sadoleto's Letter to the Genevans and Calvin's Reply* (edited by John C. Olin; New York: Fordham University Press, 2000).

—. *Calvin's Sermons upon Genesis taken by a swifte writer as he preached them* (Denis Raguenier, 1559 – MS.Bod.740: the Bodleian Library, Oxford).

—. *Concerning Scandals* (1550) (translated by John W. Fraser; Edinburgh: Saint Andrew Press, 1978).

—. *Ioannis Calvini Opera quae supersunt omnia* [CO] (Corpus Reformatorum: Brunswick: Schwetschke et Filium, 1863–1900).

—. *Johannis Calvini, Opera Selecta*, volumes 1–5 [OS] (edited by P. Barth and W. Niesel; Munich, 1952–1970).

—. *Letters*, 4 volumes (edited by J. Bonnet; translated by Marcus R. Gilchrist; Philadelphia: Presbyterian Board, 1858).

—. *Lettres françaises*, 2 volumes (edited by J. Bonnet; Paris: Meyrueis, 1854).

—. *Sermons on Isaiah's Prophecy of the Death and Passion of Christ* (translated and edited by T.H.L. Parker; London: James Clarke, 1956).

—. *Sermons on 2 Samuel, chapters 1-13* (translated by Douglas Kelly; Edinburgh: Banner of Truth, 1992).

—. *Sermons on the Beatitudes* (translated by Robert White; Edinburgh: Banner of Truth, 2006).

—. *Sermons on the Book of Micah* (edited and translated by Benjamin W. Farley; Phillipsburg: P&R, 2003).

—. *Sermons on the Ten Commandments* (edited and translated by Benjamin W. Farley; Grand Rapids: Baker, 1980).

—. *The Institutes of the Christian Religion* (edited by J.T. McNeill; translated by F.L. Battles; Philadelphia: Westminster, 1960).

Luther, Martin, *Luther: Letters of Spiritual Counsel* (edited by Theodore G. Tappert; Vancouver: Regent College, 2003).

Meyer, Sebastian, *In apocalypsim Johannis Apostoli* (Zürich: Froschouer, 1559).

Noll, Mark A. (ed.), *Confessions and Catechisms of the Reformation* (Leicester: APOLLOS, 1991).

Secondary works

Alexander, J.H., *Ladies of the Reformation* (Harpenden: Gospel Standard Strict Baptist Trust, 1978).

Armstrong, Brian, '*Duplex cognitio Dei*, or the Problem and Relation of Structure, Form and Purpose in Calvin's Theology' in E.A. McKee / B. Armstrong (eds), *Probing the Reformed Tradition* (Louisville: Westminster / John Knox, 1989).

Augustijn, Cornelis, 'Calvin in Strasbourg' in Wilhelm H. Neuser (ed.), *Calvinus Sacrae Scripturae Professor. Calvin as Confessor of Holy Scripture* (Grand Rapids: Eerdmans, 1994), 166-177.

Badcock, G.D., *The Way of Life: A Theology of Christian Vocation* (Grand Rapids: Eerdmans, 1998).

Bainton, Roland, *Hunted Heretic. The Life and Death of Michael Servetus, 1511-1553* (Boston: Beacon, 1953).

—. *The Age of the Reformation* (New York: Van Nostrand, 1956).

—. *Women of the Reformation* (Boston: Beacon, 1974).

Baldwin, C.M., 'Marriage in Calvin's Sermons' in R.V. Schnucker (ed.), *Calviniana: Ideas and Influence of Jean Calvin* (Kirksville: Sixteenth Century Publishers, 1988), 121-129.

Balserak, Jon, *John Calvin as Sixteenth-Century Prophet* (Oxford: Oxford University Press, 2014).

Barker, William S., 'The Historical Context of the *Institutes* as a Work in Theology' in David W. Hall and Peter A. Lillback (eds), *A Theological Guide to Calvin's Institutes. Essays and Analysis* (Phillipsburg: P&R, 2008), 1-15.

Barton, F.W., *Calvin and the Duchess* (Louisville: Westminster / John Knox, 1989).

Battles, F.L., '*Calculus Fidei*: Some Ruminations on the Structure of the Theology of John Calvin' in R. Benedetto (ed.), *Interpreting John Calvin* (Grand Rapids: Baker, 1996), 139-178.

—. 'The First Edition of the *Institutes of the Christian Religion* (1536)' in R. Benedetto (ed.), *Interpreting John Calvin* (Grand Rapids: Baker, 1996), 91-116.

—. 'True Piety According to Calvin' in R. Benedetto (ed.), *Interpreting John Calvin* (Grand Rapids: Baker, 1996), 289-306.

Beal, Rose M., 'Priest, Prophet and King: Jesus Christ, the Church and the Christian Person,' in Gerard Mannion and Eduardus Van der Borght (eds), *John Calvin's Ecclesiology. Ecumenical Perspectives* (London: T&T Clark, 2011), 90-106.

Beeke, Joel R., 'Calvin on Piety' in D.K. McKim (ed.), *The Cambridge Companion to John Calvin* (Cambridge: Cambridge University Press, 2004), 125-152.

—. 'Making Sense of Calvin's Paradoxes on Assurance of Faith' in D. Foxgrover (ed.), *Calvin Studies Society Papers, 1995, 1997* (Grand Rapids: Calvin Study Society, 1998), 13–30.

Benedict, Philip, 'Settlements: France' in Thomas A. Brady, Heiko A. Oberman and James D. Tracy (eds), *Handbook of European History 1400-1600. 'Late Middle Ages, Renaissance and Reformation'* (Leiden: Brill, 1995), 385-415.

Biéler, André, *La Pensée Economique et Sociale de Calvin* (Geneva: Librairie de l'Université, 1959).

—. *L'homme et la femme dans la morale calviniste: la doctrine réformée sur l'amour, le marriage, le celibate, le divorce, l'adultère et la prostitution, considerée dans son cadre historique* (Geneva: Labor et Fides, 1961).

—. *L'Humanisme Social de Calvin* (Geneva: Labor et Fides, 1961).

—. 'Man and Woman in Calvin's Ethic,' *Reformed and Presbyterian World* 27 (1963), 357-363 (also published as 'Mann und Frau in Calvins Ethik,' *Der deutsche Hugenott* 28 (1964), 69-74).

Billman, K.D. and D.L. Migliore, *Rachel's Cry: Prayer of Lament and Rebirth of Hope* (Cleveland: United Church Press, 1999).

Blaisdell, C.J., 'Calvin's and Loyola's Letters to Women' in R.V. Schnucker (ed.), *Calviniana: Ideas and Influence of Jean Calvin* (Kirksville: Sixteenth Century Journal Publishers, 1988), 235-253.

—. 'Calvin's Letters to Women: The Courting of Ladies in High Places,' *Sixteenth Century Journal* 13 (1982), 67-85.

—. 'The Matrix of Reform: Women in the Lutheran and Calvinist Movements' in R.L. Greaves (ed.), *Triumph over Silence: Women in Protestant History* (Westport: Greenwood, 1985), 13-44.

Bohatec, J., *Calvin und das Recht* (Feudingen: Buchdruck und Verlags-Anstalt, 1934).

Bonivard, F., *Advis et devis de l'ancienne et nouvelle police de Genève* (Geneva: J.G. Fick, 1865).

Boulton, Matthew Myer, *Life in God. John Calvin, Practical Formation, and the Future of Protestant Theology* (Grand Rapids: Eerdmans, 2011).

Bouwsma, William J., 'Calvin and the Dilemma of Hypocrisy' in P. de Klerk (ed.), *Calvin and Christian Ethics* (Grand Rapids: Calvin Studies Society, 1987).

—. *John Calvin. A Sixteenth Century Portrait* (New York: Oxford University Press, 1988).

—. 'The Peculiarity of the Reformation in Geneva' in Steven Ozment (ed.), *Religion and Culture in the Renaissance and Reformation* (16th Century Publications, 1989), 65-76.

Brake, W.P. Te, *Shaping History. Ordinary People in European Politics, 1500–1700* (Berkeley: University of California Press, 1998).

Brown, Delwin, *Boundaries of Our Habitations: Tradition and Theological Construction* (New York: Sate University of New York, 1994).

Butin, Philip W., 'Reformed Ecclesiology and Trinitarian Grace According to Calvin,' *Studies in Reformed Theology and History* 2.1 (1994), 1-52.

—. *Revelation, Redemption and Response. Calvin's Trinitarian Understanding of the Divine-Human Relationship* (Oxford: Oxford University Press, 1995).
Canlis, Julie, 'Beyond Tearing One Another to Pieces. Union with Christ in Reformed Scholarship,' *Journal of Reformed Theology* 8.1 (2014), 79-88.
—. *Calvin's Ladder. A Spiritual Theology of Ascent and Ascension* (Grand Rapids: Eerdmans, 2010).
Carew-Hunt, R.N., *Calvin* (London: Centenary, 1933).
Chadwick, O., *The Early Reformation on the Continent* (Oxford: OUP, 2001).
— *The Reformation* (Harmondsworth: Penguin, 1984).
Chidester, David, *Christianity. A Global History* (London: Penguin, 2000).
Cocke, W.E., 'Luther's View of Marriage and Family,' *Religion in Life* 42 (1973), 103-16.
Collinson, P., 'The Late Medieval Church and its Reformation (1400–1600)' in J. McManners (ed.), *The Oxford History of Christianity* (Oxford: OUP, 1993), 243–76.
Compier, Don H., *John Calvin's Rhetorical Doctrine of Sin* (Lewiston: Edwin Mellen, 2001).
Cottret, Bernard, *Calvin. A Biography* (Grand Rapids: Eerdmans / Edinburgh: T&T Clark, 2000).
Crisp, Oliver D., *Retrieving Doctrine. Explorations in Reformed Theology* (Milton Keynes: Paternoster, 2010).
Crouzet, Denis, *Jean Calvin: Vies parallèles* (Paris: Fayard, 2000).
Crowther, Kathleen M., *Adam and Eve in the Protestant Reformation* (New York: Cambridge University Press, 2010).
Davis, T.J., 'Images of Intolerance: John Calvin in 19th Century History Textbooks,' *Church History* 65 (1996), 234-248.
De Koster, Lester, *Light for the City. Calvin's Preaching, Source of Life and Liberty* (Grand Rapids: Eerdmans, 2004).
Denis, Philippe, 'La Prophétie dans les Églises de la Réforme au xvie siècle,' *Revue d'Histoire ecclésiastique* 72 (1977), 289-316.
Douglass, Jane Dempsey, *Women, Freedom and Calvin* (Philadelphia: Westminster, 1985).
Eßer, H.H., 'Zur Anthropologie Calvins: Menschenwürde-Imago Dei zwischen humanistischen und theologischen Ansatz' in H.-G. Geyer, *et al.*, (eds), *Wenn nicht jetzt, wann dann?* (Neukirchener, 1983), 269-281.
Edgar, William, 'Ethics: The Christian Life and Good Works according to Calvin (3.6-10, 17-19)' in David W. Hall and Peter A. Lillback (eds), *A Theological Guide to Calvin's Institutes. Essays and Analysis* (Phillipsburg: P&R, 2008), 320-346.
Edmondson, Stephen, *Calvin's Christology* (Cambridge: Cambridge University Press, 2004).
—. 'The biblical structure of Calvin's *Institutes*,' *Scottish Journal of Theology* 59.1 (2006), 1-13.
Eire, C.M.N., 'Antisacerdotalism and the Young Calvin' in P.A. Dykema / H.A. Oberman (eds), *Anticlericalism in the Late Medieval and Early Modern Europe* (Leiden: Brill, 1994), 583–603.

Elwood, Christopher, 'Calvin, Beza and the Defense of Marriage in the Sixteenth Century' in David Foxgrover (ed.), *Calvin, Beza and Later Calvinism* (Grand Rapids: Calvin Studies Society, 2006), 11-34.

Farley, M.A., 'Sexual Ethics' in J.B. Nelson and S.P. Longfellow (eds), *Sexuality and the Sacred* (London: Mowbray, 1994).

Ferguson, Sinclair B., 'Calvin the Man: A Heart Aflame' in J.R. Beeke and G.J. Williams (eds), *Calvin. Theologian and Reformer* (Grand Rapids: Reformation Heritage, 2010), 7-24.

Forde, Gerhard O., *On Being a Theologian of the Cross. Reflections on Luther's Heidelberg Disputation, 1518* (Grand Rapids: Eerdmans, 1997).

Friedman, Jerome, *Michael Servetus: A Case Study in Total Heresy* (Geneva: Librairie Droz, 1978).

Fulop, Timothy E., 'The Third Mark of the Church? – Church Discipline in the Reformed and Anabaptist Reformations,' *Journal of Religious History* 19.1 (1995), 26-42.

Gamble, Richard C., 'Calvin's Controversies' in Donald K. McKim (ed.), *The Cambridge Companion to John Calvin* (Cambridge: Cambridge University Press, 2004), 188-203.

Ganoczy, Alexandre, 'Calvin's Life' in Donald K. McKim (ed.), *The Cambridge Companion to John Calvin* (Cambridge: Cambridge University Press, 2004), 3-24.

—. *The Young Calvin* (translated by David Foxgrover and Wade Provo; Edinburgh: T&T Clark, 1987).

Garcia, Mark A., *Life in Christ. Union with Christ and Twofold Grace in Calvin's Theology* (Eugene: Wipf and Stock, 2008).

George, Timothy, *Theology of the Reformers* (Nashville: Broadman, 1988).

Gerrish, Brian A., 'Sovereign Grace. Is Reformed Theology Obsolete?' *Interpretation* 57 (2003), 45-57.

Gilligan, Carol, *In a Different Voice* (Cambridge: Harvard University Press, 1982).

Gleason, Elizabeth G., 'Catholic Reformation, Counter Reformation and Papal Reform in the Sixteenth Century' in T.A. Brady, H.A. Oberman and J.D. Tracy (eds), *Handbook of European History 1400-1600, Late Middle Ages, Renaissance and Reformation*, volume 2, 'Visions, Programs and Outcomes' (Leiden: Brill, 1995), 317-345.

Godfrey, W. Robert, 'The Counsellor to the Afflicted' in Burk Parsons (ed.), *John Calvin. A Heart for Devotion, Doctrine and Doxology* (Lake Mary: Reformation Trust, 2008), 83-93.

Greef, Wulfert de, 'Calvin's Writings' in Donald K. McKim (ed.), *The Cambridge Companion to John Calvin* (Cambridge: Cambridge University Press, 2004), 41-57.

—. *The Writings of John Calvin. An Introductory Guide* (translated by Lyle D. Bierma; Grand Rapids: Baker / Leicester: APOLLOS, 1993).

Gregory, Brad S., *Salvation at Stake. Christian Martyrdom in Early Modern Europe* (Cambridge: Harvard University Press, 1999).

Grimm, H.J., *The Reformation Era 1500-1650* (New York: Macmillan, 1954).

Bibliography

Haight, Roger, 'Calvin's Contribution to a Common Ecclesial Spirituality' in Henk van den Belt (ed.), *Restoration through Redemption: John Calvin Revisited* (Leiden: Brill, 2013), 159-170.

—. 'John Calvin and Ignatius Loyola on an Ecclesial Spirituality of Social Engagement' in Gerard Mannion and Eduardus Van der Borght (eds), *John Calvin's Ecclesiology. Ecumenical Perspectives* (London: T&T Clark, 2011), 31-49.

Hall, B., 'The Reformation City', *Bulletin of the John Rylands Library* (1971/2), 103–48.

Hall, C.A.M., 'With the Spirit's Sword' (unpublished doctoral thesis, Basel University, 1968).

Hall, D.W., 'Calvin's circle of friends: propelling an enduring movement' in Michael Parsons (ed.), *Reformation Faith. Exegesis and Theology in the Protestant Reformations* (Milton Keynes: Paternoster, 2014), 190-204.

—. *The Genevan Reformation and the American Founding* (New York: Lexington, 2003).

Harkness, G., *John Calvin: The Man and his Ethics* (Abingdon, New York, 1981).

Harman, Allan M., 'Speech about the Trinity: with Special Reference to Novatian, Hilary and Calvin,' *Scottish Journal of Theology* 26.4 (1973), 385-400.

Heinze, Rudolph W., *Reform and Conflict. From the Medieval World to the Wars of Religion, AD 1350-1648* (Grand Rapids: Baker, 2005).

Helm, Paul, *John Calvin's Ideas* (Oxford: Oxford University Press, 2004).

Henderson, Henry F., *Calvin in his Letters* (Eugene: Wipf and Stock, 1996).

Hendrix, Scott, *Recultivating the Vineyard. The Reformation Agendas of Christianization* (Louisville: WJKP, 2004).

—. 'Rerooting the Faith: The Reformation as Re-Christianization,' *Church History* 69 (2000), 558-577.

Hesselink, I. John, *Calvin's First Catechism. A Commentary* (Louisville: Westminster John Knox, 1997).

—. 'Calvin's Theology' in Donald K. McKim (ed.), *The Cambridge Companion to John Calvin* (Cambridge: Cambridge University Press, 2004), 74-92.

Hillerbrand, Hans J., *The Reformation. A Narrative History Related by Contemporary Observers and Participants* (Grand Rapids: Baker, 1979).

Hörcsik, Richard, 'John Calvin in Geneva, 1536-38. Some Questions about Calvin's First Stay at Geneva' in Wilhelm H. Neuser (ed.), *Calvinus Sacrae Scripturae Professor: Calvin as Confessor of Holy Scripture* (Grand Rapids: Eerdmans, 1994), 155-165.

Hourticq, D., *Calvin, mon ami* (Geneva: Labor et Fides, 1963)

Hughes, P.E., 'John Calvin: The Man Whom God Subdued' in J.I. Packer (ed.), *How Shall They Hear?* (Stoke-on-Trent: Tentraker, 1960), 5-10.

Hughes, R.A., *Lament, Death, and Destiny* (New York: Peter Lang, 2004).

Jelsma, Auke, *Frontiers of the Reformation. Dissidence and Orthodoxy in Sixteenth Century Europe* (Aldershot: Ashgate, 1998).

Jensen, Peter F., 'Calvin, Charismatics and Miracles,' *Evangelical Quarterly* 51.3 (1979), 131-144.
Jewett, Paul K., *Man as Male and Female* (Grand Rapids: Eerdmans, 1976).
Johnson, Phillip R., 'The Writer for the People of God' in Burk Parsons (ed.), *John Calvin. A Heart for Devotion, Doctrine and Doxology* (Orlando: Reformation Trust, 2008), 95-108.
Johnson, Stephen M., '"The Sinews of the Body of Christ." Calvin's Concept of Church Discipline,' *Westminster Journal of Theology* 59 (1997), 87-100.
Jones, Serene, *Calvin and the Rhetoric of Piety* (Louisville: Westminster John Knox, 1995).
Kagay, D. and L.J.A. Villalon (eds), *Final Argument: The Imprint of Violence on Society in Medieval and Early Modern Europe* (Woodbridge, UK: Boydell, 1998).
Kaplan, Benjamin J., *Divided by Faith. Religious Conflict in the Practice of Toleration in Early Modern Europe* (Cambridge: Harvard University Press, 2009).
—. '"For they will turn away thy sons": the practice and perils of mixed marriage in the Dutch Golden Age' in M.R. Forster and B.J. Kaplin (eds), *Piety and Family in Early Modern Europe. Essays in Honour of Steven Ozment* (Aldershot: Ashgate, 2005), 115-133.
Karant-Nunn, Susan, '"Gedanken, Herz und Sinn": Die Unterdrückung der religiösen Emotionen' in B. Jussen and C. Koslofsky (eds), *Kulturelle Reformation: Sinnreformationen in Umbruch 1400–1600* (Göttingen, Vandenhoeck & Ruprecht, 1999).
—. *The Reformation of Ritual. An Interpretation of Early Modern Germany* (London: Routledge, 1997).
Keck, D., 'Sorrow and Worship in Calvin's Geneva: their place in Family History' in M.R. Forster and B.J. Kaplan (eds), *Piety and Family in Early Modern Europe. Essays in Honour of Steven Ozment* (Aldershot: Ashgate, 2005), 201-218.
Kelly, Douglas, 'The Transmission and Translation of the Collected Letters of John Calvin,' *Scottish Journal of Theology* 30.5 (1977), 429-437.
Kearsley, R., 'Calvin and the Power of the Elder: A Case of the Rogue Hermeneutic' in A.N.S. Lane (ed.), *Interpreting the Bible. Historical and Theological Studies in Honour of David F. Wright* (Leicester: APOLLOS, 1997).
Kim, Yosep, *The Identity and the Life of the Church. John Calvin's Ecclesiology in the Perspective of his Anthropology* (Eugene: Pickwick, 2014).
Kingdon, Robert M., *Adultery and Divorce in Calvin's Geneva* (Cambridge, Mass: Harvard University, 1995).
—. *Geneva and the Coming Wars of Religion in France (1553-1563)* (Geneva: Librarie Droz, 1956).
—. *Geneva and the Consolidation of the French Protestant Movement (1564-1572)* (Geneva: Librarie Droz, 1967).

Bibliography

—. 'International Calvinism' in T.A. Brady, H.A. Oberman and J.D. Tracy (eds), *Handbook of European History 1400–1600. Late Middle Ages, Renaissance and Reformation* (Leiden: Brill, 1995), 229–247.

—. (ed.), *Registers of the Consistory of Geneva in the Time of Calvin*, volume 1 (Grand Rapids: Eerdmans / Meeter Center for Calvin Studies, 1996).

—. 'The Episcopal function in Protestant churches in the sixteenth and seventeenth centuries' in Bernard Vogler (ed.), *Miscellanea Historiae ecclesiasticae VIII. Colloque de Strasbourg, Septembre 1983* (Brussels: Nauwelaerts, 1987), 207-220.

—. 'The First Calvinist Divorce' in R.A. Mentzer (ed.), *Sin and the Calvinists. Morals Control and the Consistory in the Reformed Tradition* (Kirksville: Sixteenth Century Journal, 1994), 1-13.

—. 'Was the Protestant Reformation a Revolution? The Case of Geneva' in idem. (ed.), *Transition and Revolution: Problems and Issues of European Renaissance and Reformation History* (Minneapolis: Burgess, 1974), 53–107.

Klauber, Martin I., 'Servetus, Michael (1511-53)' in Trevor A. Hart (ed.), *The Dictionary of Historical Theology* (Grand Rapids: Eerdmans / Carlisle: Paternoster, 2000), 520-522.

Koenigsberger, H.G. and G.L. Mosse, *Europe in the Sixteenth Century* (London: Longman, 1968).

Kolb, Robert, 'God's Gift of Martyrdom: The Early Reformation Understanding of Dying for the Faith,' *Church History* 64.3 (1995), 399-411.

Kraus, Hans-Joachim, 'The Contemporary Relevance of Calvin's Theology' in D. Willis and M. Welker (eds), *Toward the Future of Reformed Theology* (Grand Rapids: Eerdmans, 1999), 323-338.

Lambert, T., 'Preaching, Praying and Policing the Reform in Sixteenth-Century Geneva' (unpublished doctoral dissertation, University of Wisconsin-Madison, 1998).

Larson, M.J., 'John Calvin and Genevan Presbyterianism', *Westminster Theological Journal* 60 (1998), 43–69.

Lazareth, W.H., *Luther on the Christian Home* (Philadelphia: Muhlenburg, 1960).

Lee, S.-Y., 'Calvin's understanding of Pietas' in W.H. Neuser and B.G. Armstrong (eds), *Calvinus Sincerioris Vindex* (Kirksville: Sixteenth Century Journal Publishers, 1997), 225-240.

Leith, John, 'Calvin's Theological Realism and the Lasting Influence of his Theology' in D. Willis and M. Welker (eds), *Toward the Future of Reformed Theology* (Grand Rapids: Eerdmans, 1999), 339-345.

Lindberg, Carter, *The European Reformations* (Oxford: Blackwell, 1996).

Linder, Robert D., 'Brothers in Christ: Pierre Viret and John Calvin as Soul-Mates and Co-Laborers in the Work of the Reformation' in David Foxgrover (ed.), *Calvin Studies Society Papers 1995, 1997* (Grand Rapids: Calvin Studies Society, 1998), 134-158.

Lowther, Roland J., 'The Holy Spirit, Holy Scripture and the Holy Reader: The Moral Dimension of the Spirit's "Secret Testimony",' *Scottish Bulletin of Evangelical Theology* 32.1 (2014), 51-62.

—. *The Praxis of Living by the Spirit. A Reformed Practical Pneumatology* (unpublished doctoral dissertation: University of Queensland, Brisbane, 2013).

Mannion, Gerard, 'Calvin and the Church: Trajectories for Ecumenical Engagement Today – Volume Introduction' in Gerard Mannion and Eduardus Van der Borght (eds), *John Calvin's Ecclesiology. Ecumenical Perspectives* (London: T&T Clark, 2011), 1-30.

Matheson, Peter, *Argula von Grumbach. A Woman's Voice in the Reformation* (Edinburgh: T&T Clark, 1995).

—. *The Imaginative World of the Reformation* (Edinburgh: T&T Clark, 2000).

McGrath, Alister E., *A Life of John Calvin. A Study in the Shaping of Western Culture* (Oxford: Blackwell, 1990).

—. *In the Beginning* (New York: Anchor, 2002).

—. 'John Calvin and Late Medieval Thought. A Study in Late Medieval Influences upon Calvin's Theological Development,' *Archiv für Reformationsgeschichte* 77 (1986), 58-79.

McIntyre, John, *The Shape of Pneumatology. Studies in the Doctrine of the Holy Spirit* (Edinburgh: T&T Clark, 1997).

McNeill, J.T., *The History and Character of Calvinism* (London: Oxford University Press, 1954).

Millet, Olivier, *Calvin et la dynamique de la parole: Étude de rhétorique réformée* (Geneva: Editions Slatkine, 1992).

—. 'Le theme de la conscience libre chez Calvin' in *La liberté de conscience (xvie-xviie siècles)* (Geneva:Droz, 1991), 21-37.

Moeller, B., *Imperial Cities and the Reformation* (Philadelphia: Fortress, 1972).

—. 'What was Preached in German Towns in the Early Reformation?' in C.S. Dixon (ed.), *The German Reformation* (Oxford: Blackwell, 1999).

Monheit, M.L., 'The ambition for an illustrious name: Humanism, Patronage, and Calvin's Doctrine of the Calling,' *Sixteenth Century Journal* 23 (1992), 267-287.

Monter, William, 'Heresy Executions in Reformation Europe, 1520-1565' in Ole Peter Grell and Robert W. Scribner (eds), *Tolerance and Intolerance in the European Reformation* (Cambridge: Cambridge University Press, 1996), 48-64.

Moon, Byung-Ho, *Christ the Mediator of the Law. Calvin's Christological Understanding of the Law as Rule of Living and Life-Giving* (Milton Keynes: Paternoster, 2006).

Muller, Richard A., *The Unaccommodated Calvin: Studies in the Foundation of a Theological Tradition* (New York: Oxford University Press, 2000).

Mullett, Michael A., *Calvin* (London: Routledge, 1989).

—. *John Calvin* (Abingdon: Routledge, 2011).

Murstein, B.I., *Love, Sex and Marriage Through the Ages* (New York: Springer, 1974).

Bibliography

Naef, H., *Les Origines de la Réforme à Genève* (Geneva: La Société d'Histoire et d'Archéologie de Genève, 1936).

Naphy, William G., 'Baptism, Church Riots and Social Unrest in Calvin's Geneva', *Sixteenth Century Journal* 26 (1995), 87–97.

—. *Calvin and the Consolidation of the Genevan Reformation* (Louisville: John Knox, 2004).

—. 'Calvin's Church in Geneva: Constructed or Gathered? Local or Foreign? French or Swiss?' in Irena Backus and Philip Benedict (eds), *Calvin and His Influence, 1509-2009* (Oxford: Oxford University Press, 2011), 102-118.

—. 'Calvin's Geneva' in Donald K. McKim (ed.), *The Cambridge Companion to John Calvin* (Cambridge: Cambridge University Press, 2004), 25-37.

—. 'Calvin's Letters: Reflections on their Usefulness in Studying Genevan History,' *Archiv für Reformationsgeschichte* 86 (1995).

—. 'Church and State in Calvin's Geneva' in David Foxgrover (ed.), *Calvin and the Church. Calvin Studies Society Papers 2001* (Grand Rapids: Calvin Studies Society, 2002), 13-28.

Needham, N.R., *2000 Years of Christ's Power.* Part 3 'Renaissance and Reformation' (London: Grace Publications Trust, 2004).

Nestingen, James Arne, 'Challenges and Responses in the Reformation,' *Interpretation* 46.3 (1992), 250-260.

Nicolls, D., 'The Theatre of Martyrdom in the French Reformation,' *Past and Present* 121 (1988).

Oberman, Heiko A., 'Calvin and Farel: the Dynamics of Legitimation in Early Calvinism,' *Journal of Early Modern History* 2.1 (1998), 32-60.

—. 'Initia Calvini: The Matrix of Calvin's Reformation' in Wilhelm H. Neuser (ed.), *Calvinus Sacrae Scripturae Professor: Calvin as Confessor of Holy Scripture* (Grand Rapids: Eerdmans, 1994), 113-154.

—. *The Dawn of the Reformation* (Grand Rapids: Eerdmans, 1992).

Old, H.O., *The Reading and Preaching of the Scriptures in the Worship of the Church*: volume 4 (Grand Rapids: Eerdmans, 2002).

Oliphint, K. Scott, 'A Primal and Simple Knowledge (1.1-5)' in David W. Hall and Peter A. Lillback (eds), *A Theological Guide to Calvin's* Institutes. *Essays and Analysis* (Phillipsburg: P&R, 2008), 16-43.

Olsen, Jeannine E., 'The Friends of John Calvin: The Budé Family' in David Foxgrover (ed.), *Calvin Studies Society Papers 1995, 1997* (Grand Rapids: Calvin Studies Society, 1998), 159-168.

Olsen, V.N., *The New Testament Logia on Divorce. A Study of their Interpretation from Erasmus to Milton* (Tübingen: Mohr, 1971).

Oyer, J.S., 'The Reformers Condemn the Anabaptists' in J.D. Roth (ed.), *They Harry the Good People out of the Land* (Goshen: Mennonite Historical Society, 2000), 3-16.

Ozment, Steven, *The Age of Reform 1250-1550. An Intellectual and Religious History of Late Medieval and Reformation Europe* (New Haven: Yale University Press, 1980).

Parker, T.H.L., *Calvin. An Introduction to his Thought* (London: Geoffrey Chapman, 1995).

—. *John Calvin. A Biography* (Philadelphia: Westminster, 1975), 118.
Parsons, Burk, 'The Humility of Calvin's Calvinism' in Burk Parsons (ed.), *John Calvin. A Heart for Devotion, Doctrine and Doxology* (Lake Mary, Fl: Reformation Trust, 2008), 1-17.
Parsons, Michael, '"Let us not . . . call God to account." John Calvin's reading of some difficult deaths' in Michael Parsons (ed.), *Aspects of Reforming. Theology and Practice in Sixteenth Century Europe* (Milton Keynes: Paternoster, 2013), 202-216.
—. *Luther and Calvin on Grief. Life Experience and Biblical Text* (Lewiston: Edwin Mellen, 2013).
—. (ed.), *Reformation Faith. Exegesis and Theology in the Protestant Reformations* (Milton Keynes: Paternoster, 2014).
—. *Reformation Marriage. The Husband and Wife Relationship in the Theology of Luther and Calvin* (Eugene: Wipf and Stock, 2011).
—. 'Review of G. Mannion & E. Van der Bought, *John Calvin's Ecclesiology* (Edinburgh: T&T Clark, 2011)' in *The Baptist Quarterly* 44 (2012), 442-443.
—. (ed.), *Since we are Justified by Faith. Justification in the Theologies of the Protestant Reformation* (Milton Keynes: Paternoster, 2012).
Partee, Charles, *Calvin and Classical Philosophy* (Leiden: Brill, 1977).
—. 'Calvin and Experience,' *Scottish Journal of Theology* 16.2 (1973), 169-181.
Pattison, Bonnie, *Poverty in the Theology of John Calvin* (Eugene: Wipf and Stock, 2006).
—. 'The suffering church in Calvin's *De Scandalis*: an exercise in Luther's *Theologia Crucis*? in Michael Parsons (ed.), *Since we are Justified by Faith. Justification in the Theologies of the Protestant Reformation* (Milton Keynes: Paternoster, 2012), 117-37.
Perrot, A., *Le visage humain de Calvin* (Geneva: Labor et Fides, 1986).
Peterson, Eugene H., *Under the Unpredictable Tree. An Exploration in Vocational Holiness* (Grand Rapids: Eerdmans, 1992).
Pettegree, Andrew, *Reformation and the Culture of Persuasion* (Cambridge: Cambridge University Press, 2005).
—. (ed.), *The Reformation of the Parishes: The Ministry and the Reformation in Town and Country* (Manchester: Manchester University, 1993).
—. 'The spread of Calvin's thought' in Donald K. McKim (ed.), *The Cambridge Companion to John Calvin* (Cambridge: Cambridge University Press, 2004), 207-224.
Pfeiffer, C.W., 'Heinrich Bullinger and Marriage' (unpublished doctoral thesis, St Louis University, 1981).
Piuz, A.-M. and L. Mottu-Weber, *L'économie genevoise de la Réforme à la fin de l'Ancien Régime, xvie-xviiie siècles* (Geneva: Georg, Société d'histoire et d'archéologie de Genève, 1990).
Reinis, A., *Reforming the Art of Dying. The* ars moriendi *in the German Reformation (1519–1528)* (Aldershot: Ashgate, 2007).

Bibliography

Reymond, Robert L., *John Calvin. His Life and Influence* (Geanies House, Fearn: Christian Focus, 2000).

Richardson, Kurt A., 'Calvin on the Trinity' in Sung W. Chung (ed.), *John Calvin and Evangelical Theology. Legacy and Prospect* (Milton Keynes: Paternoster, 2009), 32-42.

Rilliet, J., *Le Vrai Visage de Calvin* (Toulouse: Pensée / Privat, 1982).

Robinson, Marilynne, 'The Polemic Against Calvin: The Origins and Consequences of Historical Reputation' in David Foxgrover (ed.), *Calvin and the Church. Calvin Studies Society Papers 2001* (Grand Rapids: Calvin Studies Society, 2002), 96-122.

Roelker, N.L., 'The Appeal of Calvinism to French Noblewomen in the Sixteenth Century,' *Journal of Interdisciplinary History* 2 (1972), 391-418.

—. 'The Role of Noblewomen in the French Reformation,' *Archiv für Reformationsgeschichte* 63 (1972), 168-195.

Roget, A., *Histoire du Peuple de Genève depuis la Réforme jusqu'a l'escalade* (Nieuwkoop: B. de Graaf, 1976 – original 1870–83).

Ruff, J.R., *Violence in Early Modern Europe 1500–1800* (Cambridge: Cambridge University Press, 2001).

Safley, Thomas M., (ed.), *A Companion to Multiconfessionalism in the Early Modern World* (Leiden: Brill, 2011).

—. *Let No Man Put Asunder* (Kirksville: Sixteenth Century Journal Publishers, 1984).

Schilling, Heniz, 'Reform and Supervision of Family Life in Germany and the Netherlands' in R.A. Mentzer (ed.), *Sin and the Calvinists. Morals Control and the Consistory in the Reformed Tradition* (Kirksville: Sixteenth Century Journal, 1994), 15-61.

Schreiner, Susan, '"The Spiritual Man Judges all Things": Calvin and the Exegetical Debates about Certainty in the Reformation' in R.A. Muller and J.L. Thompson (eds), *Biblical Interpretation in the Era of the Reformation* (Grand Rapids: Eerdmans, 1996), 189-215.

—. *The Theater of his Glory: Nature and the Natural Order in the Thought of John Calvin* (Durham: Labyrinth, 1991).

—. *Where Shall Wisdom be Found? Calvin's Exegesis of Job from Medieval and Modern Perspectives* (Chicago: University of Chicago Press, 1994).

Selderhuis, Herman J., *John Calvin. A Pilgrim's Life* (Downers Grove: IVP Academic, 2009).

—. *Marriage and Divorce in the Thought of Martin Bucer* (Kirksville: Thomas Jefferson University Press, 1999).

Selinger, Susanne, *Calvin Against Himself. A Study in Intellectual History* (Hamden: Archon, 1984).

Shenk, Richard A., 'Is marriage among the sacraments? Were Luther and Calvin wrong?' in Michael Parsons (ed.), *Reformation Faith. Exegesis and Theology in the Protestant Reformations* (Milton Keynes: Paternoster, 2014), 105-121.

Smeeton, Donald D., 'Calvin's Conflict with the Anabaptists,' *Evangelical Quarterly* 54.1 (1982), 46-54.

Spierling, Karen E., 'Friend or Foe. Reformed Genevans and Catholic Neighbors in the Time of Calvin' in R.C. Zackman (ed.), *John Calvin and Roman Catholicism. Critique and Engagement. Then and Now* (Grand Rapids: Baker, 2008), 79-98.

—. *Infant Baptism in Reformation Geneva. The Shaping of a Community, 1536–1564* (Aldershot: Ashgate, 2005).

—. 'Women, Marriage and Family' in David M. Whitford (ed.), *The T&T Clark Companion to Reformation Theology* (London: T&T Clark, 2012), 178-196.

Spijker, Willem van 't, 'Calvin's Friendship with Bucer: Did it make Calvin a Calvinist?' in David Foxgrover (ed.), *Calvin Studies Society Papers 1995, 1997* (Grand Rapids: Calvin Studies Society, 1998), 169-186.

Spinks, Bryan, 'The Sacraments' in David M. Whitford (ed.), *The T&T Clark Companion to Reformation Theology* (London: T&T Clark, 2012), 123-142.

Spitz, L.W., *The Protestant Reformation. 1517-1559* (New York: Harper and Row, 1985).

Stanford Reid, W., 'John Calvin, Pastoral Theologian,' *Reformed Theological Review* 42.3 (1982), 65-72.

Starn, Randolph, 'The Early Modern Muddle,' *Journal of Early Modern History* 6.3 (2002), 296-307.

Stauffer, Richard, *Dieu, la creation et la providence dans le predication de Calvin* (Berne: Peter Lang, 1978).

—. *L'humanité de Calvin* (Neuchâtel: Delachaux and Niestlé, 1964).

—. 'Un Calvin inconnu: le prédicateur de Genève', *BHPF* 4 (1978).

Steinmetz, David C., *Calvin in Context* (Oxford: Oxford University Press, 1995).

—. 'The Intellectual Appeal of the Reformation,' *Theology Today* 57.4 (2001), 459-472.

Stetina, Karin Spiecker, *The Fatherhood of God and the Use of Feminine Imagery in John Calvin's Thought* (Milton Keynes: Paternoster, 2016).

Storms, Sam, 'Living with One Foot Raised: Calvin on the Glory of the Final Resurrection and Heaven,' in John Piper and David Mathis (eds), *With Calvin in the Theater of God. The Glory of Christ and Everyday Life* (Illinois: Crossway, 2010), 111-132.

Strohm, Christoph, 'Beobachtungen zur Elgenart der Theologie Calvins' *Evangelische Theologie* 69.2 (2009), 85-100.

Sytsma, D.S., 'The Exegetical Context of Calvin's Loci on the Christian Life,' *Calvin Theological Journal* 45.2 (2010), 243-255.

Takeshi, Takasaki, 'Calvin's Theology as Pastoral Theology,' *Reformed Review* 57.3 (1998), 220-241.

Talbot, Mark R., 'Bad Actors on a Broken Stage: Sin and Suffering in Calvin's World and Ours,' in John Piper and David Mathis (eds), *With Calvin in the Theater of God. The Glory of Christ and Everyday Life* (Illinois: Crossway, 2010), 59-63.

Thomas, Derek, *Calvin's Teaching on Job. Proclaiming the Incomprehensible God* (Geanies House, Scotland: Mentor, 2004).

—. 'Who was John Calvin?' in Burk Parsons (ed.), *John Calvin. A Heart for Devotion, Doctrine and Doxology* (Orlando: Reformation Trust, 2008), 19-30.

Thompson, John L., 'Calvin as a biblical interpreter' in Donald K. McKim (ed.), *The Cambridge Companion to John Calvin* (Cambridge: Cambridge University Press, 2004), 58-73.

—. '"*Creata ad Imaginem Dei, Licet Secundo Gradu*": Woman as the Image of God According to John Calvin,' *Harvard Theological Review* 81 (1988), 125-414.

—. *John Calvin and the Daughters of Sarah* (Geneva: Librarie Droz, 1992).

Thompson, Mark D., 'Calvin on the Mediator' in Mark D. Thompson (ed.), *Engaging with Calvin. Aspects of the Reformer's legacy for today* (Nottingham: APOLLOS, 2009), 106-135.

Torrance, Thomas F., *The Hermeneutics of John Calvin* (Edinburgh: Scottish Academic Press, 1988).

—. *Trinitarian Perspectives* (Edinburgh: T&T Clark, 1994).

Van den Berg, M.A., *Friends of Calvin* (Grand Rapids: Eerdmans, 2006).

Van der Kooi, Cornelius, 'Life as Pilgrimage. The Eschatology of John Calvin' in Henk van den Belt (ed.), *Restoration through Redemption: John Calvin Revisited* (Leiden: Brill, 2013), 185-198.

Van der Walt, B.J., 'Woman and Marriage: In the Middle Ages, in Calvin and in our own time' in B.J. van der Walt (ed.), *John Calvin's Institutes: His Opus Magnum* (Potchefstroom: Potchefstroom University for Christian Higher Education, 1986), 184-238.

Vorster, J.M., 'Calvin and Human Dignity' in Henk van den Belt (ed.), *Restoration through Redemption: John Calvin Revisited* (Leiden: Brill, 2013), 215-229.

Vosloo, Robert R., 'The Displaced Calvin: "Refugee Reality" as a Lens to Re-Examine Calvin's Life, Theology and Legacy,' *Religion and Theology* 16.1/2 (2009), 35-52.

Wadkins, Timothy H., 'A Recipe for Intolerance: A Study of the Reasons behind John Calvin's Approval of Punishment for Heresy,' *Journal of the Evangelical Theological Society* 26.4 (1983), 431-441.

Walker, W., *John Calvin* (New York, Putnam, 1906).

Wallace, P.G., *The Long European Reformation. Religion, Political Conflict, and the Search for Conformity, 1350–1750* (Basingstoke, UK: Palgrave MacMillan, 2004).

Wallace, R.S., *Calvin, Geneva, and the Reformation. A Study of Calvin as Social Reformer, Churchman, Pastor and Theologian* (Edinburgh: Scottish Academic, 1988).

Walters, Gwyn, *The Sovereign Spirit. The Doctrine of the Holy Spirit in the Writings of John Calvin* (Edinburgh: Rutherford House, 2009).

Wandel, Lee Palmer, *The Reformation. Towards a New History* (Cambridge: Cambridge University Press, 2011).

Ward, Haruko Nawata, 'Martyrdom' in David M. Whitford (ed.), *The T&T Clark Companion to Reformation Theology* (Edinburgh: T&T Clark, 2012), 332-351.

Watanabe, Nobuo, 'Calvin's Second Catechism: Its Predecessors and its Environment' in Wilhelm H. Neuser (ed.), *Calvinus Sacrae Scripturae Professor: Calvin as Confessor of Holy Scripture* (Grand Rapids: Eerdmans, 1994), 224-232.

Watt, Jeffrey R., 'The Marriage Laws Calvin Drafted for Geneva' in Wilhelm H. Neuser (ed.), *Calvinus Sacrae Scripturae Professor. Calvin as Confessor of Holy Scripture* (Grand Rapids: Eerdmans, 1994), 245-255.

Wendel, F., *Calvin: The Origins and Development of his Religious Thought* (London: Collins, 1965).

Wiley, David N., 'Calvin's Friendship with Guillaume Farel' in David Foxgrover (ed.), *Calvin Studies Society Papers 1995, 1997* (Grand Rapids: Calvin Studies Society, 1998), 187-204.

Wolterstorff, N., 'The Wounds of God. Calvin's Theology and Social Injustice,' *Reformed Journal* 37 (1987), 14–22.

Wood, John Hasley, Jr., 'Making Calvin Modern: Form and Freedom in Abraham Kuyper's Free Church Ecclesiology' in Gerard Mannion and Eduardus Van der Borght (eds), *John Calvin's Ecclesiology. Ecumenical Perspectives* (London: T&T Clark, 2011), 169-184.

Wright, D.F., 'Calvin's Pentateuchal Criticism: Equity, Hardness of Heart, and Divine Accommodation in the Mosaic Harmony Commentary,' *Calvin Theological Journal* 21 (1986), 33-55.

—. 'Calvin's Role in Church History' in Donald K. McKim (ed.), *The Cambridge Companion to John Calvin* (Cambridge: Cambridge University Press, 2004), 277-288.

Zachman, Randall C., 'Restoring Access to the Fountain: Calvin and Melanchthon on the Task of Evangelical Theology' in David Foxgrover (ed.), *Calvin Studies Society Papers 1995, 1997* (Grand Rapids: Calvin Studies Society, 1998), 205-228.

—. *Image and Word in the Theology of John Calvin* (Notre Dame: University of Notre Dame, 2007).

—. 'What Kind of a Book is Calvin's *Institutes*?' in *John Calvin as Teacher, Pastor, and Theologian. The Shape of his Writings and Thought* (Grand Rapids: Baker, 2006), 77-102.

Author Index

Alexander, J.H.,   34
Armstrong, Brian,   3
Augustijn, Cornelis,   13

Badcock, G.D.,   13
Bainton, R.H.,   4, 34, 101
Baldwin, C.M.,   30
Balserak, Jon,   53
Barker, William,   56, 72
Barton, F.W.,   31
Battles, Ford Lewis,   31, 51, 55, 57, 59, 62, 68
Beeke, Joel,   133, 138
Beal, Rose M.,   170
Benedict, Philip,   51
Biéler, André,   12, 30, 41
Billman, K.D.,   124
Blaisdell, C.J.,   1, 31
Bohatec, J.,   31
Bonnet, Jules,   129, 131, 147
Bonivard, F.,   10
Boulton, Matthew M.,   160, 165, 166
Bouwsma, William J.,   10, 34, 42, 56, 74, 118, 140, 141
Brown, Delwin,   63, 144
Butin, Philip,   119, 168

Campbell, Jennifer,   163
Canlis, Julie,   119, 169
Carew-Hunt, R.N.,   34
Chadwick, Owen,   9
Chidester, David,   11
Cocke, W.E.,   30
Collinson, P.,   10
Compier, Don H.,   57, 60, 61, 62, 73
Cottret, Bernard,   8, 12, 29, 41, 42, 47, 50, 51, 61, 64, 72, 75, 77, 78, 81, 88,100, 101, 102, 103, 104, 105, 113, 116, 118, 144
Crisp, Oliver,   140
Crouzet, D.,   11

Davis, T.J.,   100
de Greef, Wulfert,   50
de Koster, Lesyer,   12, 168, 170
Douglass, Jane Dempsey,   30

Edgar, William,   34
Edmondson, Stephen,   50, 104
Eire, C.M.N.,   10
Elwood, Christopher,   33

Ferguson, Sinclair B.,   3, 134
Forde, Gerhard O.,   145
Friedman, J.,   101
Fulop, Timothy E.,   117

Gamble, Richard C.,   76, 101, 115
Ganoczy, Alexandre,   11, 75, 78, 97, 121
George, Timothy,   11, 76, 100, 119, 121
Gerrish, Brian,   7, 99, 166
Gleason, Elizabeth G.,   75
Godfrey, W. Robert,   2, 159
Gregory, Brad S.,   144, 162
Gustafson, J.M.,   31

Haight, Roger,   161, 169
Hall, B.,   10
Hall, C.A.M.,   31
Hall, D.W.,   10, 27, 50
Harkness, G.,   13, 33
Harman, Allan M.,   119
Helm, Paul,   140
Heinze, Rudolph W.,   75, 101, 122
Henderson, Henry,   1, 2, 44, 111, 114, 115, 122
Hendrix, Scott,   9
Hesselink, John I.,   55
Hillerbrand, H.,   101, 102, 103, 148
Hörcsik, Richard,   64
Hourticq, D.,   2, 43, 130

Hughes, P.E., 2
Hughes, R.A., 124, 125, 131

Jelsma, Auke, 143
Jenson, Peter F., 69
Johnson, Phillip R., 64
Johnson, Stephen M., 117
Jones, Serene, 50, 51, 62, 63, 64, 69

Kagay, D., 12
Kaplan, Benjamin J., 144
Karant-Nunn, Susan, 137, 141
Kearsley, R., 12
Keck, David, 46, 140, 141
Kelly, Douglas, 1
Kim, Yosep, 76
Kingdon, R.M., 9, 12, 21, 168, 169
Klauber, Martin I., 104
Kolb, Robert, 143, 144, 145
Kraus, Hans-Joachim, 7

Lambert, T., 11
Larson, M.J., 11
Lazareth, W.H., 30
Leith, John, 4-6, 51
Lillback, Peter A., 50
Lindberg, Carter, 10, 15, 95, 101
Linder, Robert D., 26, 41, 130

Mannion, Gerard, 79, 80, 96-97, 114
Matheson, Peter, 144
McGrath, Alister E., 1, 3, 9, 10, 11, 13, 34, 55, 56, 57, 58, 78, 101, 114, 115, 117
McIntyre, John, 119
McNeill, J.T., 95, 118
Meyer, Sebastian, 147
Migliore, Daniel L., 124
Millet, Oliver, 117
Moeller, B., 9
Monheit, Michael, 13, 31
Monter, William, 114, 144
Moon, B.-H., 104

Muller, Richard A., 56
Mullett, Michael, 11, 29, 31, 39, 55, 58, 67, 76, 82, 85, 97, 98, 100, 101, 115, 118, 131

Naef, H., 10
Naphy, William, 3, 10, 12, 19, 100, 101, 117
Needham, N.R., 11, 42, 75, 102, 116, 118
Nestingen, James A., 167
Nicolls, D., 51, 143, 160

Oberman, Heiko A., 23, 51, 77, 78
Old, H.O., 9
Olin, John C., 74, 75, 76, 77
Olsen, Jeannine, 129
Olson, V.N., 30
Oyer, J.S., 61
Ozment, Steven, 12, 29

Parker, T.H.L., 12, 51, 55, 56, 73, 101, 119
Parsons, Michael, 2, 14, 30, 32, 34, 39, 43, 47, 84, 85, 91, 99, 124, 125, 131, 133, 135, 143, 145
Partee, Charles, 140, 160
Pattison, Bonnie, 67, 106, 152, 162, 167
Perrot, A., 2, 43, 130
Peterson, Eugene H., 162, 165
Pettegree, Andrew, 9, 146, 147, 167
Pfeiffer, C.W., 30

Reid, Stanford, 2
Reinis, A., 141
Reymond, Robert L., 36, 101
Richardson, Kurt A., 119
Rilliet, J., 10
Robinson, M.A., 100, 116
Roget, A., 10
Ruff, J.R., 12

Author index

Safley, Thomas M., 144
Schilling, Heinz, 33
Schreiner, Susan E., 68, 140
Selderhuis, Herman J., 15, 30, 33, 34, 36, 39, 42, 47, 75, 78, 83, 96, 100, 101, 118, 133, 135, 140
Selinger, Susanne, 9, 25, 120
Smeeton, Donald D., 61
Spierling, Karen E., 11, 12, 34, 46, 74
Spitz, L.W., 31
Stauffer, Richard, 2, 42, 140
Steinmetz, David, 71
Stetina, Karin Spiecker, 28
Storms, Sam., 142
Strohm, Christoph, 2
Sytsma, D.S, 56

Takeshi, Takasaki, 2
Talbot, Mark R., 141
Tappert, Theodore G., 145
TeBrake, W.P., 9
Thomas, Derek, 115, 140
Thompson, John L., 3, 30
Torrance, Thomas, F., 105, 119

Van den Berg, M.A., 130, 135

van der Kooi, Cornelius, 138
van der Walt, B.J., 30
van't Spijker, Willem, 27
Villalon, L.J.A., 12
Vorster, J.M., 141
Vosloo, Robert R., 9

Wadkins, T.H., 101, 103, 118, 119, 121
Walker, W., 95
Wandal, Lee Palmer, 33, 34, 51, 56, 143, 161
Wallace, P.G., 11
Wallace, R.S., 11
Walters, G., 92, 123, 161
Ward, Haruko N., 143, 144
Watt, Jeffrey R., 32
Wendel, F., 95
Wiley, David N., 9, 27, 35
Wolterstorff, Nicholas, 124, 136, 139
Wood, Jr., J.H., 100
Wright, David F., 33, 58, 76

Zachman, Randall C., 56, 74, 103, 106

Letters Index

Letters to the Church at Basel
November 13, 1537 52

Letters to James Bernard
March 11, 1541 25, 26

Letters to Ambrose Blaurer
February 6, 1554 104

Letters to Martin Bucer
October 15, 1541 28

Letter to the Budé family
1547 129

Letters to Heinrich Bullinger
November 8, 1542 135
Whitsuntide, 1552 147
April, 1553 139
September 7, 1553 113
November 26, 1553 113
December 30, 1553 104
February 23, 1554 104
February 27, 1554 100, 123
March 28, 1554 121
September 6, 1560 135

Letter to John Cavent
June, 1545 137

Letter to Madame de Cany
April 29, 1549 132
January, 1552 112

Letters to the brethren at Chambery
October 8, 1555 109

Letter to John Clauburger
February 28, 1556 137

Letter to Madame de Coligny
August 5, 1563 139

Letters to Francis Daniel
October 1533 52
October 13, 1536 9

Letters to Christopher Fabri
January 13, 1553 29, 40

Letters to Madame de Falais
September 18, 1545 38

Letters to Monsieur de Falais
July 4, 1546 44
October 4, 1547 46
November 16, 1546 45
November 20, 1546 139
May 1, 1547 45

Letters to William Farel
August 1538 16
August 20, 1538 26, 139
September 1538 16
October 14, 1538 26
October 24, 1538 134, 138
January 1539 134
February 23, 1539 43
March 1539 25
April 1539 26
May 19, 1539 36, 43
September 1539 18, 54, 76
December 31, 1539 52
February 6, 1540, 25, 37, 43, 54
March 1540 25
May 1540 26, 52, 54
June 21, 1540 52
October 1540 54
October 27, 1540 20
November 13, 1540 21
March 28, 1541 126
April 24, 1541 27, 136
May 4, 1541 25
July 1, 1541 52
September 16, 1541 8, 23, 27
November 11, 1541 27

Letters index

June 16, 1542   134, 138
May 1, 1545   53
January 26, 1546   53
February 13, 1546   111, 122
February 20, 1546   53
May 1, 1546   54
May 2, 1546   138
April 11, 1549   39, 130, 132
August 19, 1550   107
June 15, 1551   135
March 27, 1553   135, 139
August 20, 1553   112, 117
October 26, 1553   113, 122
July 24, 1555   155
July 1, 1558   45
September 1558   48

Letter to John Frellon
February 13, 1546   111, 122

Letter to a French gentleman
June 30, 1551   135

Letters to the Church in Geneva
October 1, 1538   17, 89-90
June 25, 1539   18

Letters to the Council in Geneva
October 23, 1540   20
November 12, 1540   22
February 19, 1541   23
September 7, 1541   23

Letter to Christopher Goodman
April 23, 1561   136

Letter to John Liner
August 10, 1552   153

Letter to Peter Martyr
March 2, 1559   137

Letters to Philip Melanchthon
January 21, 1545   54
March 5, 1555   114
August 23, 1555   114

Letters to Oswald Myconius
June 24, 1544   54

Letters to the Ministers of Neuchâtel
September 26, 1558   47

Letter to Monsieur le Curé de Cernex   68

Letters to Nicolas Parent
December 14, 1540   24

Letter to the Pastors of Basel
November 13, 1537   147

Letters to the Pastors of Frankfurt
August 27, 1553   104, 121

Letters to the Pastors of Schaffhausen
July 24, 1545   54

Letter to Denis Peloquin and Louis de Marsac
August 22, 1553   138, 147

Letter to a gentleman of Piedmont
February 25, 1554   155

Letters to prisoners in Chambery
September 5, 1555   154
October 5, 1555   156

Letters to the prisoners in Lyon
June 10, 1552   148
March 7, 1553   150
May 15, 1553   151, 171

Letter to Monsieur de Richebourg
April, 1541   125

Letter to Thomas Sollicoffre
March 28, 1553   151

Letter to Sulzer
  1553,   117
  September 8, 1553   147

Letters to Louis du Tillet
  July 10, 1538   16, 19, 24
  October 20, 1538   16, 17, 18

Letter to Godfrey Varaglia
  December 17, 1557   158, 162

Letters to Peter Viret
  May 19, 1540   25, 53
  October 8, 1540   52
  March 1, 1541   26, 27
  July 1542   38
  August 19, 1542   38, 54, 135, 137
  February 2, 1545   54
  March 15, 1545   53
  May 25, 1545   54
  February 22, 1546   44, 136
  March 8, 1546   44, 135
  May 1, 1546   54
  July 13, 1546   45
  July 15, 1546   45
  July 25, 1546   45
  June 15, 1548   38
  September 1, 1548   45, 111
  April 7, 1549   3, 38, 130
  May 10, 1551   135
  April 22, 1553   150
  August 4, 1555   155
  September 9, 1555   155

Letter to women detained in prison
  September 1557   157

Letter to the Count of Wurtemberg
  July 12, 1558   147

Scripture Index

Genesis
2.22   32
6–9   70

Exodus
31.18   93

Deuteronomy
13   120
13.12   69
13.13-15   121

1 Kings
18.17   71
18.18   71

Job   125

Psalms
13.1   124
22.1   124
91.14-15   146

Isaiah
6   136
8.14   71n.108

Matthew
7.7   109
15.14   95
16.26   82
17.5   70
24.24   69
25.34-46   153

Mark
16.20   69

Luke
22.24-25   69
23.5   71

John
7.18   69
8.50   69
16.33   146
19.7   71

Acts
6   71n.108
11   71n.108
14.3   69
15   71n.108
24.5   71

Romans
6.1   71n.108
6.15   71n.108
8.26   154
8.26-27   151
9.33   71n.108

1 Corinthians
1.10   71n.108
1.18-2.16   145
1.27-28   157
1.31   67
3.21-22   69
3.23   69
4.13   67
7.1   42-43
8.6   70

2 Corinthians
1.4   151
10.17   67
11.3   71n.108
11.14   69

Galatians
1.6   71n.108

Ephesians
6   18
6.11   18n.56

Philippians
1.6   149

1.15   71n.108
1.17   71n.108
2.13   149
2.21   71n.108
3   148

Colossians
3.20   69

1 Timothy
3.1-13   41n.61

2 Timothy
2.9-10   69
2.11   69

Hebrews
2.4   69
12.22-24   156
13.3   161

1 Peter
2.8   71n.108

2 Peter
2.18-19   71n.108
2.22   71n.108
3.16   71n.108

Persons Index

Achard, Jean,   47
Agricola, Johann,   29, 105
Alba, Martial,   147

Bartholomew, Bernhardi,   29
Bartolomâus, Bernhardi,   29
Bataille, Bertrand,   154
Baudin, Jean,   117
Baumgaertner, Sibyl,   146
Bernard, James,   25
Beza, Theodore,   135
Bucer, Martin,   16, 21, 27-28, 34, 35, 36, 43, 75, 102, 134, 171
Budé, Guillaume,   129
Budi, Mathieu de,   129
Bugenhagen, Johann,   29
Bullinger, Heinrich,   118
Bure, Idelette de,   130, 141

Calvin, Idelette,   4, 34, 34n.25, 36n.36, 38-39, 42, 43, 44, 49, 170, 171, death of,   38-39, 42, 43
Calvin, Jacques,   38
Cany, Madame de,   132
Capito,   21, 35
Caroli, Pierre,   35, 37, 118
Charles V, Holy Roman Emperor,   37, 51, 53, 115
Clauburger, Adolph,   137, 138
Courault, Augustin,   134
Crespin, Jean,   106

Daniel, Francis,   52
de la Baume, Peter,   75
de Bois, Michel,   76
de Lunz, Phillippe,   157
de Normandy, Laurent,   108
Deperius,   105
de Rouen, Marie,   46
Doletus,   105

Erasmus, Desiderius,   75
Escrivain, Peter,   147

Farel, William,   8, 9, 11, 15, 16, 18, 21, 23, 26, 28, 35, 36-37, 43, 46-49, 74, 74n.3, 76, 81, 86, 117, 120n.118, 126, 135, 171, *Sommaire et briefve declaration* (1525),   55
Farnese, Cardinal,   75
Favre, Charles,   147
Féray, Claude,   126, 136
Francis I, King of France,   4, 6, 37, 50, 51, 53, 54, 57, 65, 66, 72, 73, 166, 168

Goveanus,   105
Grossman, Gasper,   36

Henry II,   51, 73, 151
Hofmann, Melchoir,   102

Jonas, Justus,   29
Joris, David,   113n.81

Karlstadt, Andreas,   29
Knox, John,   136
Kuntz, Peter,   76

Laborie, Anthony,   154
la Fontaine, Nicolas,   112
Lambert, Francis,   29, *Somme chrestienne* (1529),   55
Lefèvre, Jacques,   51
le Moine, Robert,   117
Liner, John,   148, 153-54, 161, 169
Link, Wenceslas,   29
Luther, Katherine (von Buren),   29
Luther, Martin,   2, 13, 29, 30, 32, 33, 35, 43, 95n.125, 125, 129, 133, 135, 143, 144, 144n.9, 152, 152n.49, 160, 170, 172, *The Large Catechism* (1529),   55; *The Small Catechism* (1522),   55

Person Index

Marsac, Louis de, 138
Martyr, Peter, 116
Melanchthon, Philip, 29, 55n.32, 75, 75n.10, 115
More, Thomas, 116
Münster, Thomas, 29
Musculus, Wolfgang, 118n.105

Navihères, Peter, 147

Oecolampadius, Johann, 55n.32, 102
Olivétan, Peter Robert, 134

Peloquin, Denis, 138

Rabelais, 105
Richardot, Claude, 47
Richebourg, Charles de, 126, 129
Richebourg, Louis de, 125-126, 129, 136
Rihel, Wendelin, 76

Sadoleto, Jacopo, 4, 7, 18n.61, 67, 158, 166, 167, 169, 170
Seguin, Bernard, 147, 148

Servetus, Michael, 1n.3, 5, 6, 99, 100-123
Spalatin, George, 43
Stordeur, John, 34
Sturm, John, 35, 75
Sulzer, 117

Thorn, Lambert, 146
Tillet, Louis du, 16, 24, 25
Trigalet, John, 154
Turol, Alexandre, 46
Tyndale, William, 116

Vadian, Joachim, 134
Vernou, John, 154
Viret, Elizabeth Turtaz, 44, 130n.40
Viret, Peter, 20, 26-27, 27n.111, 28, 43, 44-46, 74n.3, 136, 171
van den Esschen, John, 145
von Grumbach, Argula, 43
von Schweckfeld, Casper, 102
Vos, Henry, 145

Wattville, Nicholas de, 130n.40

Zwingli, 35

Subject Index

Adam, 32, 32n.16
adoption, 13
Affair of the Placards, the, 51
alter Christus, 141
Anabaptists, 59, 60-61, 71, 105, 105n.28
Antichrist, 52-53
anticlericalism, 11
anxiety, 151, 157, 159
apocalyptic, 104n.25
Aquinas, Thomas, 125
atheism, 102, 105
Augsburg Confession, the, 55n.32
Augustine, 31, 66, 70n.100, 110, 124, 125, 141, 141n.96
authority, 87, 92, 93, 96

baptism, 55, 71, 103
Basel, 15, 16, 23, 23n.89, 50, 60, 113, 116
Bern, 16, 20n.69, 23n.89, 36, 76, 113, 116, 148
bifocal lens, 39-40, 41, 44, 48
boundaries, 14, 15, 64, 70

calling (vocation), 3, 32, 33, 41, 44, 78, 79, 81, 89, 97, 136, 155, 156, 159, 166, 167, 168, 169, 170
Calvin, John: anger of, 3, calling, doctrine of, 13-15, 19, 28, calling of, 4, 5, 8, 8n.3, 12, 17, 20, 21, 23, 24-25, 26, 158, 160, 162, Christ-centred, 171, commentaries, 167, *Commentary on the Psalms* (1557), 60, compassionate, 2, 3, *Concerning Scandals* (*De Scandalas*), 67, 105-10, 122, 159, 163, 164, confidence, 171, conversion, 95n.125, deference of, 3, determination, 171, ecclesiology, 167-68, 170, empathy of, 4, 5, 130, 156, 157, 159, 171, expulsion of, 4, 9, 11, 15, 18, 20n.69, 23, 24, 28, failings, 3, 171, faith, 171, God-centred, 171, grief, 2, 5, 34, 38-39, 127-28, 130, 131, health, 8, 36, 38, hope, 171, humanity, 1, 2, inadequacy of, 3, 8, 17, 21, 25-28, insight of, 3, *Institutes* (1536), 50, 51, 54, 55, 56, 57-73, *Institutes* (1539), 50, 56, *Institutes* (1543), 50, 103, *Institutes* (1559), 1, 2, 4, 13, 50, 60, *Institutes* (French 1560), 50, 60, *La Forme des Prieres et chantz ecclesiastiques* (1542-43), 33n.19, *Les ordonnances ecclesiastiques* (1541), 33n.20, letters, 1, 2, 3, marriage, doctrine of, 31-34, 40-43, ministry, 8, 16n.47, 21, 36, 38, 39, 42, 48, passionate, 2, pastoral, 2, 5, 6, 18, 19, 44, 47, 97, 103, 107, 112, 113, 120, 122-123, 127, 133, 141, 147, 159, 163, 166, 171, pastoral theology, 2, poverty, 44, 67, Reader of Holy Scripture, 9, *Responsio ad Sadoletum*, 76, realism of, 4-5, recall of, 3, 8, 23, 24, sermons, 2, strengths, 3, teaching, 1, theology, 2, 5, 13, 32, vulnerability of, 3, 16, 21, 133, 134, 136, 141, 171, weakness of, 2, 3, 5, 171, writings, 1, 2
Catholic Church, the, 85, 86, 86n.69, 87, 88, 94, 95, 97, 99
cercle de Meaux, 51
certainty, 133, 163

Subject index

Chambery, 143, 147, 154, 160
Christ, 4, 6, 13, 20, 39, 41, 68, 68n.93, 69, 70, 71, 82, 83, 84-85, 86, 88, 89, 90, 91, 93, 94, 98, 99, 104, 108, 133, 136, 138, 139, 142, 145, 146, 149, 152, 153, 158, 162, 163, 164, 165, 166, 167, 168, 168, 170, 171, blood of, 91, 92, 170, centrality of, 84-85, 91, 94, 98, cross of, 91, 92, 94, 165, 170, 171, death of, 91, 92, 170, deity, 119, fellowship with, 139, glory of, 91, grace, 138, humanity, 102, identification with, 146, incarnation, 104n.22, mercy, 139, obedience of, 91, 92, reign of, 146, resurrection of, 146, righteousness of, 92, sacrifice of, 91, 92, 170, sonship, 102, suffering, 146, sufficiency of, 92, triumph, 146, victory, 152, virtue of, 92
Christology, 103
church, 85-89, 90, 120
Church Fathers, 102, 109, 117
city, 4
comfort, 18, 152
community, 5, 13, 33, 40, 63, 64, 128, 144, 149, 151, 154, 156n.69, 157, 161, 161n.95, 165, 168, 169
companionship, 32, 38-39, 40, 41n.61, 42, 48
confession, 96
confidence, 96, 97, 99, 133, 137, 151, 152
conscience, 93, 95, 103n.19
Consilium de emendala ecclesia, 75
consolation, 150
coram Deo, 66, 89, 127, 153
Council of Trent, 76
Cyprian, 70n.100

Diet of Augsburg, 55n.32
Diet of Ratisbon, 23
duty, 14, 17, 22

ecumenism, 77, 79, 80
edification, 5, 6
Elijah, 2n.5, 71
eschatology, 6, 151, 152, 158, 160, 163
eternal life, 138, 160
Eve, 32, 32n.16
Eucharist (Lord's Supper), the, 15, 33, 55, 58, 71, 74
excommunication, 15
experience, 5, 6, 91, 121, 124, 125, 130, 136, 137, 145, 147n.26, 149, 151, 152, 156, 158, 159, 160, 166, 167, 168, 172

faith, 5, 13, 67, 68n.94, 72, 77, 78, 79, 82, 82n.47, 83, 84-85, 91, 92, 93, 96, 98, 110, 125, 127, 132, 133, 137, 138, 139, 141, 142, 144, 152, 156, 158, 159, 160, 163, 167, 168
family, 2, 3
fear, 95
Flood, the, 70
forgiveness, 88, 166, 169
Frankfurt, 121
friendship, 43-44

Geneva, 2, 3, 8-13, 16, 19, 35, 40, 41, 44, 45
Council of Two Hundred, the, 74
General Council, the, 74
Little Council, the, 74, 76
God, 5, 6, 13, 24, 32, 90, 96, 98, 119, 137, 139-41, 160, 165-66, 167, 167n.9, 169, 170, 171, 172, anger of, 18, 83, 91, 170, experience of, 4, 5, faithfulness, 166, Father, 38, 127, 129, 132, 133, 137, 142,

151, 155, 156, 159n.87, 160, 163, 166, fear of, 6, glory of, 6, 32, 66, 90, 98, 120, 166, goodness, 105, 127, 137n.76, grace of, 4, 6, 41, 48, 67, 68, 72, 87, 91, 96, 98, 99, 103, 107, 109, 111, 131, 132, 133, 137, 140, 148, 151, 152, 153, 155, 156, 157, 158, 166, 167, 168, 171, 172, Guardian, 155, 156, Judge, 15, 69, 88-89, 93, 95, 99, judgement of, 15, 68, 69, 88, 94, 99, justice, 59, 96, 127, King, 59, 66n.80, knowledge of, 165-66, love of, 46, 48, 137, 145, 151, 156, 171, mercy of, 18, 87, 88, 91, 92, 95n.125, 103, 140, 170, mystery, 127, omnipotence, 140, power, 64, 67, 152, 157, 158, 171, presence, 148, 150, 151, 167, promises of, 149, 150, 160, 167, 168, protection of, 149, 152, 160, providence of, 5, 6, 64, purposes of, 6, 32, 43, 128, 155, 156, 168, 169, Trinity, the, 103, 104, 117, 156
'good works' 85
gospel, the, 10, 45, 52, 56, 68, 69, 71, 72, 90, 91, 94, 95, 106, 108, 109, 136, 145, 146, 152, 153, 163, 166, 169, 171
grief, 2, 4, 5, 6, 99, 126, 166, 167, 168, 169, 171

heresy, 93-94, 100, 104, 105-10, 114, 120, 121
Holy Spirit, the, 18, 87, 88, 89, 90, 93, 96, 98, 99, 102, 104, 109, 111, 129, 138, 141n.94, 149, 150, 151, 152, 153, 153, 154, 156, 157, 160, 161n.93, 162n.100, 167, 169
hope, 5, 18, 87, 94, 157, 162, 166, 168
human nature, 84

humility, 15, 18

iconoclasm, 11
image of God (*imago Dei*), 6, 40

judgement, 86, 95
justification by faith, 77, 78, 79, 84-85, 91, 92, 96, 103

kingdom of God (or Christ), the, 19, 66, 70, 73, 128, 145, 152n.44

Lausanne, 45, 46
lament, 124
Leipzig, 146
love, 85-86, 91
Lyon, 143, 147-54, 160

marriage, 2, 3, 4, 6, 29-31, 55, 166, 169, 170, 171, 172
martyrs (martyrdom), 4, 5, 39, 39n.50, 42, 58, 60, 63, 87, 99, 138, 143, 144-46, 153, 154, 155, 158, 158n.81, 161, 162, 163, 169, 170, 171
miracles, 58, 68, 69
modesty, 15, 72

Neuchâtel, 23, 46
Nicaea, Council of, 104

obedience, 15, 59, 62, 85, 87, 88, 92, 94, 162, 166
office, 15, 19, 22
Oratories of Divine Love, 75
Orbe, 45
order (*ordo*), 31, 33, 40

pantheism, 104
pardon, 87
Paris, 144, 147, 157
patience, 72
patriarchy, 2, 41n.58, 43, 46, 49
Pelagian theology, 85
Penances, 87

Subject index

persecution, 4, 51-54, 60, 62, 64, 67, 68-69, 72, 91, 94, 99, 109n.61, 144, 145, 146, 157n.74, 163, 164, 166, 167, 168
perseverance, 15, 149, 159, 162, 166, 168
piety, 6, 36, 41, 57, 61, 84, 90, 94, 98, 110, 121, 125, 127, 129, 133, 141, 170
plague, the, 126
politics, 3
prayer, 5, 18, 39, 53, 126, 151, 154, 157, 162
preaching, 3, 69, 70, 91, 93, 94, 155, 170
predestination, 100, 137
pride, 15
prophet, 94
providence, 124, 127, 139n.89, 140, 150, 155, 156, 159, 163

reconciliation, 91, 170
redemption, 84, 94
Reformation, the, 8, 9-10, 29, 50, 52, 58, 64, 82, 159n.85, 165
regeneration, 13, 86
remedium peccati, 32, 32n.16, 40
repentance, 96
reprobation, 103n.19
resurrection, 94, 142, 152, 162
rhetoric, 4, 17, 25, 59, 60, 61-62, 62n.62, 63, 65, 66, 67, 71-72, 80, 81, 82-84, 96, 97
righteousness, 91, 92, 99, 108, 163

sacraments, 3, 55
saints, the, 95n.123
salvation, 13, 28, 77, 79, 82, 83, 84-85, 86, 87, 88, 89, 90, 91, 92, 93, 96, 97, 98, 105, 118, 119, 120, 121, 137, 152, 166, 167, 171
sanctification, 5, 85, 119

Satan (the devil), 18, 59, 69, 71, 92, 106, 107-109, 109n.62, 111, 113, 120, 122, 146, 156
scandal(s), 47, 48
Schaffhausen, 113, 116
schism, 93-94
self-denial, 133
sin, 14, 91, 92, 103, 107, 121, 125, 171
Sorbonne, the, 51, 52
Stoicism, 129, 133, 141, 159
Strasbourg, 12, 15, 16, 20, 21, 21n.81, 23, 23n.89, 27, 34, 37, 41, 44, 54, 76, 78
subordination, 31
suffering, 146, 152n.49, 155, 158, 160, 163, 165, 167

temporal kingdom, the, 62
Ten Commandments, the, 93
theology of the cross (*theologia crucis*), 67, 145, 152, 170
transformation, 6
trust, 140, 151, 168
truth, 87, 89, 92, 93, 96, 98, 109, 110, 120, 144, 145, 149, 150, 152, 155, 157, 157n.78, 161, 162, 163, 169, 172

unity, 86, 90, 94, 96

violence, 12, 46

wedding, 32-33, 36
witnesses, 150, 152, 155, 161, 162, 162n.96
Word, the, 4, 11, 12, 18, 22n.84, 59, 71, 79, 83, 90, 92, 93, 94, 96, 98, 103n.19, 110, 114, 142, 145, 145n.11, 162n.100, 166, 169, 172
'works', 92, 98
worship, 33, 34, 70, 84, 89, 94, 98, 121

Zurich, 16, 23n.89, 35, 113, 116

www.ingramcontent.com/pod-product-compliance
Lightning Source LLC
Chambersburg PA
CBHW070257230426
43664CB00014B/2560